LAW'S MISTAKES

A VOLUME IN

The Amherst Series in Law, Jurisprudence, and Social Thought

EDITED BY

Austin Sarat

Martha Umphrey

Lawrence Douglas

LAW'S MISTAKES

Edited by
Austin Sarat
Lawrence Douglas
and
Martha Umphrey

University of Massachusetts Press
Amherst & Boston

Printed in the United States of America

ISBN 978-1-62534-193-8 (paper); 192-1 (hardcover)

Designed by Jack Harrison
Typeset in Scala and Gill Sans
Printed and bound by Maple Press, Inc.

Library of Congress Cataloging-in-Publication Data

Law's mistakes / Edited by Austin Sarat, Lawrence Douglas, and Martha Umphrey.
pages cm. — (Amherst series in law, jurisprudence, and social thought)
Includes bibliographical references and index.
ISBN 978-1-62534-193-8 (pbk. : alk. paper) — ISBN 978-1-62534-192-1 (hardcover : alk paper) 1. Judicial error—United States. I. Sarat, Austin, editor. II. Douglas, Lawrence, editor. III. Umphrey, Martha Merrill, editor.
KF9756.L39 2016
347.73'12—dc23

British Library Cataloguing-in-Publication Data

A catalogue record for this book is available from the British Library.

For my son Ben

(A.S.)

Contents

Acknowledgments

We are grateful to our Amherst College colleagues Clara Altman, David Delaney, Nasser Hussain, and Adam Sitze for their intellectual companionship. We thank our students in Amherst College's Department of Law, Jurisprudence, and Social Thought for their interest in the issues addressed in this book. Finally, we would like to express our appreciation for generous financial support provided by Amherst College's Corliss Lamont Fund.

LAW'S MISTAKES

The Legal Treatment of Mistakes
An Introduction

AUSTIN SARAT, LAWRENCE DOUGLAS,
AND MARTHA UMPHREY

From false convictions to botched executions, from erroneous admission of evidence in a criminal trial to misunderstandings that arise in the process of creating contracts, law is awash in mistakes. Mistakes are unintentional deviations from expected practices or are the results of intentional actions that produce unintended negative consequences. They may become part of a process of response and correction or are accepted as an inevitable cost of action. Mistake is distinguishable from misconduct, which involves an intentional violation of rules or practices.

Some mistakes are external to law itself—for example, errors in an agreement made by two private parties; others are made by legal actors in the course of their work, such as a policeman failing to obtain a search warrant where one is required. *Law's Mistakes* seeks to understand the things that law counts, or recognizes, as mistakes and the way it responds to them. In addition, this book identifies the jurisprudential and political perspectives that underlie different understandings of what is or is not a legal mistake.

Perhaps the most dramatic and best known examples of mistakes concern the conviction and sentencing of innocent people in capital cases.[1] Exonerations from death row have become increasingly common: since 1973, more than 150 people in twenty-five states have been released from death row by evidence of their innocence.[2] These exonerations possess enormous power in the debate about the death penalty and raise important questions about the reliability of the legal system itself. Mistakes of the kind that have recently plagued the death penalty system are a repeated staple of American history. From the largely unknown Tulsa Race Riots of 1921,[3] to the infamous 1930s case of the Scottsboro Boys,[4] to the lynching of the young African American teenager Emmitt Till,[5] to the 1983 case of Rolando Cruz,[6] from the 1977 conviction of Leonard Peltier[7] to the 1984 trial of Darryl Hunt,[8] the last century witnessed more than its share of mistakes as well as miscarriages of justice. Faulty eyewitness identifications, false confessions, biased juries—these as well as the politicization of prosecution and the pervasive fact of racial bias in the criminal justice system make error a legal commonplace not only in capital cases but throughout the legal system.

Sometimes law's mistakes arouse indignation and spur calls for redress. At other times law seems to be relatively tolerant of mistakes, even when they may lead to the most dramatic consequences. Thus in *Herrera v. Collins,* Chief Justice William Rehnquist held that the Court did not need to grapple with the question of whether a person facing execution actually might be innocent.[9] The Court, Rehnquist said, need be concerned only with the question of whether or not a defendant had received a fair, technically efficient, and procedurally sound trial.

Recounting the procedural history of Herrera's case, Rehnquist wrote:

> In February 1992, petitioner lodged the instant habeas petition—his second—in federal court, alleging, among other things, that he is innocent of the murders of Rucker and Carrisalez, and that his execution would thus violate the Eighth and Fourteenth Amendments. In addition to proffering the above affidavits, petitioner presented the affidavits of Raul Herrera, Jr., Raul Sr.'s son, and Jose Ybarra, Jr., a schoolmate of the Herrera brothers. Raul Jr. averred that he had witnessed his father shoot Officers Rucker and Carrisalez and petitioner was not present. Raul Jr. was nine years sold at the time of the killings. Ybarra alleged that Raul Sr. told him one summer night in 1983 that he had shot the two police officers. Petitioner alleged that law enforcement officials were aware of this evidence, and had withheld it in violation of *Brady v. Maryland,* 373 U.S. 83 (1963).[10]

The question of innocence was irrelevant, however. As Rehnquist wrote:

> Petitioner asserts that the Eighth and Fourteenth Amendments to the United States Constitution prohibit the execution of a person who is innocent of the crime for which he was convicted. This proposition has an elemental appeal, as would the similar proposition that the Constitution prohibits the imprisonment of one who is innocent of the crime for which he was convicted. After all, the central purpose of any criminal justice is to convict the guilty and free the innocent. See *United States v. Nobles,* 422 U.S. 225, 230 (1975). But the evidence upon which petitioner's claim of innocence rests was not produced at his trial, but rather eight years later. In any system of criminal justice, "innocence" or "guilt" must be determined in some sort of judicial proceeding. Petitioner's showing of innocence, and indeed his

> constitutional claim for relief based upon that showing, must be evaluated in light of the previous proceedings in this case, which have stretched over a span of 10 years.[11]

Denying Herrera's claim of actual innocence, Rehnquist observed:

> All of these constitutional safeguards, of course, make it more difficult for the State to rebut and finally overturn the presumption of innocence which attaches to every criminal defendant. But we have also observed that "[d]ue process does not require that every conceivable step be taken, at whatever cost, to eliminate the possibility of convicting an innocent person." *Patterson v. New York*, 432 U.S. 197, 208 (1977). To conclude otherwise would all but paralyze our system for enforcement of the criminal law.[12]

In what follows we offer a sampling of a few of the kinds of mistakes found in American law rather than a comprehensive overview of law's mistakes. We do so to show both the complexity of the subject and the variability that attends law's response to mistakes.

Responding to Law's Mistakes: Burdens of Proof

Rhenquist's attitude toward mistake—namely, that it is part of the fabric of law and not crippling to its integrity—is reflected both in evidentiary rules and burdens of proof as well as in the so-called harmless error rule. As is well known, in civil litigation the plaintiff must prove that an event is more probable than not in order for it to be regarded as proven[13]—that is, if any piece of evidence has a probability greater than 50 percent of supporting a fact, then a jury and/or judge must treat that fact as true. Moreover, the plaintiff is required to prove his/her case by the preponderance of evidence.[14] This standard means that civil litigation may be rife with mistakes.

In other kinds of cases the evidentiary burden is expressed as clear and convincing evidence. This requires a party to prove that an event is substantially more likely than not. And, in criminal cases, the state must prove its case beyond a reasonable doubt. Here there is the least tolerance for mistake. The cost of a false positive in which a defendant would be wrongly convicted is treated as greater than the cost of a false negative in which a guilty defendant is found acquitted.[15]

Moreover, in all trials the probability of two independent events occurring together is the product of their respective marginal probabilities.[16] If the probability of a defendant being liable depends on two elements occurring together, then the likelihood that both occur together is the probability of one event, p(A), multiplied by the probability of the other event, p(B). That is to say that p(A&B) = p(A) x p(B). Where the standard of proof is the preponderance of the evidence, the probability that both events occurred together has to exceed 50 percent to satisfy the "more likely true than not true" requirement. Therefore, p(AB) = p(A) x p(B) must also be equal to 0.5. As simple as it sounds, this requires very high probabilities that A and B occurred in order for their joint occurrence to be more likely than not.

But judges and juries rarely think this way; instead, cases are decided "element by element, with each element decided on a more-probable-than not basis."[17] Juries typically consider each element separately, find each to be more probable than not, and then assume each occurred with full certainty before moving to the next element. As a result, they may find a defendant liable even if the joint probabilities are far below the 50 percent necessary to satisfy preponderance of evidence standard.[18] This way of deciding cases illustrates the ubiquity of mistakes in ordinary trials and their embeddedness in existing legal practices.

Responding to Law's Mistakes: Harmless Error

Another example of this phenomenon is provided by the harmless error rule.[19] Over the course of the twentieth century, American law shifted its understanding of the meaning of fair trials from a highly procedural one to one that is much more substantive. At the start of the last century, appellate courts automatically reversed convictions if even minor technical errors occurred in a trial.[20] Indeed, the chance of reversal for any error was sufficiently great that defense attorneys would themselves create, or allow, technical errors.

To stop this kind of manipulation of the legal system, in 1919 Congress passed §269 of the Judicial Code. This said that only errors that "affect the substantial rights of the parties" may be grounds for reversal and gave appellate judges greater discretion by recognizing that a fair trial did not require procedural perfection.[21] This was the first step toward the creation of an idea of harmless error.

During the last one hundred years an enormous body of case law developed that articulated the meaning and consequences of harmless error. That body of law is underpinned by the distinction between constitutional and nonconstitutional errors, though the harmless error rule itself makes no such distinction.[22] Even after the creation of the federal harmless error rule in 1919, there remained a per se rule of automatic reversal for constitutional error in federal courts.

When the Supreme Court first directly interpreted the harmless error rule in *Kotteakos v. United States,* constitutional errors were categorically excluded from its analysis.[23] *Kotteakos* concerned improper jury instructions in a conspiracy case. The Court did not establish a general presumption for evaluating harmless errors, deciding instead that it was the appellate court's job to determine the effect of an error on a jury's decision, regardless of whether other evidence was sufficient for conviction.[24] The appellate court must be able to "say, with fair assurance, . . . that the judgment was not substantially swayed by the error," and if there is "grave doubt" as to the effects of the error, then the conviction must be reversed.[25] At the same time, *Kotteakos* exempted from its analysis errors "in regards to a constitutional norm or a specific command of Congress" and thus perpetuated the idea that constitutional errors could never be harmless.[26]

Many state courts, however, rejected this view and were willing to find constitutional errors harmless.[27] In 1967, the Supreme Court held for the first time that constitutional errors could be harmless.[28] Such an error could be harmless, the Court said, if the beneficiary of the mistake (typically the prosecution) could prove beyond a reasonable doubt that the error did not contribute to the verdict.

After *Chapman v. California,* the harmlessness of constitutional errors was determined on a case-by-case basis until, in the 1991 case of *Arizona v. Fulminante,* the Supreme Court created a new test for determining the kinds of constitutional errors that could be subject to harmless error analysis under the *Chapman* test.[29] Fulminante was a suspect in his stepdaughter's murder. While in federal prison for committing another crime, he confessed to an FBI informant that he had killed his stepdaughter. He confessed again once he was out of prison and was later tried and convicted of the murder. Fulminante appealed on the grounds that his confession was coerced and should not have been admitted into evidence. The Court agreed that the first confession had been coerced, but ruled that, owing to the second uncoerced confession, the error had been harmless and the conviction should stand.[30]

Justice Rehnquist offered a new formula for analyzing constitutional errors, dividing those errors into two categories: structural errors and trial errors. Structural errors, he noted, require automatic reversal, while trial errors are subject to harmless error analysis. An error is structural if it affects "the framework within which the trial proceeds."[31] A trial error, on the other hand, is an error "which occurred during the presentation of the case to the jury, and which may therefore be quantitatively assessed in the context of other evidence presented in order to determine whether its admission was harmless beyond a reasonable doubt."[32] Rehnquist's opinion expanded the kinds of constitutional errors that can be found harmless.

While scholars disagree about what the correct standard for evaluating errors should be, they now seem to agree that, in American courts, mistake often is not fatal.[33] The view that Rehnquist articulated in *Herrera,* that due process does not require procedural perfection, has become the prevailing one.

Responding to External Mistakes

The trend toward increased tolerance of mistake that characterized the harmless error rule and mistakes made by legal actors has not characterized the legal treatment of mistakes made by citizens and private parties. To illustrate this fact, we briefly discuss mistakes in contract and criminal law.

Contracts

Mistakes in contracts may occur when what the contract says does not accurately reflect what the parties intended—that is, when there is "an objective agreement or declarations of will, but the subjective intentions of the parties are not in agreement."[34] Yet, the dominant theory of contract law, embodied in the first Restatement of Contracts, published in 1932,[35] was an objective theory that "has nothing to do with the actual state of the [contracting] parties' minds."[36] Under the objective theory a contract could be binding even if the expression of a party's intent was mistaken.[37]

American contract law also traditionally distinguished between mutual and unilateral mistakes. Mutual mistake occurs when both parties are mistaken about something that, according to the first *Restatement,* "vitally affects the basis upon which they contracted."[38] For example, if a jeweler buys what he and the seller both believe to be a topaz for one dollar, when in fact the topaz is a diamond worth many times that amount, a mutual mistake has occurred.[39]

A unilateral mistake, in contrast, is recognized by only one party. Many unilateral mistakes involve errors in bidding. Suppose A answers an advertisement by B for construction bids and sends B a $50,000 bid. B accepts the bid. A then discovers that in his pre-bid calculations, he failed to take into account some material that costs an additional $10,000. This is an example of unilateral mistake, as only A made a mistake.[40]

Courts have been much more likely to grant rescission or reversal in cases of mutual mistake than in cases of unilateral mistake.[41] According to the first *Restatement,* while a mutual mistake "vitally affects the basis upon which the contract was made," unilateral mistakes are cause for rescission only if the error was recognizable by the other party and was about something so "vital" that if the mistake had been mutual, the contract would be voidable.[42]

The *Restatement (Second) of Contracts,* published in 1981, departs substantially from the first *Restatement* and offers greater relief from mistake. Today, "rules that once afforded a qualified promise of individual [and contractual] autonomy are employed instead to police the fairness of the contractual exchange."[43] In addition, the *Second Restatement* also creates more liberal rules for rescission in cases of unilateral mistake. It says:

> A contract entered into by one party under a mistake which has a material affect on the agreed exchange can be avoided by him if he does not bear the risk of the mistake, and either (a) enforcement of the contract against him would be unconscionable, or (b) the other party caused the mistake or had reason to know of it. A party bears the risk of the mistake if he has, expressly or implicitly, assumed it, or if under the circumstances it is reasonable for the court to assign it to him.[44]

Unlike the first Restatement, in which it was necessary that the mistake be known to both parties for rescission, the Second Restatement opened the door to granting relief in cases of contractual mistake that previously would have been enforced. Unilateral mistakes can now be rescinded if enforcement would be unconscionable.

Yet Allan Farnsworth identifies three ways that modern contract law limits relief from mistake: risk, countervailing concerns, and fault. A mistaken party who bears the risk of mistake, even if mutual, will not usually be able to rescind a contract.[45] Countervailing concerns are interests of persons other than the claimant. These are public concerns, regarding the efficiency of the judicial system.[46] Negligence or fault on the part of the party making the mistake can also prevent rescission of contracts.[47] Despite these impediments to relief and rescission, the general trend in the treatment of mistake in contract law, unlike the treatment of mistake in the context of the harmless error rule, has been toward granting more relief where mistakes are made.

Criminal Law

In the determination of criminal liability, the law's treatment of mistake is based on two separate questions. First, what is the relationship between mistake and the individual's culpability? Second, are there conflicting legal objectives that should keep the mistake from being treated as exculpatory? Traditionally, the common law articulated these concerns in two maxims: ignorantia juris non excusat and ignorantia facti excusat, and, by 1680, in Great Britain mistakes of fact would excuse the defendant, whereas mistakes of law would not.[48]

Over time, particularly in the last century, this sharp dichotomy between mistakes of fact and law has eroded. While the old maxims still hold some force, the law has become more tolerant of mistake of law defenses and less tolerant of mistake of fact defenses. These shifts can be understood in part as responses to broader changes in the landscape of the criminal law.

At the heart of the treatment of mistake in criminal law is *mens rea*. Mistakes traditionally could be exculpatory only if they "negated the criminal mind."[49] A mistake of fact generally fulfills this condition because the person's flawed conception of reality means that he is not morally culpable.

Yet defenses based on mistake of fact are restricted in two ways. One form of restriction involves the requirement that mistakes of fact must be "honestly entertained [and] based upon *reasonable* grounds."[50] The other restriction came with the development of strict liability crimes in the first half of the twentieth century. Strict liability crimes include various sexual offenses, bigamy, adultery, embezzlement, and narcotics sale, among others.[51]

The old maxim regarding mistakes of law had its origins in the belief that they did not have the same relation to moral guilt as mistakes of fact. Ignorance or mistake of law could not be an excuse because "most laws [were] also generally sins."[52] People were expected to know when an action was inherently wrong. Whether they knew of the act's legal status was irrelevant.

Although a presumption of the knowledge of an act's moral status might be applicable to a few basic felonies such as murder and rape, applying a blanket presumption to today's criminal law seems indefensible. Modern criminal law has become increasingly technical and complex and filled with numerous regulatory provisions having no obvious moral content (for example, no parking rules, complex tax laws). Recognizing that mistake or ignorance of law actually does in many cases negate the criminal mind, both legislatures and courts have allowed greater congruence between this understanding of culpability and the law's treatment of mistakes.

On the legislative side, this is reflected in the addition of special mental elements to the statutory definitions of some crimes. When a crime, such as larceny, requires proof of "specific intent" rather than merely general intent, a mistake of law may excuse by negating that element of the crime. Thus the mental element required to commit larceny is "not merely the intent to do the *actus reus,* but also the intent to steal—the *animus furandi.*"[53] Likewise, requirements that a crime be committed maliciously, corruptly, willfully, or knowingly are all elements of crimes that can be negated by a showing of mistake of law.

If the law was solely concerned with ensuring that only those morally culpable for their crimes were punished, then any honest mistake, regardless of whether it was of law or of fact, or was patently unreasonable, would negate the criminal mind. However, even as the willingness to allow mistakes to exculpate has grown, there are policy concerns that push in the opposite direction.

Among those policy concerns are the belief that it is impractical for courts to determine if someone is actually ignorant of the law, that an interest in making the people "know and obey" the law outweighs an interest in individual justice, and that because mistakes of law can be understood as challenging the official interpretation of the law, allowing the mistake of law defense would place the opinions of private parties on a par with official interpretations and would, as a result, undermine the rule of law.[54]

As the preceding discussion of burdens of proof, harmless error rules, and mistake in contract and criminal law illustrates, there are no uniform guidelines for determining when and how law polices or responds to mistakes. There is, if you will, no consistent law of mistake. Each area of law has its own way of dealing with mistakes that changes over time.

The chapters that follow offer a broad jurisprudential and political context for understanding law's mistakes and how law responds to mistakes in the social world.[55] Drawing on various sources and offering various examples, they offer us a glimpse of the variability attending the legal treatment of mistakes as well as a sense of the contingencies and tradeoffs associated with the way law treats and regards mistakes. The work that follows identifies instances when mistakes have serious legal consequences even while it illustrates the limitations of the idea of mistake in describing legal phenomena. In addition, it considers whether some mistakes are built into the very fabric of law's structures and systems and whether other legal values do, and should, override the correction of mistakes.

The first chapter, by Stewart Motha, describes standards for deciding whether legal actions should be regarded as mistakes or errors. In Motha's view, it is the distinctive responsibility of law to investigate mistakes, whether its own or those that occur beyond its purview, but he worries that law often fails in this calling. One type of error for which law should take responsibility is *mistaken judgment,* decisions and outcomes that we would not affirm in retrospect.

Motha also identifies what he calls *forgetful judgments,* those that occur with a lapse in memory. He argues that amnesty is an example of a state-sanctioned forgetful judgment in the interest of reconciliation. Among other things, his chapter examines the practices of amnesty in South Africa and notes that amnesty tries to avoid two mistakes, one of which involves forgetting past crimes, the other of which involves letting those crimes dictate present practices.

Motha next takes up *indefensible judgments.* Such judgments, he argues, are mistakes born both of a lack of attention to context and a lack of imagination. To void making indefensible judgments, law must go beyond "the prison house of fact." Law's mistakes, he says, frequently arise from its inability or unwillingness to do so.

Legal judgment, Motha says, requires looking over the horizon. Justice is something that we never quite experience, something just beyond our comprehension. Mistakes are best understood as problems of judgment, problems that arise from a dearth of imagination and a lack of interest in the future. Law's mistakes, he concludes, arise from an insistence on the priority of the present and an unwillingness to forge new temporal horizons.

The second chapter, by Kanul Parker, provides a very different account of the causes of mistaken judgments. It does so offering a reading of what Parker calls Alexander Bickel's jurisprudence of "mood." In this jurisprudence, mistaken judgments arise from failures to distinguish the spheres of law and political democracy. Mistakes in this context are not specific to particular cases, or areas of law, but rather arise from a particular approach to jurisprudence.

Parker examines the influences that shaped Bickel's jurisprudence, particularly the thought of Oliver Wendell Holmes. Contrary to the ahistorical beliefs of the late nineteenth and early twentieth centuries, Holmes argued that law was excessively invested in a "blind imitation of the past" and thus was not rooted in reason. Bickel, Parker notes, tried to navigate around two mistakes: one involved failing to *recognize* the overlapping of law in history and the other failing to *overcome* the overlapping of history and law. Bickel wanted law to embody a "mood" that balanced continuity with change.

Starting with the decision in *Brown v. Board* and the era of the Warren Court, the law, in Bickel's view, went astray. The Warren Court, he felt, moved in the direction of establishing unequivocal principles that would bring certainty and clarity to law. The quest for clarity is, for Bickel, the source of law's mistakes. Moreover, the Warren Court tried to shape the future as opposed to letting the future unfold in its own way. Bickel believed that the law fell into error when it focused on reaching particular substantive results rather than more modestly policing procedural processes.

As Parker understands it, Bickel's jurisprudence of mood does not help us identify particular instances of mistaken judgments. It focuses instead on general orientations toward law, preferring modesty over ambition, vagueness over clarity, procedure over substance. Parker concludes that Bickel is particularly useful in warning of the dangers of scientific rationality as a template for legal decisions.

Jordan Steiker's chapter offers a distinctly anti-Bickelian perspective on law's mistakes by elevating substance over procedure. Steiker outlines the law's traditional approach to mistakes, which, he contends, is highly procedural. In the domain of criminal justice this may achieve a kind of formal purity, but it neglects substantive errors in actual sentencing.

Warren Court jurisprudence exemplified this search for formal purity but left defendants with no means to challenge the length of their sentences or the substantive nature of the "justice" done in their case. Cases such as *Hutto v. Davis*[56] and *Harmelin v. Michigan*[57] illustrate this fact, holding that there are no constitutionally mandated proportionality limits on punishment.

Steiker notes that the tendency to police procedural errors while ignoring substantive mistakes is vividly illustrated in the jurisprudence of the death penalty. Judges have generally been concerned with procedural safeguards as opposed to evaluating the proper use of the death penalty, if any. *Herrera v. Collins,* Steiker argues, exemplifies the elevation of procedure over substance in capital cases.

Steiker outlines some of the consequences of the focus on procedural rather than substantive error. He observes that the high visibility of procedure gives a false impression of fairness in the court system. In addition, courts forgo reviewing punishment because of the difficulty of delineating standards for excessive punishment. Steiker concludes that we need to focus more on substantive mistakes, even if this requires the articulation of new normative commitments and the further development of existing ones.

For Jody Madeira the problem of mistakes is less a problem of the nature of our normative commitments or their interpretation than it is one of the nature of the organizations within which mistakes happen. To focus on normative commitments is to ignore the factors that determine whether they can, and will, be realized. Madeira argues that we should turn to organization theory to help understand why legal mistakes happen and how law responds to them.

Her chapter uses the example of botched lethal injections to explore the value of organization theory. Four factors, she suggests, must be present for any organization to best handle mistakes: clear objectives, competent personnel, respect for expertise, and feedback practices. The system of lethal injection, Madeira argues, currently is deficient with regard to all four of these factors. This has resulted in a system in which "mistakes are inherent, and perhaps now endemic."

Lethal injection was first introduced in Oklahoma in 1977. Chosen without much consideration or deliberation, the method soon spread to dozens of other states. Legal challenges to lethal injection culminated in *Baze vs. Rees,* which upheld the method unless state protocols "presented an 'objectively intolerable' risk of serious harm." Since *Baze* new problems have arisen. Foreign and U.S. drug companies have stopped providing drugs used in lethal injection to corrections departments, forcing states to rely on riskier, unregulated sources for the drugs. Additionally, professional medical associations have tried to prevent doctors from participating in lethal injection procedures. This has forced untrained and unqualified personnel to administer the medical procedure.

What Madiera labels "dark side" organization studies explore how decisions that seem irrational and deviant outside of an organization are not regarded as such internally because they conform to organizational culture and goals. While botched executions are viewed by the media and the public as "*preventable* mistakes," Madeira considers them to be types of organizational deviance explained by the "dark side" framework. Imperfect knowledge and poor feedback loops create organizational stress and result in more mistakes and more botched executions.

No protocol, Madeira suggests, can prevent mistakes from occurring. However, needed improvements have not been made after repeated problems. Review of protocols has been inadequate, and state secrecy prevents public scrutiny of how these protocols are implemented. States and corrections respond to repeated failures by aligning their actions with existing organizational norms. This contributes to a culture of mistake in which botched executions are viewed by actors within the death penalty system as unproblematic or unfortunate instead of unacceptable.

In the end, Madeira recognizes that mistakes are inevitable in lethal injection. However, she worries that mistakes have become so commonplace as to suggest misconduct. Distinguishing between mistake and misconduct requires transparency. Only with a transparent political and institutional system can we change the culture of mistake in lethal injection reforms. For Madeira, the consequences of inaction are too high: "we cannot allow society and its institutions . . . to become complacent about botched executions, and must actively prevent execution mistakes from becoming yet another banal evil."

Sonali Chakravarti takes up a very different aspect of the criminal justice system, focusing on law's attitude toward hung juries—namely, the occasions when jurors cannot arrive at a verdict of guilty or not-guilty. Her chapter explores the question of whether a hung jury should be considered a mistake. She says that a mistake is "an outcome that reveals a breakdown in the procedures of the trial or undermines the tenets of the adversarial justice system."

Chakravarti discusses the use of the so-called Allen charge when juries appear to be hung. The availability of the Allen charge, she observes, suggests that law regards hung juries as mistaken outcomes that should, if at all possible, be avoided. Chakravarti is a critic of the use of the Allen charge in criminal cases. She regards it as coercive, seeking to push juries toward a verdict and also as a violation of the presumption of innocence. Like Robert Burns, she believes that each trial develops its own structure of judgment and that the judge should respect rather than shape that distinctive structure. The Allen charge gives the judge power to expedite a process or force a conclusion. It unduly intrudes on the appropriately insular world of a jury.

Chakravarti characterizes the Allen charge as itself a mistake of law, an intrusion at a point when jurors are fatigued, and frustrated and are at their most vulnerable. It is a failure to recognize that the legitimate plurality of the jury and the fact that because jurors come from different life-worlds, they will interpret and perceive evidence in ways that need not, in every case, lead to agreement. Hung juries, Chakravarti concludes, provide a valuable brake on punitiveness in American criminal justice, which, like Steiker, she regards as a regrettable and mistaken tendency of our era.

The fact of plurality that is at the heart of Chakravarti's analysis of the hung jury is also central to Paul Berman's discussion of mistakes in a system of overlapping, sometimes contradictory laws. In a world with multiple legal jurisdictions, it is difficult to decide how to balance, what Berman calls "individual claims of justice" with "systemic justice." Revisiting Rehnquist's concern in *Herrera,* though in a very different context, Berman asks whether erroneous judgments should be recognized and enforced between states and between different countries. "These are cases," he says, "that involve not necessarily an obvious legal or factual mistake, so much as the inevitable pluralism of values that arise when legal systems interact with other systems that may operate based on different laws and principles of justice."

In the American context, the Full Faith and Credit Clause of the Constitution calls on each state to respect the judgments reached by judicial tribunals and state legislatures in other states even where those judgments and legislative actions seem to be mistaken. The Supreme Court, Berman notes, has ruled that erroneous judgment issued in one state must nonetheless be honored by another to preserve systemic integrity. Turning from the domestic context to the enforcement of foreign judgments, Berman sees a similar conflict between individual and systemic justice.

Applying foreign judgments domestically may cause conflict because of differences in laws and norms and judgments that in the view of one nation may be mistaken. The Second Restatement of Conflict of Laws states that a judgment rendered by a foreign nation will typically be valued the same as a judgment rendered by a fellow state. And, in fact, rarely do domestic courts avoid enforcing foreign rulings as long as the ruling does not violate fundamental values. Courts must, Berman argues, think about more than enforcing the "correct" judgment in a world with widely divergent notions of what is correct.

For Berman, recognizing and honoring legal plurality means that one legal system may have to enforce what it regards as mistaken rulings from other systems. Berman, however, does not argue that all mistaken judgments must be enforced, for at times individual justice must take precedence. But this should not be the default position. "Because people and corporate activities cross borders, because actions in one location can have consequences elsewhere, and because assets are often spread throughout the globe," Berman notes, "we see many situations in which a tribunal in one legal system is asked to recognize and enforce the judgment of a tribunal in a different legal system. In those cases, there may be a legal decision that is correct in one system, but the question is whether that judgment should be recognized and enforced by a different system that sees the decision as mistaken according to its own laws or norms."

In the end Berman presents us with a question: "Should a mistaken judgment be recognized?" He offers a nuanced answer that requires weighing the severity of the mistake and its effects on legal principles against the importance of "comity," legal reciprocity in a pluralistic system of justice. Berman places great importance on such reciprocity and believes that living with mistakes is the price we pay for living in a world with multiple legal jurisdictions.

Taken together, the work collected in *Law's Mistakes* offers an overview of significant arguments/contests about the way in which law handles / should handle mistakes. It examines the fraught, contested, and evolving relationship between law and mistake. It offers templates for thinking about what mistakes can tell us about the aspirations and limits of law and for understanding how our imagining of law is enabled and shaped by its juxtaposition to a condition labeled mistake.

NOTES

We are grateful for the skilled assistance of Haley Cambra, Joshua Ferrer, Laura Merchant, Juan Gabriel Delgado Montes, Keshav Pant, Samuel Rosenblum, and Sarah Smith.

1. See Richard Moran, "The Presence of Malice," *New York Times*, August 2, 2007. In Moran's view, "mistakes are good-faith errors—like taking the wrong exit off the highway, or dialing the wrong telephone number. There is no malice behind them. However, when officers of the court conspire to convict a defendant of first-degree murder and send him to death row, they are doing much more than making an innocent mistake or error. They are breaking the law."

2. This material is taken from Charles J. Ogletree Jr. and Austin Sarat, Introduction to *When Law Fails: Making Sense of Miscarriages of Justice*, ed. Ogletree and Sarat (New York: New York University Press, 2009), 1–2. See also Death Penalty Information Center, "Innocence and the Death Penalty," available at www.deathpenaltyinfo.org.

3. See, for example, "Tulsa Race Riot: A Report by the Oklahoma Commission to Study the Tulsa Race Riot of 1921," February 28, 2001, available at www.ok-history.mus.ok.us /trrc/freport.htm.

4. The Scottsboro Boys were a group of nine African American teenagers who were charged with allegedly raping two white girls on a train in Tennessee in 1931. See Clarence Norris and Sybil Washington, *The Last of the Scottsboro Boys* (New York: G. P. Putnam's Sons, 1979); Dan T. Carter, *Scottsboro: A Tragedy of the American South* (Baton Rouge: Louisiana State University Press, 1979).

5. Emmett Till traveled from Chicago to visit relatives in Mississippi in 1955 and was lynched for allegedly whistling at a white woman. See Stephen J. Whitfield, *A Death in the Delta* (Baltimore: Free Press, 1988); Mamie Till Mobley, *The Death of Innocence* (New York: Random House, 2003); Clenora Hudson-Weems, *Emmett Till: The Sacrificial Lamb of the Civil Rights Movement* (Troy, MI: Bedford Books, 1994).

6. Rolando Cruz was wrongly convicted of the kidnapping, rape, and murder of a nine-year-old girl in Illinois. Cruz was pardoned in 2002 by Governor George Ryan.

7. Leonard Peltier was convicted of the murder of two FBI agents during a shootout in South Dakota in 1975. He is currently serving two consecutive life sentences.

8. Darryl Hunt was wrongly convicted of the 1984 murder of a newspaper reporter, Deborah Sykes. He was later exonerated by DNA evidence.

9. *Herrera v. Collins*, 506 U.S. 290 (1993).

10. Ibid.

11. Ibid.

12. Ibid.

13. The material that follows was prepared for inclusion in this book by Juan Gabriel Delgado Montes (memo to Austin Sarat, July 15, 2014). See also Kevin Clermont and Emily Sherwin, "A Comparative View of Standards of Proof," 50 *American Journal of Comparative Law* (2002): 243–75, at 251.

14. Charles Nesson, "The Evidence or the Event? On Judicial Proof and the Acceptability of Verdicts," 98 *Harvard Law Review* (1985): 1357–92.

15. See Clermont and Sherwin, "A Comparative View of Standards of Proof," 251.

16. Nesson, "The Evidence or the Event," 1385.

17. Ibid., 1386.

18. Ibid.

19. The material that follows was prepared for inclusion in this book by Samuel Rosenblum and Laura Merchant (memo to Austin Sarat, July 27, 2013).

20. For instance, in *State v. Campbell*, 109 S.W. 706 (1908), the Missouri Supreme Court reversed a conviction for rape despite convincing evidence against the defendant because the word "the" was omitted from the charging indictment.

21. The full text of §269 reads: "On a hearing of any appeal, certiorari, writ of error, or motion for a new trial, in any case, civil or criminal, the court shall give judgment after an examination of the entire record before the court, without regard to technical errors, defects, or exceptions which do not affect the substantial rights of the parties." This language is currently found in 28 U.S.C. §2111.

22. See Stephen A. Saltzburg, "The Harm of Harmless Error," 59 *Virginia Law Review* (1973): 988–1032, at 999.

23. *Kotteakos v. United States*, 328 U.S. 750 (1946).

24. Ibid., 764.

25. Ibid., 765.

26. Ibid., 764–65.

27. Saltzburg, "The Harm of Harmless Error," 1012–13, citing *Fahy v. Connecticut*, 375 U.S. 85.

28. *Chapman v. California,* 386 U.S. 18 (1967).
29. *Arizona v. Fulminante,* 499 U.S. 279.
30. Ibid., 287, 303.
31. Ibid., 310.
32. Ibid., 307.
33. See Steven M. Shepard, "The Case against Automatic Reversal of Structural Errors," 117 *Yale Law Journal* (2008): 1180–1214; and James Edward Wicht, "There Is No Such Thing as a Harmless Constitutional Error: Returning to a Rule of Automatic Reversal," 73 *BYU Journal of Public Law* (1997): 73–109.
34. Hoffman F. Fuller, "Mistake and Error in the Law of Contracts," 33 *Emory Law Journal* (1984): 41–92, 43.
35. For a discussion of the *First Restatement,* see Andrew Kull, "Unilateral Mistake: The Baseball Card Case," 70 *Washington University Law Review* (1992): 57–84.
36. Oliver Wendell Holmes, *Common Law* (Cambridge: Harvard University Press, 2009), 279.
37. Ralph A. Newman, "Relief for Mistake in Contracting," 54 *Cornell Law Review* (1968): 232–48, at 232.
38. Ibid., 232, quoting §502 of the original *Restatement of Contracts.*
39. Fuller, "Mistake and Error in the Law of Contracts," 58, discussing *Wood v. Boynton,* 64 Wis. 265, 25 N.W. 42 (1885).
40. Ibid., 74, quoting *Restatement of Contracts* §503 illustration 1 (1932).
41. Newman, "Relief for Mistake in Contracting," 237.
42. Ibid., 232–33.
43. Kull, "Unilateral Mistake," 59.
44. Fuller, "Mistake and Error in the Law of Contracts," 75, quoting from §§293–300 of the *Second Restatement.*
45. See §§293–300 of the *Second Restatement.* For a full discussion of risk, see E. Allan Farnsworth, *Alleviating Mistakes: Reversal and Forgiveness for Flawed Perceptions* (Oxford: Oxford University Press, 2004), 148–63.
46. Farnsworth, *Alleviating Mistakes,* 166.
47. Ibid., 183–98.
48. Edwin R. Keedy, "Ignorance and Mistake in the Criminal Law," 22 *Harvard Law Review* (1908): 75–96, at 76.
49. Ibid., 82.
50. Rollin M. Perkins, "Ignorance and Mistake in Criminal Law," 88 *University of Pennsylvania Law Review and American Law Register* (1939): 35–70, at 55.
51. Farnsworth, *Alleviating Mistakes,* 109–10. Scholars such as H. L. A. Hart, George Fletcher, and Michael S. Moore, as well as the Model Penal Code, have criticized strict liability crimes, because they offer no forgiveness for mistakes.
52. Livingston Hall and Selig J. Seligman, "Mistake of Law and Mens Rea," 8 *University of Chicago Law Review* (1941): 641–83, at 644, quoting Holmes, *Common Law.*
53. Perkins, "Ignorance and Mistake in Criminal Law," 45.
54. See Hall and Seligman, "Mistake of Law and Mens Rea." See also Rebecca Northey, "Expanding the Mistake of Law Doctrine: United States v. Barker," 57 *Boston University Law Review* (1977): 882–905, at 884.
55. The material that follows was prepared for inclusion in this book by Haley Cambra, Joshua Ferrer, Keshav Pant, and Sarah Smith.
56. *Hutto v. Davis,* 454 U.S. 370 (1982).
57. *Harmelin v. Michigan,* 501 U.S. 957 (1991).

1
Mistaken Judgments

STEWART MOTHA

Gauguin famously deserted his family in France to go and paint in Tahiti. Although his abandoned wife and children continued to suffer, this morally objectionable desertion might be retrospectively justified, as it was the beginning of a creative life. The modern condition apparently features a subject whose decisive will and choices drive their destiny. We leave parents, lovers, and communities in search of what lies beyond. Whether we later believe these are mistakes or the conditions of a fulfilling life depends on how it all turns out in the end. Can we approve of these choices, judge them not to be mistaken, if the overall life is affirmed? Such questions are the subject of a book by R. Jay Wallace, *The View from Here: On Affirmation, Attachment, and the Limits of Regret.*[1] It is a work of moral philosophy that asks whether there are any limits to hand-wringing and regret about the past.[2]

How should past actions be judged? Moving this question from the register of moral philosophy to that of juridical and political judgment, this essay examines the problem of doing justice to past mistakes and errors.[3] Are past mistakes and errors merely contingent (to be judged on their contextual conditions and the passions and will of the agent of action), or can they be judged transhistorically through a transcendent measure? In the discussion that follows this question is reframed as a wider problem of what it means to judge in the wake of mistakes that no one would wish to affirm after the event.

Judging past actions and omissions of individuals or states is what the law is regularly called on to do. However, the juridical significance of mistake and error is not straightforward. Other than in the law of contract, law hardly addresses what might be called mistake or error at a deeper jurisprudential level. Something more than mistake/error is usually necessary to attract legal sanction. Transgressing the law in modern positivist legal systems shifts the agent of action beyond the register of mistake and error, right and wrong, and into categories such as responsibility and guilt/innocence. However, these categories cannot expunge deeper moral and ethical questions about the mistakes, errors, and wrongs that lie behind actions that are later translated into crimes that are prosecuted and punished.

Mistaken judgments are decisions and actions we would not retrospectively affirm. We do not have the luxury of acting differently in the first instance. The harm cannot be remedied. Often enough, if an act is successfully prosecuted as a crime, a conviction would result in a punishment being declared. But in some cases that is not the end of the matter. The fact of punishment, or indeed amnesty for political crimes, does not bring the problem of judgment to a close. The ripples of violence can return long after a sentence is declared or amnesty is granted. Judgment is thus a transhistorical problem—an eternal return of the call for responsibility and justice.

What the mistaken judgments discussed in this chapter reveal is not so much the errancy of the person being judged, but the limited imagination brought to bear on the problem of judging itself. A mistaken judgment might be an untimely one—too hasty, without all the facts, knowledge of context, pleadings, or understanding of the standards and norms to be applied. I extend the notion of mistaken judgments to consider *forgetful judgments* as a form of mistake (where forgetting is the condition and interruption of memorial practices in the South African post-apartheid setting). A judgment that fails to understand the relationship between remembering and forgetting—*forgetful judgment*—will be examined through a South African Constitutional Court case about the extent of "forgetting" that follows from amnesty for political crimes (the *McBride* case).[4] *McBride* considered whether it is lawful for a person who has been convicted of murder but granted amnesty to still be called a "murderer" without defamation of character. I will also consider *indefensible judgments* (where the act of judging itself seems indefensible). This is the problem of judgment where children kill. How should children who kill be judged? Are their actions closer to being "mistakes" rather than crimes for which they are responsible? In *feminist judgments* we encounter judging as the "work" of critique. Here the critical encounter with a past judicial decision seeks to address gender bias, but risks subordinating the act of judgment to what may have an actual impact on the "real world" of judging. How does such instrumentality affect the task of critical judgment? What is the relationship between the imagination and the work of judging? Some would deny that such a relationship even exists. It is commonplace for judges who believe that they "simply apply the law"—to treat judgment as a "technique" of arranging rules in a hierarchical relationship to facts and circumstances. If legal judgment is brought under scholarly and critical scrutiny in order to point out and correct erroneous, biased, gendered formulations of the law, what should be the parameters of that exercise of judgment-as-critique? What is perceived to be the "real" work of judging, and how should critical legal scholarship engage with the practice of judgment? Each of these forms of judgment either address a mistake by an individual agent or by the judicial process itself. The discussion explores the encounter between judging and doing justice to past mistakes.

What Is a Mistake?

We should begin by examining the difference, if any, between "mistake" and "error." Among the acerbic debates around deconstruction in literary studies and philosophy in the early 1980s was an exchange between Stanley Corngold, professor of German and comparative literature at Princeton, and Paul de Man, professor of humanities at Yale.[5] In an essay published in Critical Inquiry, Corngold asserted that there is a distinction between "mistake" and "error," but that the force of this polarity is lost in de Man's inattention to the difference. De Man, replying in a letter published alongside Corngold's essay, claims that he was not aware of such a distinction between mistake and error, and that in any case such a polarity could not be a stable binary. For Corngold,

> [e]rror is not *mistake*. The concept of the mistake is usable, perhaps, within the restricted teleology of pragmatic acts or within the quasi-rigorous language of scientific description. Mistakes (or what de Man sometimes calls "mere error") are without true value: trivial, in principle corrigible according to a norm already known. But the skew of error implies a truth.[6]

Corngold concludes that in de Man the usefulness of the concept of error "disappears utterly."[7] De Man replied, acknowledging his inattention to the difference between mistake and error, but refusing to accept the existence of such a binary:

> I am grateful to Stanley Corngold for having pointed out a polarity (error/mistake) that I have not explicitly thematized in these terms. If "mistake" is random and contingent (of the order of "can" or "may") and "error" is systemic and compulsive (of the order of "must"), then I have stated, in a variety

> of terminologies, the impossibility of ever coming to rest on one or the other side of this distinction.[8]

This exchange between Corngold and de Man is brought to bear on wider political concerns in a recent essay by Marc Redfield.[9] Corngold had asserted that mistake is accidental and contingent, whereas error suggests the realm of judgment. Error conforms or deviates from a norm, and relates to some order of truth. However, as Redfield points out, error, as its root in the Latin *errare* indicates, could mean both to "wander freely" and "to wander from the right path."[10] Error could then be said to "contain mistake within it."[11]

As Redfield has put it, de Man's troubling of the difference between mistake and error is relevant to questions of sovereignty and the political because they reveal how "unstable the difference between contingency and compulsion, or randomness and systematicity" can be.[12] Acts of political will and violence, or exercises of sovereign force and power, might on the one hand be judged as random or contingent contesting forces at a particular point in time. However, judging acts of violence or sovereign power may also throw open the "systematicity"—the structures of law and the state that compel violence and counterviolence.

In the first form of judgment we turn to below—what I term "forgetful judgment"—the relationship between systematicity and violence is posed very much as Redfield has described it. That is, we encounter a case about an act of violence acknowledged to be a (contingent) mistake by the perpetrator, but one performed in the process of undoing a systemic form of state violence (a systematicity that compels counterviolence). The system was the violent apartheid state. The mistaken judgment concerned, on the one hand, the counterviolence deployed to overthrow apartheid, and on the other, how that counterviolence would in turn be judged after the passage of time. In the process of violence and counterviolence, many innocent people lost their lives or were maimed, injured, or otherwise violated. Was this "collateral" violence a mistake? And how should such actions be judged retrospectively?

Forgetful Judgment

In the 1980s, Robert McBride was a member of Umkhonto we Sizwe ("Spear of the Nation"), the armed wing of the African National Congress (ANC). On 14 June 1986, McBride and other operatives carried out a car-bomb attack on Magoo's Bar and Why Not Restaurant located on the beach front in Durban, South Africa. The attack killed three young women and injured sixty-nine others. They were all civilians. The attack was a departure from the ANC strategy of attacking inanimate targets such as strategic infrastructure, or security and military facilities. McBride was convicted of murder and sentenced to death for his part in these attacks. In 1988 he lost an appeal against his death sentence. He later received a reprieve and was released from prison in 1992.

As South Africa moved beyond the era of formal apartheid, it confronted the problem of state violence and counterviolence. Decades of state-sponsored brutality and the violent resistance to apartheid had left people traumatized. The polity nonetheless sought a future beyond violence and retribution. The apartheid state, the ANC, and other combatants negotiated a compromise. It was a pact for peace that remains contested to this day. Rather than vengeance and retributive justice, South Africa attempted to become "reconciled" to its past—the verb more aptly describing what is at stake in "reconciliation."

In exchange for information about the "truth" of violent events, perpetrators would be granted amnesty as long as the violence was shown to be politically motivated. The Promotion of National Unity and Reconciliation Act of 1995 was a central instrument of that process. Section 20(10) of that Act provided that once a person has been granted amnesty for an offense committed with a political objective, the conviction would be deemed not to have taken place:

> Where any person has been convicted of any offence constituted by an act or omission associated with a political objective in respect of which amnesty has been granted in terms of this Act, any entry or record of the conviction shall be deemed to be expunged from all official documents or records and the conviction shall for all purposes, including the application of any Act of Parliament or any other law, be deemed not to have taken place.[13]

McBride applied for amnesty in 1997 and was granted it in April 2001. In 2003 he became a candidate for head of metro police in Ekurhleni, one of South Africa's largest municipalities.

South Africa has had to confront what many "transitional" societies face—the problem of judging past acts of violence that are both contingent to the conflict and conditions of the past, as well as foundational of the present and future. State violence and the counterviolence that undoes it condition the present and future. In what register, and from what perspective, will past acts, omissions, mistakes, or errors be judged in the present and future?

The Citizen newspaper opposed McBride's appointment as head of police. In September and October 2003 it published articles contending that McBride was unsuitable for appointment because he was a criminal and murderer, and as he had in 1998 been arrested on suspicion of gun-running. An editorial of the newspaper read as follows:

> Robert McBride's candidacy for the post of Ekurhuleni Metro Police Chief is indicative of the ANC's attitude to crime. They can't be serious. He is blatantly unsuited, unless his backers support the dubious philosophy: set a criminal to catch a criminal. Make no mistake, that's what he is. The cold-blooded multiple murders which he committed in the Magoo's Bar bombing put him firmly in that category. Never mind his dubious flirtation with alleged gun-dealers in Mozambique. Those who recommended him should have their heads read. McBride is not qualified for the job. If he is appointed, it will be a slap in the face for all those crime-battered folk on the East Rand who look to the government for protection.[14]

Following these publications, McBride sued for defamation. What is at stake in characterizing McBride as a murderer and criminal? The editorial is explicit about whose credibility is being judged—it is the competence of the ANC government. It is not only McBride and his suitability for chief of police but also the competence of the rulers of the newly democratic South Africa that is being contested. Judging McBride's suitability also served as a proxy for judging the new black-majority government.

President Mbeki weighed into the controversy. On 17 October 2003 he wrote to point out the nature of McBride's actions as a form of revolutionary counterviolence:

> I do not know whether Mr McBride was ever or is interested to be Chief of Ekurhuleni Metropolitan Police. I do not know whether he has the competence to serve in this capacity. What I know is that it would be fundamentally wrong that he is denied the possibility to be appointed to any position, simply because of what he did during our struggle for liberation, for which he apologised and for which he was granted amnesty.[15]

Once McBride was appointed as police chief, *The Citizen* newspaper repeated its views in a manner that McBride claimed was defamatory and injured his reputation:

> *We believe we performed a civic duty on September 10 by alerting readers to the possibility that Robert McBride could be named Ekurhuleni's Metro Police chief. We said he was not the right person for the job. We maintain that view, as do a great many readers.* But obviously a decision had already been taken. President Mbeki even devoted one of his lengthy Internet messages to defending McBride and attacking The Citizen. *The bomber has support in high places,*

> *but that doesn't detract from the evil of his multiple murders, or make him a suitable policeman.* His appointment speaks volumes about the ANC's attitude to crime. God help Ekurhuleni. (Portions alleged to be defamatory in italics.)[16]

The law of defamation allows for the defense of fair comment. Was it a fair comment to call McBride a "criminal" and a "murderer" when the Reconciliation Act had specified that the grant of amnesty, at least in the South African setting, would see convictions "expunged for all purposes" and the "conviction would be deemed not to have taken place"? Is calling McBride a murderer true or false? Is it a claim of fact or a (fair) opinion or comment? Much more is at stake in these questions than whether to adopt a literalist reading of a statute.

Judging the concomitants of amnesty is in more than one sense a problem of *forgetful judgment.* Amnesty is a juridical form of state-sanctioned forgetting. In *McBride* the Constitutional Court of South Africa faced the problem of judging the extent of this forgetfulness. While no one would reasonably suggest that amnesty wipes the slate clean, there is a need for a reflective treatment of how the process of amnesty was socially and politically constitutive in South Africa. That is, amnesty was part of a package of transitional measures that moved South African society from an impasse of violence and counterviolence.

How are we to judge the political status of an act of violence? Does amnesty alter the status and character of the act of killing, or the perpetrator who committed it? For Justice Cameron, who wrote the leading judgment in the *McBride* case, the truth is a "compilation" of "collective memory."[17] The interpretation of the statute urged by McBride hampers this collective compilation of the "truth" of the past. If the family of the victims and wider society are unable to characterize McBride as a "murderer," then the reconciliation process, the truth of events gathered through the amnesty process, freedom of expression, the dignity of the bereaved, and the integrity of their memory would be undermined.[18] But what are the limits and dangers of a truth that is validated on the basis that it is "collective memory"? And in this case, it is a collective memory that now comes to be sanctioned by the force of law.

According to the Khulumani Support Group, a victims' advocacy organization that intervened as amicus curiae in the defamation proceedings, the ability of victims and others to call McBride a "murderer" is central to the existence of "victims" and "perpetrators," and to the fact that a "crime" took place:

> Khulumani has joined this case because the implication, if McBride wins, is to nullify the struggle of thousands of Khulumani's members in telling the truth about their experiences during apartheid. It would mean that no one who received amnesty may be called a "murderer" or a "torturer." Hence, members of Khulumani would no longer either be "victims" of crimes that no longer "exist"—just as the perpetrators would no longer be identified as "perpetrators."
>
> This is silly, insulting and false. A killer is a killer, and the crime remains the crime. The fact that a perpetrator received amnesty cannot deny the very fact of the act. Amnesty simply means that the person's conviction is removed, and he or she is no longer guilty in terms of the law. It cannot mean that the act never happened and that therefore the person is no longer a killer.[19]

It is true that amnesty does not result in the undoing of the act of killing, or the pain, injury, suffering, and death that it has caused. The question, however, is whether the fact of suffering and injury, including the status of "victim," are heterogeneous to the crime and its moral and juridical status. McBride's assertion that he should not be called a "murderer" is not dependent on denying that the car bomb he set off caused death, injury, and suffering. No one can deny that the crime happened, that a finding of guilt was made, a conviction registered, or that victims of that crime exist. What are the conditions of victimhood? It would be too comforting to think that victimhood is a condition that has a single author.[20]

For the court, McBride was convicted for committing the crime of murder. But curiously, the meaning of "murder" does not depend, on the court's view, on a conviction. "Murderer" is an appellation of ordinary language that attaches to particular facts—although it also carries a technical meaning in law. Justice Cemeron resorted to ordinary language to conclude that McBride engaged in the unlawful intentional killing of another. The court was keen to hold on to the reach and potency of amnesty—that it is not only convicted killers, but the secret operatives of the "deep state" that were lured to give information about unlawful killings. Convicted killers could not be given a benefit that was not afforded to those who were not convicted of a crime.

The implications of section 20(10) of the Reconciliation Act had already been addressed by the Constitutional Court in *Du Toit v. Minister for Safety and Security*.[21] In that case a police officer who had received amnesty for a conviction asserted that he should be exempt from another statutory provision that would deem him to be discharged from the police service if convicted of a crime. The court held that amnesty "does not obliterate all the direct legal consequences of conduct in respect of which amnesty is granted."[22] Judgments in the *Du Toit* and *McBride* cases assert that there is no stable and uniform meaning to "amnesty."

Justice Cameron in *McBride* surrenders his capacity to determine the intrinsic meaning of amnesty. His judgment emphasized the instrumental role of amnesty in the South African setting. Amnesty was granted to perpetrators of violence so as to extract the truth that victims and their families would need in order to engage in "national transition and reconciliation."[23] Amnesty becomes the lure or enticement for truth-telling:

> The two decisions [*AZAPO*, and *Du Toit*] set up signposts to the main questions before us. Each emphasizes the instrumental role of amnesty—it was not an end in itself, but a means to the end of national transition and reconciliation. They establish that truth-telling, as a means to these ends—and hence the offer of amnesty—lay at the base of the moral and operational structure of the TRC. They further establish that amnesty has no necessary meaning or intrinsic effect: its operation depends on history, context, and statutory wording."[24]

"Truth" is taken to be the "fact" of McBride's conviction. If he committed acts of violence that resulted in a conviction of murder—that is the fact that constitutes the "truth." This is the "true statement" (McBride is a "murderer") that Cameron J sets out to uphold: "In addressing the legal consequences of conviction only, section 20(10) does not presume to have linguistic effect, or to govern the discourse that arises from the conviction."[25]

But acts of violence that result in a conviction of murder are not simply historical facts with a stable linguistic meaning. There is indeed a wider discourse regarding a conviction for murder than what is literally stated in the statute on amnesty. That wider discourse must surely open the problem of judging past events as counterviolence and not simply as "murder." Amnesty is a form of state-sanctioned forgetting. While Cameron concedes that the operation of amnesty depends on history and context—he *forgets* that it was more than the instrumental nature of the statute that he was called on to interpret as a judge in this case. He was also judging the process of violence and counterviolence; he was judging the systematicity of the past, and the conditions of the present.

Justice Cameron summarized the reasons for not accepting McBride's arguments thus:

> There are at least four reasons why Mr McBride's argument cannot prevail. First, it depends on a literal and a contextual approach, which runs counter to the decision in *Du Toit v Minister for Safety and Security* [2010] 2 LRC 623.

> Secondly, it is inimical to truth-telling, which was one of the moral bases of the transition from the injustice of apartheid to democracy and constitutionalism. It is hardly conceivable that a statute premised on the necessity of truth-telling in pursuit of national unity and reconciliation should operate so as to render the truth false. Thirdly, the interpretation fails to give weight to the right of freedom of expression. Fourthly, it overreaches the benefits Mr McBride earned when he sought and was granted amnesty: it would disturb the delicate interplay of benefit and disadvantage the statute reflects, thereby also creating an untenable anomaly in that only those convicted, but not those never charged, would gain immunity from truthful description of their deeds.[26]

The court's decision is reduced to judging the status of amnesty in the present, rather than recognizing that this is where history-as-instrumentality fails. At this moment the past "comes together in a flash" in the present in the sense that Walter Benjamin characterized it.[27] One cannot judge the perniciousness of the assertions leveled at McBride today, and the "fairness" of characterizations of him as "criminal" and "murderer," without revisiting the context in which the acts of violence were committed.

Is the act of violence for which McBride had been tried, convicted, and granted amnesty aptly characterized as a mistake? If it was a mistake, there was still the additional need to place that mistake within the wider "systematicity" of apartheid in which it arose. The Constitutional Court did none of this. McBride had expressed regret for his actions in relation to the killing and injury of civilians. He was granted amnesty by the TRC. What was at stake in the defamation proceedings was how the law would judge an act of counterviolence—albeit one for which the perpetrator had expressed regret.[28] While McBride was not being retried for the crime in this instance, determining the consequences of amnesty needed to consider the nature of a political mistake in the context of the state-system that was being challenged at the time. And the court needed to be cognizant of the fact that, at least in part, the birthing of the post-apartheid state was facilitated by the amnesty process and the political violence that preceded it.

The culpability of perpetrators of criminal acts is not ordinarily seen as either a mistake or an error. The errancy of the accused may well follow from a moral mistake, miscalculation, or disregard for the harm done to another's person or property. And yet, the law is usually concerned only with establishing the "truth" of certain "facts"—that the accused intentionally committed the act, and that there were no mitigating circumstances that would attenuate or set aside their responsibility. Once responsibility is established, a punishment usually follows. This is a banal and thoughtless approach to judging.

What other elements should the court have considered? McBride was responding to stories of police brutality and heightened repression when he set out to detonate the car bomb.[29] He was an MK operative, and was involved in selecting targets and carrying out attacks: "If they want war, I am going to give them war. That's what was going through my mind."[30] He had initially selected a large glass-fronted building as a high-profile target. Matthew Lecordier, his accomplice in the attack, gave evidence as a state witness against McBride. Lecordier's response when McBride informed him of the initial target was that he would be "wasting 50 kg's of explosives" there, and suggested that McBride take the bomb to the Marine Parade "because the people want White destruction."[31] McBride then argued with Lecordier, stating that it was not the policy of the ANC to attack white people as such. But in the end he succumbed, and the bomb was placed at a more populous location, resulting in the deaths and injuries. The Constitutional Court did not revisit this moment of "mistaken judgment" on McBride's part. It is an omission that cements the court's forgetful judgment.

The trial court and Supreme Court of Appeal considered the extenuating circumstances surrounding the bombing in the original trial and appeal proceedings when McBride was sentenced to death (a conviction from which he later received a reprieve). McBride was born in 1963, and in accordance with the race classification laws of the time was classified as "Coloured." His father, Derrick McBride, was also classified as "Coloured," and had become politically active and was present at the meeting that produced the Freedom Charter of 1955. This political radicalism, and activism against a history of marginalization, was passed onto his son. He "encouraged his son to read the political and history books which were available in their home and he imparted to his son his own political ethos, including his hatred of White people." He told his son that "he (had) never come across a White man in history who (had) done anything honest."[32] McBride had grown up in a poor "Coloured" ghetto created by the Group Areas Act. He had attempted to "try for White," attending a white university, playing for a white rugby club, and having a fair-haired "white-looking" girlfriend. These efforts were never successful, and McBride regularly received racist taunts.

When the judges confirming the death penalty considered whether there were any extenuating circumstances, their inquiry turned on whether there were circumstances that would morally rather than legally mitigate the crime.[33] Corbett JA cited the trial judges' reasoning for the finding of no extenuating circumstances:

> We live in a country in which unhappily many of the normal incidents of freedom have been inhibited or removed by legislation in which long years of White domination have blurred the fine edges of moral judgment. The real dilemma that confronts this bench is derived from the simple proposition that according to any morally acceptable code in any civilised country you do not punish persons presumed to be innocent for the sins of those who offend you. We do not know what were the political affiliations of Angel ique Pattenden, Marchelle Gerrard or Emily van der Linde. To kill them for what you believe to be the sins of a government is to offend as surely against the primary moral code as those you believe to have offended, and to punish them for a skin presumed to be White is as racist as the very propositions that Accused no 1 opposes. In reaching this conclusion we, the majority, take into account all the aspects of the Accused's personal history that have been placed before us. The influence of his father which he rejected and then re-embraced, the inferior educational and other institutional facilities, the petty indignities inflicted on him by Whites, the inadequacy of any constructive protest machinery and then by the national emergency with its effect on the friends of Accused no 1 and the family of Accused no 2, and finally the persuasions of Lecordier. We have given all these factors weight. They explain that we must ask ourselves whether they give to the Accused's actions a sufficient modicum of excuse. The act, the explosion of an enormous bomb in the environment where it could cause massive injury to a large number of people is a gross, callous and atrocious act. The victims, I emphasise, were not faceless representatives of an oppressing authority. They were real people with families and a right to have their own vision of the future.[34]

The Supreme Court of Appeal went onto confirm the death penalty. As we observed above, McBride later received a reprieve and amnesty for political crimes.

When considering the extent of amnesty and whether McBride could lawfully be called a "murderer," Justice Cameron made no reference to the facts and circumstances considered in the appeal from the death penalty. What bearing might they have had? Would the context have given a better sense of the car bombing as a form of counterviolence, albeit one that could be judged to be mistaken? What scope should there be to recognize the final selection of target as a horrible miscalculation or an error of judgment? These are questions opened by the fact of being granted amnesty for a political crime. They were not presented as justiciable in the defamation proceedings. But they are precisely the questions that haunt the South African polity. Whatever is said of McBride's actions, the judgment of the Constitutional Court, when it came to judge retrospectively whether McBride can lawfully be called a murderer, placed too much emphasis on the instrumental reasons for being granted amnesty. More than the concomitants of amnesty were at stake in this case. The court needed to examine how a mistake should be judged in the context of the systematicity of apartheid and the counterviolence deployed to tear down that state. That counterviolence constituted post-apartheid South Africa. The Constitutional Court has conveniently forgotten that.

Indefensible Judgment

Some mistakes have no defense. This indefensibility is both a feature of the contingency of such acts, and the limits of the imagination when it comes to judging them. What is an indefensible mistake and how is it to be judged?

The English poet Blake Morrison wrote a remarkable book recounting his firsthand experience of attending the trial of Robert Thompson and Jon Venables (T & V)—two ten-year-old boys who, in February 1993, kidnapped, tortured, and killed two-year-old James Bulger in Liverpool, England.[35] Bulger's body was then left on railway tracks, where it was further mutilated. T & V were tried and found guilty of murder in an adult court. While the trial process addressed the usual questions that establish the "facts" that led to the "truth," such as "who, how, where, and when," Morrison attended the legal proceedings, and in a brave and moving account of his own life as a child and parent, asked "why."

For Morrison, trying to answer "why" seemed to require some leap of empathy, or speculation: "from the churningly gruesome facts of the case into more general thoughts of what it means to be a child—and a parent." For that inquiry, "all roads seemed to lead inward, to the imagination."[36] Without the capacity of the imagination to cast the "facts" as components of an overall narrative of acts or omissions undertaken by "responsible" agents, a trial would be impossible. And, arguably, it was a lack of imagination on the part of the authorities and a wider society that created the spectacle of two children being tried in an adult court for a crime haunted by the fact that many adults had been in contact with these children on that terrible day as they marched James Bulger to his death. Judgment and imagination ought to be inseparable but are all too often conveniently held apart.

At the heart of Morrison's book is the problem of what it means to judge—especially to pass judgment on children. The cruelty of children, their fantasies, the fables by which we (all children once) greet and understand the world are invoked to understand what it would mean to judge the killers of two-year-old James Bulger. The experts who gave evidence were simply asked to confirm whether T & V were capable of telling right from wrong.[37] There was no assistance to T & V from *doli incapax*—the ancient exculpation whereby one is deemed not to possess sufficient discretion to have criminal intention. Instead, it was decided that T & V had acted with adult consciousness.[38]

A sexual motive had been suggested in the interrogation of T & V—they had been questioned about why they undressed James Bulger; whether they touched his genitals, and whether batteries had been inserted into his anus. There was no conclusive evidence about this, but much speculation about a sexual motive in the undressing and torture of the toddler.

Throughout the book Morrison keeps returning us to his own family life and childhood. How much responsibility should we take for the cruelties we commit as children? Morrison recounts the sexual explorations of children in games like "Doctors and Nurses." The touching, poking, and prodding are undecidably conscious and innocent.[39] These are ways of exploring our desires. It is also the beginning of inflicting our desires on others.

How are we to judge what children or adolescents do to each other? Morrison returns to his own actions as a child and adolescent.[40] The year is 1967 and he is at the party of fourteen-year-old Lucy Kerrigan. Her parents are out for the night, and a group of girls and boys start those common social interactions that happen in the absence of parental supervision. They are drinking, getting drunk. Lucy kisses a boy while he nonchalantly discusses football with his mates. They kiss some more and move to the broom cupboard under the stairs. Before long the first boy is out and a second enters. Then a third—it's Morrison himself:

> Her blouse is open and I feel her breasts and slip my hands under her skirt. She isn't wearing knickers or tights: they must be what I am standing on. She pushes her tongue deeper into me as I push my hand deeper into her. Is the wetness her own desire or the sperm of Mick Turner and Pat Connolly? I know what I am supposed to do next, but it's only between her and me and the stairs. She'll regret it. I'll regret it.[41]

A fourth, fifth, sixth, and seventh boy follow. Is this the "gang rape" of a minor? It is asserted that she was not forced, but she was drunk. Morrison did not have intercourse with her, but others did, and rather than intervene to prevent it, he joined in. Is he morally or legally guilty? As he reflects on these events during the trial of T & V, Morrison imagines himself being cross-examined about his own childhood cruelties. There is, as with T & V, "no defense." The verdict, Guilty.

What kind of judgment is involved in determining that there is no defense? And what bearing does the question of "why" have on this judgment? The judge in T & V's trial characterized their actions as "unparalleled evil."[42] Terry Eagleton begins his book *On Evil* with a discussion of the T & V case, and comments on how calling what happened "evil," as the trial judge and other commentators did, makes the event unintelligible.[43] We can of course recall another famous discussion of the "banality of evil" and the judgment that Hannah Arendt rendered in the postscript of *Eichmann in Jerusalem*.[44] Arendt issued the death penalty in that imaginary judgment, perceptively uniting the "as if" and the limits of imaginary judgment.

Morrison's book is perspicaciously titled *As If.* As we will shortly see, the relationship between the law and the "as if" is a long one. The "as if" and judging is even more intimately connected. As Morrison puts it:

> *As if.* The trope used to be enlarging, wondrous, a means of seeing beyond our noses, an escape from the prison house of fact. *As if:* it was the sound the swing made as it scythed us upward through the air, the whisper of dreams and lovely promises. Much virtue in *as if.* Now, in kids' mouths, it means the opposite. Earthbound skepticism and diminution: tell me about it, dream on, get real. Not hope but the extinction of hope. *As if:* not a candle to light us to bed, but a chopper to chop off our heads.[45]

Morrison's treatment of the T & V case deftly weaves these two strands of the "as if." The hunt for a "socially determined cause" for the killers' depravity is not enough. Carefully lined up facts tell us nothing. The boys' mistake (what is achieved by calling it that?) points to a deeper errancy in law—the loss of the ability to imagine beyond "the prison house of fact." The T & V case manifests a low point in the role of the imagination in judging. But what is the relationship between the "as if" and the law?

We can trace the "as if" back to Kant's *Critique of Pure Reason*.[46] Here the "as if" designates the consciously false, illusory knowledge, or legal fiction. Kant's concern was the lawless origins of law, and so he urged members of a civil state to proceed "as if" the law was legitimately grounded on reason.[47] Hans Kelsen later took up this motif when he proposed the *Grundnorm* by way of a regressive attribution of the legal order to a higher norm.[48] Kelsen was following in the wake of neo-Kantians of the nineteenth century such as Hans Vaihinger.[49] In the twentieth century, literary theorists like Frank Kermode and poststructural philosophers like Jacques Derrida deployed the "as if" in critical engagements with literary texts and sovereign events.[50]

How is the "as if" central to sociolegal and critical legal approaches to judgment? The "as if" plays a central role in projects as varied as writing feminist judgments (Rosemary Hunter et al.), challenging the binary between nature and the social (Bruno Latour), elaborating the agency of things (Jane Bennett), or championing the primacy of rhetoric and aesthetics for justice (Marianne Constable and Linda Meyer). However, the "as if" is not an empty signifier, or benign heuristic device. From the outset the "as if" was deployed as law's facade, masking law's violence and originary lack. However, as Kant also taught us, a truly responsive judgment is not possible without a sense of awe and wonder—of being arrested by the sublime which is often experienced through aesthetic forms. The "as if" is central to the task of judgment, but it is not benign. It is useful to differentiate between approaches to the imaginary and judgment that are attentive to the demands of justice, and ones that collude with the governmental exigencies of the state. In what follows I examine this difference by comparing social scientific approaches to judging with ones informed by the humanities.

Judging with and against the Real and Apparent Worlds

Law's mistakes have variously been attributed to structural social causes. There are many instantiations of how social power or domination have been seen as the underlying social cause or structure of legal disputes and their resolution. It would be useful at this point to examine an example of how sociolegal scholars engage the underlying gendered determination of law. How does justice as a problem of judgment get displaced in the social scientific approach to law?

The rise of social scientific approaches to law have marginalized questions of justice in the name of the "impact" of research, "enterprise value," or "social relevance." Critical projects and progressive politics are not immune from social scientification—as with the "feminist judgments" project I discuss here.[51] While I fault the feminist judgments project for being too narrow in addressing the problem of justice, the more expansive critical approaches are not without shortcomings. We cannot leave judgment—and *valuing,* which is inherent to it—as open, infinite, and potentially (in)calculable. The problem of judgment is one of sense as "value." I want to suggest that the illusory (fiction) is a source of "sense"—a response to the crisis of "value" in this time between myth and nihilism.[52]

Marianne Constable's work interrogates how different conceptions of the social haunt various approaches to the study of law. According to Constable, a critical legal approach need not, must not, seek some *social* cause outside the phenomenon being studied.[53] That is the affliction of the sociology of law for which law itself is social, and law's maladies are to be explained by this or that social relation. For Constable, law, like philosophy and language, reveals worlds. But being-in-the-world poses the problem of being-with, being-in-common—another way of posing the problem of justice at the heart of plural existence. There is then an unavowable community (Blanchot)[54]—but this is a sociality that cannot be made at one with justice lest it repeat all the totalitarian disasters where society and justice were written with the same sign.

In Rosemary Hunter, Clare McGlynn, and Erika Rackley, eds., *Feminist Judgments,* a group of feminist legal scholars were gathered to write counterfactual feminist judgments in landmark legal cases.[55] Departing from what the convenors/editors of the project call "academic critiques," workshops were held in which participants engaged in " 'real world' exercises of judgment-writing," subject, they say, to the "various constraints that bind appellate judges, including fidelity to the judicial oath, respect for existing legal principles, and consciousness of the impact of decisions on the parties and the broader community."[56] The project was intended to "inaugurate a new form of critical legal scholarship"[57]—presumably one that has more "impact" than what the editors term "academic critique." Input was drawn from "invited judges, lawyers and activists who provided practical information, expert comments and 'reality checks' on the draft judgments, as well as insights into the issues involved in some of the cases and the potential value of the feminist judgments from an advocacy perspective."[58] As familiar accounts by critical legal studies claim, judges, especially at appellate level, "make" rather than "find" the law.[59] This informs the feminist judgments project, which sees in this interpretative openness the opportunity for a feminist consciousness or philosophy to "legitimately come into play."[60] The project seeks to develop the practice of writing judgments as a form of critical scholarship, a "new method of legal critique."[61] While this new critique is proposed as a theoretical and methodological opening, its limits are immediately asserted.

The feminist judgments project treats judging as a "constrained and bounded genre,"[62] beholden to the apparently undemocratic and unaccountable character of appellate courts. The ideal or Nietzschean "real" world has indeed been abolished. A priority was to make the judgments "as plausible as possible to potentially skeptical lawyers and judges"[63]—that is, for the feminist judgments to mirror the actual world, for critique and "reality" to become one. And so, here, as with Nietzsche's sixth stage in his account of the history of metaphysics in *Twilight of the Idols*—the difference between the ideal and the actual has been abolished, but we are left with a new nihilism of abolishing the true/just in the name of reality (the perceived actuality of judging).[64] This "critical" venture involved, to quote Hunter et al., taking "judgment writing largely as a given" and "not rethinking it as a practice in any significant way" (6). We are left, then, with a critical approach to judging that is inattentive to justice from beyond, or indeed from this world (the refusal to attend to the instance, event, or practice of judgment).

The *Begum* case was one of around twenty-three judgments rewritten by a feminist judge in the project. In *R (Begum) v. Headteacher and Governors of Denbigh High School,* the dispute was between Shabina Begum, a minor of nearly fourteen years when the dispute began, and Denbigh High School in Luton.[65] The school prevented Shabina Begum from wearing the *jilbab* when she attended, but denied that it had excluded her from the school. She was, according to the school, asked to conform to a "uniform policy" (wear the *shalwar kameeze* and/or other forms of dress including a *hijab*), which had been drawn up, the school claimed, in a manner sensitive to Muslim girls and their religious beliefs, and after wide consultation. Shabina Begum argued that she had been excluded, and had thus been denied her Art. 9 right and freedom to manifest her religious belief. She also contended that she had been denied her right to education, but this was not pursued later on appeal. Once Art. 9 is engaged, and not all judges agreed that it was, the question was whether the interference was authorized by law, and justified as necessary in a democratic society. The majority of the House of Lords concluded that there had been no interference with the right guaranteed in Art. 9 to manifest the practices and observances of Shabina Begum's religious beliefs. She could have gone to another school nearby which permitted her to wear the *jilbab,* they reasoned. She was regarded as "contracting out" of her Art. 9 right. Lord Nicholls and Baroness Hale, in the minority on this point, stated that there was an interference with Begum's Art. 9 rights but argued that the interference was justified under Art. 9(2).

In the process of rewriting the *Begum* decision as a feminist judgment, this parodic performance of fictional judging, this "as if," Maleiha Malik writes:

> the interference [with Art. 9 rights] is justified not because Shabina Begum's dress is an aspect of "extremist" Islam or because the majority of Muslim school girls are happy with the uniform, but because the UK Parliament is pursuing the permissible purpose of "pluralism" by allowing decisions about religious accommodation to be made at a local level. In this case, the school has provided clear evidence that making accommodation to Shabina Begum's convictions with regard to religious dress would lead to adverse consequences for its effectiveness and efficiency.[66]

While Malik disagreed with the majority view in the actual case that Shabina Begum had effectively contracted out of her right by not going to another school, she agreed with the outcome of exclusion on the grounds that it is a permissible infringement under Art. 9(2) of the European Convention of Human Rights. The local experts and officials were left to determine the extent of what is permissible in a plural society. Social cohesion, the rule of experts, and the critic's valuation of a particular pluralism have determined the character of the autonomy, freedom, and equality experienced by Shabina Begum.

What kind of "work" of judging is involved here? If "law" is also to be regarded as a discipline of the humanities, what has this project said about justice for Shabina Begum? Is the fictional judgment-as-parody of the feminist judge a constative or performative? How is law to be united with critique in this highly circumscribed performance of judgment? At the heart of the feminist judgments project was a laudable attempt to contest the underlying gendered social determinants of judging. But is the social so readily accessible and "correctible"? And what is the relationship between something called the "social" (apparently self-evident and present to the critic) and the practice of judgment?

Bruno Latour offers an approach that displaces the very possibility of external social "causes" of legal practices and decisions. Latour seeks the dynamism of (social) worlds. His approach is attentive to dynamic flows and connections that are not captured by the usual categories of modernity such as human, consciousness, or subjectivity. The event of judgment in his *The Making of Law* is a forensic undoing of the legal decision as a singular event.[67] Driven by the conviction that "we have never been modern," he looks not at what we are but how we are becoming. Latour does not seek a theory of being, but a method for understanding the contingency of networks where all things—human, animal, bacteria, paperclips, files, or architectural columns (all actants)—have agency. He is nonetheless attentive to justice. For law to speak justly, he tells us, it must first hesitate. This quivering law discloses the madness of the deconstructable decision Derrida spoke about. However, in studying the assemblage of contingent relations, what is one to make of that social, national, civilizational, sovereign sensibility that law often deploys as the ground of its "pragmatic compromise" called judgment? The social haunts law here in the sense that it matters little "how" an assemblage of *actants* become a legal decision if the "reasonableness" of that decision or its justice is posed and contested in social and political terms. How might the study of networks of contingent beings be drawn on to address a question of social and political justice? Is "social justice" the oxymoronic phrase here?

Jane Bennett's work offers a Latourian possibility of judging. In her essay "The Solar Judgment of Walt Whitman" she treats judgment as an act of discriminatory selection, one that is akin to the Zarathustrian quest to "learn how to suspend the will to judge and punish and create the alternative pleasures of art, science, philosophy."[68] Bennett is inspired by Whitman and Bergson, and especially the lines from the former's 1855 Preface to *The Leaves of Grass,* in which the poet is attributed the quality of being able to "*judge not as the judge judges but as the sun falling around a helpless thing.*" Other poems by Whitman such as "By Blue Ontario's Shore" repeat this quality of the poet to judge:

Whitman celebrates the poet who:

> . . . is no arguer, he is judgment, (Nature accepts him absolutely,)
> He judges not as the judge judges but as the sun falling round a helpless thing.
> As he sees the farthest he has the most faith,
> His thoughts are the hymns of the praise of things,
> . . .
> He sees eternity in men and women, he does not see men and women as dreams or dots. (Section 10, 137–50)[69]

So judging not as the judge judges involves being as "generous as the sun, as accepting of the things he encounters as Nature is of him"—and "Nature accepts him Absolutely."[70] As Bennett goes onto explain:

> The poet receives without prejudice all types of bodies, "whoever you are!": enslaved man at auction; farmer's wife; workman; Jew; son or daughter of China, Slavic empire, Damascus, Rome, Naples, Persia, or Greece; prisoner; helpless infant or old person; tires of carts, boot-soles, horses, snow-sleighs,

> rous'd mobs, and impassive stones. Solar judging must be also farsighted, both in the sense of anticipating that things will become otherwise than they are and in the sense of taking a big-picture or wide-angled point of view. When the poet looks out on the world, he sees not fixed entities or "dots," but an "eternity" of fibers stretched out over time. This is not a landscape of individuals but of pulsating threads that are always interacting, tangling, joining and snapping off."[71]

Here objects speak and participate—they are the wider context of human judgment. In terms borrowed from Bruno Latour, these objects are actants—things that are the source of action, effectivity, and with the capacity to alter the course of events. Whitman's law would judge not as the judge judges (certainly not like Hunter et al.'s feminist judge) but will "judge as the sun falling around a helpless thing." This signals a new materialism in which materiality is a "living force" of both humans and nonhumans.[72] That is to say, this judge will "consider everything," as the sun falls on everything. Here the objects as actants articulate their force through what Bennett calls a "middle voice." The middle voice is neither decisive nor a mere affect (for example, Whitman, "I sing myself"). It is not clear what is subject in these statements, what is agentive, what has force, what is the event: "I," "sing," "myself," or "happens."[73] Bennett's suggestion, then, is that the judge "**periodically inhabit** the role of falling sun, and this accepting, nonranking illumination may reveal things as possessing a certain performativity or what Whitman calls 'the pulsation in all matter, all spirit, throbbing forever, eternal systole and diastole of life in all things.' "[74]

However, this combination of (decentered) will and imagination is not without profound dangers. Frank Kermode addresses this problem when he combines the insights of Nietzsche, Vaihinger, and Wallace Stevens on how fiction helps us to make sense of the world:

> After Nietzsche it was possible to say, as Stevens did, that "the final belief must be in fiction." This poet to whom the whole question was of perpetual interest, saw that to think in this way was to postpone the End—when the fiction might be said to coincide with reality—for ever; to make of it a fiction, an imaginary moment when "at last" the world of fact and the *mundo* of fiction shall be one. Such a fiction—the last section of *Notes Toward a Supreme Fiction* is, appropriately, the place where Stevens gives it his fullest attention [. . .] *Mundo* is itself such a fiction.[75]

But if literary fictions are the same as all others, what is to be done with their "dangerous relations"?[76] For Nietzsche "the falseness of an opinion is not any objection to it," and all that matters is "how far the opinion is life-furthering, life-preserving, and species-preserving."[77] What happens when this opinion and imagination are combined with the will to further a genocidal or extremist project, such as furthering the "German race," the "American people," or any other of God's chosen ones? Kermode puts the conundrum well when he says that nature can always be made to comply with our fictions, which can be tested by their success in the world: "The validity of one's opinion of the Jews can be proved by killing six million Jews."[78]

Linda Meyer's *Justice as Mercy* addresses the significance of the imagination when confronting the problem of judgment.[79] A simplified Kantian position, Meyer argues, has become a legal "catechism" or "Kanticism." She draws on the later Kant of the *Critique of Judgment,* as well as Heidegger and Levinas, to give an account of the relationship between justice and grace. The problem with Kanticism is that it fails to see that reason emerges in the context of our plural existence. Reason is not the "glue" that links one person to another. Mercy does not follow rules of reason and cannot be universalized. It is our being in ethical community that is the given, and reason is derived from our coexistence.

Kant's account of judgment was driven by the conviction that reason is an assumption—and that the gap between reason and nature needed to be bridged. The application of rational principles to the world is what Kant called "judgment."[80] This judgment cannot be brought under a rule—for if it were a rule it would in turn demand guidance from judgment.[81] Judgment is thus a practiced talent and cannot be taught.[82] As Meyer emphasizes, imagination is an "arresting faculty" that makes us "passive" so we can have the space to take in the world when making a judgment:

> Our desire for order, pattern, form, and simplicity, for a world that makes sense as though it were designed by an intellect like our own, is the aesthetic core of judgment. Kant notes that when we discover such unities, we experience spontaneous pleasure and satisfaction, common to all human beings.[83]

The sublime, the sense of awe, "the feeling of disjunction between ourselves and the world, the feeling of not being at home in the world, the feeling that the world is beyond our power to comprehend" gives us an intimation of infinity.[84] In making judgments we should strive by way of this idea even though we cannot experience or understand it. Justice is an encounter with this experience of the sublime even though it "evades our grasp."[85]

Conclusion

In the space available here I have only been able to open what is a larger project on the phenomenology of legal judgment. I have focused largely on judgments that would be regarded as mistakes. The difficulty distinguishing between a mistake and an error points to larger problems in legal historicity. The problem of doing justice in the wake of systemic violence and counterviolence reveals the extent of the problem. An individual mistake cannot be separated from the structures of violence and counterviolence. The *McBride* case is a productive site for considering what remains unresolved when law decides that it covers the field of judgment. If McBride's crime had been cast as a mistake or error rather than a "forgivable" political crime, how would we judge it differently? This problem of judgment is unavowable. The eternal return of the mistake as a problem of judgment forces open, once again, the closure that amnesty for political crimes attempted to effect. The South African Constitutional Court's conclusion that the "truth" of the crime can be determined by the facticity of the act of killing was yet another instrumental gesture that defers the problem of judgment. A judgment reduced to the instrumental objectives of transitional justice cannot rid itself of the structures of violence and counterviolence. The forgetful judgment (of the South African Constitutional Court) did not address the deeper questions thrown up by Robert McBride's mistaken judgment.

To judge is to imagine. Lodged within a judgment is the "as if" that presumes to separate cause from context, and measure the difference between responsibility and mitigation. Violence cannot be judged without asking "why." The mistaken judgment does not have a stable presence that can be accessed, confined, and be critically evaluated. In order to judge, a narrative of events must be composed, and the relevant norm must be brought to bear on the singular event. Judgment as a critical genre—in the sense that the feminist judgments project approached it—must not be confined to the instrumentality of "impact." Law's errancy does not have one stable and containable structural cause. While the incalculable judgment encounters the limit of making a decision—this cannot be prescribed by a scientific method. To judge is to risk being mistaken.

NOTES

I am grateful for the opportunity I had to discuss this chapter at the Department of Law, Jurisprudence and Social Thought at Amherst College. Karin van Marle, Tshepo Madlingozi, and Neloufer de Mel have pushed my thinking on the issues discussed here. Any errors are mine.

1. R. Jay Wallace, *The View from Here: On Affirmation, Attachment, and the Limits of Regret* (Oxford: Oxford University Press, 2013).
2. See the essay discussing Wallace by Thomas Nagel, "An Invitation to Hand-Wringing" 36 *London Review of Books* (2014): 7, 25.
3. I discuss the distinction between mistakes and errors below.
4. *The Citizen v. McBride* (2011), ZACC 11.
5. Stanley Corngold, "Error in Paul de Man," 8:3 *Critical Inquiry* (1982): 489–507; and Paul de Man, "A Letter from Paul de Man," 8:3 *Critical Inquiry* (1982): 509–13.
6. Corngold, "Error," 492. For de Man's use of "mere error," see, e.g., *Blindness and Insight: Essays in the Rhetoric of Contemporary Criticism* (New York: Oxford University Press, 1971), 109.
7. Ibid., 507.
8. De Man, "Letter," 509.
9. Marc Redfield, "Mistake in Paul de Man: Violent Reading and Theotropic Violence," in *The Political Archive of Paul de Man: Property, Sovereignty and the Theotropic*, ed. Martin McQuillan (Edinburgh: Edinburgh University Press, 2012), 103–17.
10. Ibid., 104.
11. Ibid.
12. Ibid.
13. *McBride*, para. 49.
14. Ibid., para. 10.
15. Ibid., para. 13.
16. Ibid., para. 17.
17. Ibid., para. 61.
18. Ibid., para. 62.
19. Tshepo Madlingozi, "The Right to Call a Murderer a Murderer," *Mail and Guardian*, 25 June 2010. Madlingozi's comment followed the Supreme Court of Appeal's ruling that McBride should not be called a murderer. It was this decision that was appealed to the Constitutional Court.
20. I am grateful to Tshepo Madlingozi for a productive conversation about these issues.
21. *Du Toit v. Minister for Safety and Security* [2009], ZACC 22.
22. Ibid., para. 44; *McBride*, para. 52.
23. *McBride*, para. 55.
24. Ibid.
25. Ibid., paras. 60 and 73.
26. Ibid., para. 78.
27. Walter Benjamin, *The Arcades Project* (Cambridge: Harvard University Press, 1999), convolute N, 462.
28. See evidence of relatives of the deceased, and interview with Robert McBride, South African Broadcasting Corporation, "TRC," episode 4, part 2—viewable at www.youtube.com/watch?v=yvjA_zqicFo.
29. *McBride v. The State* (Supreme Court of Appeal of South Africa, 30 March 1988, per Corbett JA) (appeal from the death sentence, which McBride lost. He was later granted a reprieve from the death penalty).

30. Ibid., 9.
31. Ibid., 11.
32. Ibid., 16–17.
33. Ibid., 21.
34. Ibid., 22–24.
35. Blake Morrison, *As If* (London: Granta Books, 1997).
36. Ibid., 24.
37. Ibid., 93–94.
38. Ibid., 94.
39. Ibid., 205.
40. Ibid., see chap. 11.
41. Ibid., 210.
42. Ibid., 229.
43. Terry Eagleton, *On Evil* (New Haven: Yale University Press, 2010), 2.
44. Hannah Arendt, *Eichmann in Jerusalem: A Report on the Banality of Evil* (London: Penguin, 2006).
45. Morrison, *As If*, 13.
46. I have previously developed this notion of the "as if" in law in Stewart Motha, "As IF: Constitutional Narratives and Forms of Life," in *Genres of Critique: Law, Aesthetics, and Liminality*, ed. Karin van Marle and Stewart Motha (Stellenbosch: SUN Press, 2013).
47. Immanuel Kant, *Political Writings*, ed. H. S. Reiss (Cambridge: Cambridge University Press, 1991); Immanuel Kant, *Groundwork for the Metaphysics of Morals*, trans. Allen W. Wood (New Haven: Yale University Press, 2002).
48. Hans Kelsen, *General Theory of Norms*, trans. M. Hartney (Oxford: Clarendon Press, 1991); Kelsen, *General Theory of Law and State* (New Brunswick, NJ: Transaction Publishers, 2006).
49. Hans Vaihinger, *The Philosophy of "As If": A System of the Theoretical, Practical, and Religious Fictions of Mankind*, trans. C. K. Ogden (Abingdon: Routledge, 1924).
50. Frank Kermode, *The Sense of an Ending: Studies in the Theory of Fiction* (New York: Oxford University Press, 1966); Jacques Derrida, "The University without Condition," in *Without Alibi*, ed. and trans. P. Kamuf (Stanford: University of Stanford Press, 2002).
51. Rosemary Hunter, Clare McGlynn, and Erika Rackley, eds., *Feminist Judgments: From Theory to Practice* (Oxford: Hart Publishing, 2010).
52. See Jean-Luc Nancy, *The Sense of the World* (Minneapolis: University of Minnesota Press, 1997).
53. Marianne Constable, *Just Silences: The Limits and Possibilities of Modern Law* (Princeton, NJ: Princeton University Press, 2005).
54. Maurice Blanchot, *The Unavowable Community*, trans. Pierre Joris (Barrytown, NY: Stationhill, 1988).
55. Hunter et al, *Feminist Judgments*.
56. Ibid., 3.
57. Ibid.
58. Ibid., 4.
59. Ibid., 5.
60. Ibid.
61. Ibid.
62. Ibid.
63. Ibid., 6.
64. Friedrich Nietzsche, "How the 'Real World' Finally Became a Fable: History of an Error," in *Twilight of the Idols* (Oxford: Oxford University Press, 1998), 20.
65. *R (Begum) v. Headteacher and Governors of Denbigh High School* [2006], UKHL

15. For a discussion, see Stewart Motha, "Veiled Women and the *Affect* of Religion in Democracy," 34:1 *Journal of Law and Society* (2007): 139–62.

66. Hunter et al., *Feminist Judgments*, 336.

67. Bruno Latour, *The Making of Law: An Ethnography of the Conseil d'État* (Cambridge, Eng.: Polity, 2010).

68. Jane Bennett, "The Solar Judgment of Walt Whitman," in *A Political Companion to Walt Whitman*, ed. John Seery (Lexington: University of Kentucky Press, 2010), 131–48, at 132.

69. Ibid., 132–33.

70. Ibid., 133.

71. Ibid.

72. Ibid., 132.

73. Ibid., 139–40.

74. Ibid., 143.

75. Kermode, *Sense of an Ending*, 36–37.

76. Ibid., 37.

77. Ibid.

78. Ibid., 37–38.

79. Linda Meyer, *Justice as Mercy* (Ann Arbor: University of Michigan Press, 2010). For a more extensive discussion of Meyer's arguments in the context of the exercise of the pardon power in South Africa, see S. Motha, "Rationality, the Rule of Law, and the Sovereign Return," 4 *Constitutional Court Review* (2011): 113–36.

80. Meyer, *Justice as Mercy*, 17.

81. Ibid.

82. Ibid., 18.

83. Ibid., 19.

84. Ibid., 22.

85. Ibid., 23.

2

How Law Should Avoid Mistakes

Alexander Bickel's Modernist Jurisprudence of "Mood"

KUNAL M. PARKER

Law's Mistakes in Terms of the Law-Politics Distinction

In this essay, I approach the subject of "law's mistakes" by exploring the attempt of a single legal thinker to work through a central problem of twentieth-century American jurisprudential thought. The thinker is the mid-twentieth-century legal scholar Alexander Bickel (1924–1974). The problem is that of conceptualizing and policing the distinction between "law" and "politics."

To legal scholars, Alexander Bickel needs little introduction. In his celebrated book *Democracy and Distrust* (1980), John Hart Ely described Bickel as "probably the most creative constitutional theorist of the past twenty years."[1] Bickel coined well-known phrases such as "the counter-majoritarian difficulty," "the passive virtues," and "the morality of consent." He is known for several major books: *The Unpublished Opinions of Justice Brandeis* (1957), *The Least Dangerous Branch: The Supreme Court at the Bar of Politics* (1962), *Politics and the Warren Court* (1965), *The Supreme Court and the Idea of Progress* (1970), and the unfinished *The Morality of Consent* (1975). From the mid-1950s until his death, furthermore, Bickel also wrote a legal column for the *New Republic* and became one of the country's leading public intellectuals.

The problem of conceptualizing and policing the law-politics distinction also needs little introduction. At one time or other, every major twentieth-century American jurisprudential school—from Sociological Jurisprudence to Legal Realism to Legal Process to Critical Legal Studies to Law-and-Economics—confronted and sought to work through this problem. Alexander Bickel was, therefore, neither the first nor the last to think through it. However, Bickel's mid-twentieth-century iteration of the problem—and his resulting sense of when law might commit mistake—possessed a special poignancy and urgency that were the legacy of late-nineteenth and early-twentieth-century interactions between the country's deeply entrenched common law sensibilities, on the one hand, and the perceived advantages and shortcomings of modernist ways of conceiving the relationship between law and democratic politics, on the other. It is therefore worth briefly situating Bickel in terms of what preceded him.

By the end of the nineteenth century, American legal thinkers had begun to challenge the dominance of the incrementalist, common lawyerly modes of thought that had held sway in the country since the American Revolution.[2] A particularly powerful critique came from Oliver Wendell Holmes Jr., whose late-nineteenth-century writings reflected a modernist historical sensibility that was increasingly gathering strength in the United States and Western Europe. For Holmes, history did not point in any particular direction. Instead, it played the iconoclastic role of dismantling the foundations of law—whether logic, reason, or the accumulated weight of the past—by revealing their merely temporal origins. This led to a breach in the wall that had traditionally separated law from politics. If all of law's pretended ahistorical foundations could be shown up as thoroughly temporal, as products of human intellection arising in historical time, how could one meaningfully distinguish between law and politics? Was law just another way of doing politics? If law was really just another form of politics, where law was made by unelected common law judges, was it not then an *illegitimate* way of doing politics?

The Holmesian breaking down of the wall between law and politics found a receptive audience among reformers of the Progressive Era, for whom the changes wrought by industrialization, urbanization, and immigration necessitated urgent solutions. Antiquated common law notions of contract, property, and tort were entirely unable, Progressive Era reformers argued, to deal with the grave problems of the new industrial economy in the United States. But a common law–centric judiciary repeatedly blocked more scientific, democratically generated legislation. The most celebrated instance of this was the case of *Lochner v. New York* (1905), in which the U.S. Supreme Court struck down a New York law regulating the length of the work day in bakeries on the ground that the law violated the U.S. Constitution's Due Process clause insofar as it inhibited the individual's freedom to contract.[3]

In order to restore to democratic majorities their rightful role in giving themselves their own laws, there began a long, complex, and contradictory assault on the common law, especially as it was joined to the U.S. Constitution by the federal courts, which showed that the common law was nothing other than a particular kind of politics. The jurisprudence associated with Legal Realism, the adherents of which often claimed Holmes as an intellectual forebear, played a critical role in this regard. By the time of the New Deal, this had resulted in the judge-made common law's—and the U.S. Constitution's—retreat before the forces of democratic politics. As the administrative state grew, democratic majorities increasingly gave themselves their own laws based on the most up-to-date scientific knowledge, relatively unimpeded by the strictures of judge-made common law.

However, beginning in the 1930s, even as the New Deal triumphed, American legal thinkers were beginning to search for a defensible notion of law amid the rubble of law reduced to politics. There were many reasons why this was considered important: disenchantment with strains within Legal Realism that embraced empiricism and eschewed moral values; nervousness engendered by the rise of a potentially overweening administrative state; and fears of legal positivism run amok provoked by the horrors of World War II. Many who had attacked common lawyerly modes of thought in the early twentieth century, most notably Dean Roscoe Pound of the Harvard Law School, now began to defend the common law. The historian Edward Purcell Jr. has shown in considerable detail how a range of legal scholars—Catholics prominent among them—also turned around World War II to Aristotelian-Thomist ideas of law that distinguished law from politics in an attempt to arrest what they considered a plunge into nihilism.[4]

From the perspective of mid-twentieth-century critics of Legal Realism, the great enemy was, of course, Holmes. Holmes had, after all, engineered the collapse of the law-politics distinction by showing that the putative ahistorical foundations of law (reason, morality, and so on) were really the product of nothing but history. As a result, society had been left without tools with which to control the excesses of democratic majorities. For mainstream American legal thinkers, however, even as the horrors of the Nazis made them newly sensitive to the dangers of abdicating responsibility for checking democratic majorities, the dark shadow of anti-democratic overreaching by common law judges could not be ignored. If it was impossible to live with the modernist historical sensibility of Holmes, it was also impossible to ignore it.

In the 1950s, one influential response to this dilemma was that of the Legal Process school. Within the historiography of American legal thought, the 1950s Legal Process school is typically remembered for seeking to redefine the legitimate space of law to consist of neutral rules of the game, whether such rules consisted of rules of procedure, rules regarding reasoned elaboration, or "principles" defined at levels of generality that would effectively place them beyond the realm of political contest. This dramatically abbreviated space of law would save law from the assaults of democratic politics and provide comfort that neutral legal results could be justified. For many scholars, the text that exemplifies the Legal Process school is Henry Hart and Albert M. Sacks's *The Legal Process,* a work widely used in American law schools in the 1950s. Taking into account the post–New Deal expansion of legislatively and administratively generated law, *The Legal Process* focused on determining "institutional competence" as a way of assigning tasks among a range of legal actors (courts, agencies, legislatures, individuals, and so on). The role of law was to be the interstitial one of specifying the procedures through which the assignment of legal tasks would be accomplished. As Hart and Sacks put it:

> These institutionalized procedures and the constitutive arrangements establishing . . . them are obviously *more fundamental* than the substantive arrangements in the structure of a society. . . . The principle of institutional settlement expresses the judgment that decisions which are the duly arrived at result of duly established procedures of this kind ought to be accepted as binding upon the whole society unless and until they are duly changed.[5]

For Morton Horwitz, The Legal Process symbolizes "the moment in postwar history at which the New Deal lawyers' conception of the 'common interest' came to be thoroughly transformed from one of substance to one of procedure."[6]

This is a highly abbreviated version of the background against which Alexander Bickel thought and wrote. Just as Bickel was embarking on his scholarly career, however, the U.S. Supreme Court's decision in *Brown v. Board of Education* (1954) erupted on the legal landscape.[7] Elite legal thinkers in the 1950s were profoundly disturbed by *Brown,* because, on the one hand, *Brown* appeared to be a judicial overreaching of the repudiated

Lochner type and, on the other hand, because *Brown* appeared from the perspective of the Legal Process school to lack the "neutrality" that was required of bona fide narrowly defined legal "principles." It is the intellectual crisis provoked by the *Brown* decision—and its implications for thinking about the law-politics distinction—that would fill Bickel's writings.

Before proceeding to a discussion of Bickel's writings, it is worth devoting a few sentences to how the idea of "law's mistakes" fits into the foregoing discussion. It should be clear that, whenever we deem law to have committed a mistake, we have decided that it is a mistake relative to some ground or basis from which we judge (a set of existent social facts, a theory of justice, logic, and so on). In confronting the question of law's mistake, in other words, we necessarily confront a prior question: a mistake relative to what? Approached through the prism of the law-politics distinction, law's mistake would be judged in terms of where a legal thinker—in this case, Bickel—locates the border that separates the legitimate sphere of law from the legitimate sphere of politics. With this border in mind, law's mistake might be that of law's exceeding *or* falling short of its appropriate role vis-à-vis democratic politics. Law might commit the serious mistake of encroaching upon the legitimate sphere of democratic politics. Or it might commit the equally serious mistake of allowing democratic politics to imperialize its own legitimate sphere. Through my reading of Bickel's identification of law's mistake in terms of his rendering of the law-politics distinction, I hope to advance a few goals: to rethink the received wisdom about mid-twentieth-century jurisprudential thought; to identify some of the ways in which common law modes of thinking were pressed into service in post–World War II America; and, finally, to lay bare Bickel's novel and paradoxical ideas about how and when law would fall into mistake.

Alexander Bickel's Modernist Jurisprudence of "Mood"

Alexander Bickel was explicitly concerned with the dilemma of mid-twentieth-century legal thinkers—namely, that of conceiving the law-politics distinction in light of a sense that it was impossible either to reject or embrace fully the implications of Holmesian thought. In his last book, The Morality of Consent (1975), Bickel expressed the problem as follows:

> "I do not know what is true," said Holmes. "I do not know the meaning of the universe." His biographer, Mark DeWolfe Howe, wondered whether our stomachs were "strong enough to accept the bitter pill which Holmes tendered us." They had better be. We had better recognize how much is

> human activity a random confusion, and that there is no final validity to be claimed for our truths. If we allow ourselves to be engulfed in moral certitudes we will march to self-destruction from one Vietnam and one domestic revolution—sometimes Marcusean and often not—to another. And yet we do need, individually and as a society, some values, some belief in the foundations of our conduct, in order to make life bearable. If these too are lies, they are, as Holmes' great contemporary, Joseph Conrad, thought them, true lies; if illusions, then indispensable ones. To abandon them is to commit moral suicide.[8]

Law had, in other words, to avoid two dangers: on the one hand, that of failing to recognize its own imbrication in history (that is, failing to learn from Holmes); on the other hand, failing to transcend its imbrication in history (that is, failing to resist Holmes). Law needed to figure out how to be, in Bickel's words, a "true lie," something simultaneously known to be a lie and nevertheless insisted upon as true. It is not inappropriate to characterize Bickel's entire oeuvre as a "how to" manual for law to achieve this goal. It was when law failed to function as a "true lie" of the kind Bickel deemed desirable that it would fall into mistake.

Bickel's writings shared many of the preoccupations of the Legal Process school, but the path he carved for himself was unique. In the 1950s and early 1960s, his writings—especially *The Least Dangerous Branch* (1962)—were intended to defend the *Brown* decision. Law had to be able to generate enduring "principles" that transcended their immediate historical and political context so that it could check democratic politics. At the same time, however, law was necessarily to be understood as the product of history and could not be held to the rigorous, restrained, and often mechanical neutrality required of it by Legal Process scholars. How, in Bickel's writings, was law to achieve both or, what amounted to the same thing, to function as a "true lie"?

I want to suggest that Bickel's "how to" manual for law relies quite self-consciously upon an aesthetic of vagueness, ambiguity, and imprecision for law to be able to function as a "true lie." The legal "principle" that must check but also enable democratic politics is self-consciously rendered blurry, its outlines rubbed out. Its power inheres precisely in the fact that it cannot be identified or realized with precision. To accomplish this, Bickel has recourse to ideas that had been circulating within common law discourses for centuries.

Reflecting the Legal Process school's emphasis on the importance of reducing law to its core "principles," Bickel argued that courts in general, and the U.S. Supreme Court in particular, had always to act on "principle."

This was an unshakable imperative and courts could not act otherwise: "When it strikes down legislative policy, [a court] must act rigorously on principle, else it undermines the justification for its power."[9]

But why endow only courts with the ability to articulate legal "principles"? Why were legislatures or executives not able to articulate binding "principles" with equal facility? Like a long generation of common lawyers who complained that legislatures routinely got things wrong, Bickel argued that legislatures were simply not up to the task of articulating bona fide legal "principles": "Not merely respect for the rule of established principles but the creative establishment and renewal of a coherent body of principled rules—that is what our legislatures have proven themselves ill equipped to give us."[10] By contrast, courts possessed "certain capacities for dealing with matters of principle that legislatures and executives do not possess."[11] Bickel hailed the unique competence of judges who, "have, or should have, the leisure, the training, and the insulation to follow the ways of the scholar in pursuing the ends of government."[12] This was a throw-back to seventeenth-century Cokean arguments that only common lawyers, by virtue of their long study, possessed the "artificiall reason" of the law.[13]

If Bickel tells us who is best equipped to declare legal "principles," in what is a legal "principle" supposed to consist? Once again, Bickel has recourse to a venerable common lawyerly device to distinguish between law and politics. Judge-declared legal "principles" maintain continuity with the past; legislative pronouncements are the pronouncements of only a discrete historical moment.[14] When judges and courts establish legal "principles" that check the sphere of democratic politics, Bickel tells us, it is to articulate "the enduring values of a society."[15] By contrast, "[l]egislation . . . is evanescent, and meant to be."[16] Law's ontology for Bickel, then, is to maintain a measure of continuity with the past that is self-consciously distinguished from the evanescent world of democratic politics.

However, Bickel readily admitted that, in a post-Holmesian universe acutely alert to the perpetual changeability of the world and the instability of law's own foundations, legal "principles" themselves could not maintain continuity for very long. They were themselves subject to the law of evanescence that defined democratic politics. Bickel puts it thus: "Everybody knows that the lifetime of applied principle is often no longer than one or two generations."[17] If judicially crafted legal "principles" are durable, in other words, they possess no more than a *relative* durability. Law checks an evanescent democratic politics by virtue of the fact that it is only relatively less evanescent.

This sense that law's durability was only relative to that of democratic politics gives us a clue to Bickel's understanding of the role of history in shaping supposedly enduring legal "principles." This is what distinguishes Bickel as a historically minded modernist legal thinker from the orthodox common lawyers of the past, whose vocabulary he drew on so freely.

Orthodox common lawyers had long claimed to be engaged in faithful repetition of the past (even as they claimed to be alert to the demands of the present and future). For Sir William Blackstone, for example, when common law judges overturned a precedent, they did not make a new law, but simply cast the over-ruled decision out from the self-identical body of the common law, to which an essential integrity and continuity was thereby restored. This is how Blackstone described the effect of over-ruling a decision:

> But even in such cases the subsequent judges do not pretend to make a new law, but to vindicate the old one from misrepresentation. For if it be found that the former decision is manifestly absurd or unjust, it is declared, not that such a sentence was *bad law*, but that it was *not law*.[18]

The position that there was a body of law "out there," timeless in its logical and moral coherence, such that no new law needed to be made, was repeated into the early twentieth century. Thus, in 1902, the Harvard legal scholar Joseph Henry Beale could state: "Wherever . . . there is a political society, there must be some complete body of law, which shall cover every event there happening."[19]

The modernist historical revolution in legal thought inaugurated by Holmes had made it difficult, if not impossible, to make such statements. Lawyers could no longer claim to be discovering "some complete body of law" that lay "out there." Bickel thus acknowledges openly that the legal "principles" articulating enduring values that can check democratic politics have a short life. They will need to be remade over and over again. This implies, of course, that they are, in the first instance, made.

The fact that legal "principles" must be made gives us a clue to Bickel's understanding of history. For Bickel, it is not just that legal "principles" are not eternal. Bickel is a thoroughgoing modernist to the extent that he believes that there is also simply no determinate historical past "out there" that we can look to in order to discover a fully formed legal "principle." Instead, the past only exists *for* us. It is ours to shape creatively to our purposes. In *The Least Dangerous Branch*, Bickel repeatedly cites the mid-twentieth-century historian Herbert Muller's *The Uses of the Past*

(1952) for the idea that "[o]ur task is to create a 'usable past,' for our own living purposes."[20] Bickel puts it thus:

> We are guided in our search of the past by our own aspirations and evolving principles, which were in part formed by that very past. When we find in history, immanent or expressed, principles that we can adopt or adapt, or ideals and aspirations that speak to us with contemporary relevance, we find at the same time evidence of inconsistent conduct. But we reason from the former, not from the frailties of men who, like ourselves, did not always live up to all they professed or aspired to. Lincoln reasoned, not from the Framers' resignation to the fact of slavery, but from the abolition of the slave trade and from the numerous manumissions, particularly in Virginia. In considering the Bill of Rights, we find worthy of note the stirrings of libertarian theory in colonial times, not the barbaric prosecutions.[21]

Thus, the turn to history to find legal "principles" that articulated enduring values was always and necessarily an active, creative endeavor that involved a range of choices. History always offered several different legal "principles," often at odds with one another, each of which was available for the judge to choose and foster. In November 1955, Bickel published a long analysis of the "Original Understanding" of the Fourteenth Amendment, in which he sought to justify the Brown decision: "The record of history, properly understood, left the way open to, in fact invited, a decision based on the moral and material state of the Union in 1954, not 1866."[22] The very phrasing of this sentence—that the record of history "left the way open to," rather than dictated such a conclusion—suggests Bickel's sense that the historical past was up for interpretation, subject to different readings.

How, then, were binding legal "principles" to be identified and chosen? Ultimately, for Bickel, the task of finding legal "principles" in the historical past—hence, the task of reading the historical record—was irreducible to science. It was a poetic endeavor. This was a more common position in mid-twentieth-century America than we might suspect. For example, in 1935, the political scientist Alpheus Mason of Princeton University wrote: "Any concrete political situation, however seemingly transparent, cannot be dealt with by reason alone; it can only be grasped by a process similar to artistic perception."[23] In this vein, Bickel, quoting the historian Herbert Muller again, insisted that "[o]ur interest in history is more poetic than practical or scientific. But . . . the very poetry of history consists in its truth."[24] Such a self-conscious invocation of the poetry of identifying legal "principles" in the past compels, if nothing else, a rethinking of the Legal Process school as engaged in an arid and apolitical task of setting narrowly defined procedural rules for the game.[25]

Bickel's conviction that canvassing the historical past for enduring legal "principles" was a profoundly poetic interpretive enterprise—in short, that the ground of binding legal "principles" was poetic truth—gives us a point of entry into his understanding of the ontology of legal "principles" that both arise in history and somehow (at least relatively) transcend it. "Principle," Bickel insisted, was an "evocative, not definitional" term; it was an "attempt . . . to locate meaning, not to enclose it."[26] Ultimately, nothing could point in any definitive justificatory way to the source of a binding legal "principle." Thus, the constitutional text, precedent, and history were merely "empirical aids." They were "sources of inspiration, instigators of reflection, producers of mood. . . . [T]hey are the setting for judgment and they condition it, but they are not its wellspring."[27] Legal "principles" thus emerged, not from a process of rational intellection, but from a "mood." We could do no better than to acknowledge that openly.

Even among legal scholars, Bickel was by no means the first to speak of law in terms of "mood." In 1930, Judge Learned Hand had written that constitutional provisions "represent a mood, rather than a command."[28] In his 1955 Harvard Law School address commemorating the two hundredth anniversary of the birth of Chief Justice Marshall, Bickel's hero and mentor, Justice Felix Frankfurter, approvingly quoted Hand for this proposition.[29] In a paper delivered before the American Philosophical Society a year earlier, Frankfurter had asserted something similar: "Judges . . . must have something of the *creative artist* in them; they must have antennae registering feelings and judgment *beyond logical, let alone quantitative, proof.*"[30]

In confirmation of the idea that legal "principles" sprang from a "mood" that could not be pinned down in terms of reason, in *The Least Dangerous Branch,* Bickel approvingly quoted the mid-twentieth-century cultural critic Dwight Macdonald, who, in a 1957 essay tellingly entitled "The Triumph of the Fact: An American Tragedy," asked the following question: How does one *prove* that Faulkner was an important artist and that J. P. Marquand was not? According to Macdonald, "it cannot be proved, [b]ut it can be demonstrated, a quite different operation involving an appeal—by reason, analysis, illustration, and rhetoric—to cultural values which critic and reader have in common, values no more susceptible of scientific statement than are the moral values-in-common to which Jesus appealed but which, for all that, exist as vividly and definitely as do mercy, humility, and love."[31]

How does one come to terms with Bickel's proposition that legal "principles" capable of binding democratic politics are the product of, and therefore are, a "mood"? I submit that the idea of law as "mood," for Bickel, is the way for law to function as a "true lie" in a democracy, which we have seen is Bickel's name for managing the law-politics distinction in the post-Holmesian world.

A "mood" is, of course, susceptible neither to rational, scientific, or moral definition nor to disaggregation into its component parts. Its strength, power, and vibrancy rest precisely in its vagueness, ambiguity, and imprecision, precisely in the fact that it can only be evoked, never proved or defined or disaggregated. Furthermore, unlike logic or reason, a "mood" cannot be demolished by showing that it is the product of nothing but history. It can recognize its location in history without being limited by it. Take, for example, the evocation of the "mood" of a particular historical period, say, the Baroque. In one sense, the "mood" of the Baroque clearly points to a specific historical period, the Baroque. In another sense, however, the power of the "mood" of the Baroque is in no way diminished by identifying its historical origins in the way that, for example, the power of Newtonian science—which claimed to embody the eternal truth of nature—would now be. In a historical world shorn of foundations, therefore, a "mood" can do work that logic or reason or historical teleology—discredited as they are—cannot do. In its relationship to democratic politics, law, by becoming "mood," can avoid (a) failing to recognize its own imbrication in history and (b) failing to transcend its own imbrication in history. It is as a "mood" that law can function as a "true lie."

Given the "mood"-like ground from which legal "principles" arose, it is not surprising that the recommended manner of their application would be such as to instantiate a "mood." It is at this juncture that common lawyerly, incrementalist modes of calibrating the imperatives of change and continuity come into play in Bickel's work. To be sure, Bickel was hardly unique among mid-twentieth-century American thinkers or their successors in pressing common law incrementalism to his ends. As the political scientist Ken Kersch has recently pointed out, modern American thinkers of various stripes—Friedrich Hayek, Christian conservatives, and law-and-economics thinkers—have all turned to common law incrementalism to bolster their positions.[32] Bickel's colleague at Yale, the political scientist Charles Lindblom, invoked the finitude of human beings' ability to know the world in extolling the virtues of incrementalism and what he called "muddling through."[33] Bickel's appropriation of the common law is, however, specific to his particular way of managing the law-politics distinction.

Bickel insisted that "mechanical application" of legal "principles" was not a possibility because "[o]ur system . . . calls for the evolution of principle in novel circumstances."[34] "The courts are concerned with the flesh and blood of an actual case." This common lawyerly focus on concrete cases could prove "an extremely salutary proving ground for all abstractions."[35] But the common lawyerly focus on concrete cases was much more than just a way of testing abstractions. Combined with the famous "passive virtues" that Bickel describes in *The Least Dangerous Branch,* the step-by-step, incremental common law method was a means of putting legal "principles" into play as "mood."

Rather than endorsing the use of legal "principles" as a blunt weapon against democratic politics, Bickel preferred what he called "the exquisite balance" between adhering to a legal "principle" and also keeping that "principle" in abeyance through recourse to common lawyerly devices.[36] Doing this was the "secret of the [Court's] ability to maintain itself in the tension between principle and expediency."[37] As he put it: "A sound judicial instinct will generally favor deflecting the problem in one or more initial cases, for there is much to be gained from letting it simmer, so that a mounting number of incidents exemplifying it may have a cumulative effect on the judicial mind as well as on public and professional opinion."[38] Legal "principles" were thus always to coexist with, indeed should only be realized through, compromise, deferral, and delay. As Bickel put it:

> [I]t is not true that in our society we are generally governed wholly by principle in some matters and indulge a rule of expediency exclusively in others. There is no such neat dividing line. There are exceptions, some of which are delineated, as we shall see, by the so-called doctrine of political questions. Most often, however, and as often as not in matters of the widest and deepest concern, such as the racial problem, both requirements exist most *imperatively* side by side: guiding principle and expedient compromise. The role of principle, when it cannot be the immutable governing rule, is to *affect* the policy of expediency.

Nothing better exemplifies this position than Bickel's assertion (channeling Justice Brandeis) that "[t]he most important thing we do is not doing."[39] "Not doing" was not, of course, abandoning the legal "principle." Far from it. It was rather a technique for letting the legal "principle" become "mood," operate as a force of vagueness, ambiguity, and imprecision, and act as a kind of slow contagion in the world that could disappear or take hold. The creeping pace of common law change was crucial in this regard.

Bickel's emphasis on the salutary vagueness, imprecision, and "mood"-like quality of legal "principles," both in their ontology and in their application, did not necessarily give rise to consistent readings. Various decisions of the Court were dismissed as errors. The *Dred Scott* case was "more than a crime; it was a blunder."[40] Similarly, *Plessy v. Ferguson* (1896) was a "grave error."[41] The same was true of the Court's early-twentieth-century pro–laissez-faire jurisprudence embodied by *Lochner.* "Serving this value [laissez-faire] in the most uncompromising fashion, at a time when it was well past its heyday, five Justices, in a series of spectacular cases in the 1920s and 1930s, went to unprecedented lengths to thwart majority will. The consequence was very nearly the end of the story."[42]

But Bickel defended *Brown* even as he criticized *Lochner:* "I would assert that the rightness of the Court's decisions in the *School Segregation Cases* can be demonstrated. . . . I would deny, however, that any similar demonstration can be or was mounted . . . to show that a statute setting maximum hours or minimum wages violates fundamental presuppositions of our society."[43] Similarly, he denied the status of valid legal "principle" to what was increasingly becoming his bête noire, the one man, one vote rule: "The principle of the *School Segregation Cases* is one that judges may hold and proclaim with present certainty, although pragmatic compromises may remain necessary for a time. But one cannot with like moral confidence proclaim the principle of equal individual representation, holding everything else to be a temporary if necessary evil."[44]

Why did *Brown* stand for a valid legal "principle," while *Dred Scott, Plessy, Lochner,* and the voting rights cases did not? After all, *Dred Scott, Plessy, Lochner,* and the voting rights cases could all be read as articulating the enduring values of their day based on a creative search of the historical record just as much as *Brown* could. How did one decide whether something did or did not constitute a valid legal "principle"? How did one decide how, when, and under what circumstances legal "principles" were to cede to expediency? Bickel does not give us very good or convincing answers.

Such inconsistencies did not mean that Bickel was not himself thoroughly convinced that law's best chance of functioning as a necessary "true lie" in a democratic society was by becoming a "mood" possessed of vagueness, ambiguity, and imprecision. But if "mood" became Bickel's way of managing the problem of the law-politics distinction, it also showed how law could commit mistake. This would happen if law lost its "mood"-like quality, if it experienced a deficit of vagueness, imprecision, and ambiguity. And this is exactly what appeared to happen, in Bickel's opinion, in the late 1960s.

From the mid-1960s until his death, a period I will characterize for the sake of convenience as the second phase of his scholarly career, Bickel retreated into political and legal conservatism. It is this Bickel that Robert Bork, then solicitor general of the United States, would hail for his contribution to "the reconstitution of a conservative intellectual tradition in this country."[45]

In part, Bickel's conservatism was the result of a visceral reaction to the nihilistic tone of some of the protest movements of the late 1960s and early 1970s. In his last book, *The Morality of Consent* (1975), Bickel quoted from a pamphlet issued by the Yippies:

> Burn your money. You know life is a dream and all our institutions are man-made illusions, effective only because you take the dream for reality. Break down the family, church, nation, city, economy, turn life into an art form and theater of the soul. What is needed is a generation of people who are freaky, crazy, irrational, sexy, angry, irreligious, childish, and mad . . . who lure the youth with music, pot, and acid . . . who redefine the normal. . . . Burn your houses down and you will be free.[46]

To someone who had worked so very hard to find an aesthetic response—namely, the vagueness, ambiguity, and imprecision of law as "mood"—to work through the conflicting pulls of opening up to history and resisting history, of expanding and restricting the spaces of democracy and law, the Yippies' bold rhetoric, and especially their willingness to throw caution to the winds and embrace an uncompromising stand, was nerve-racking. Bickel's fear and anger are evident in his response:

> Our recent revolutionists have offered us hatred. They despise and dehumanize the persons, and they condemn the concerns and the aspirations, of the vast majority of their countrymen. They have offered for the future, so far as their spokesmen have been able to make clear, the Maypole dance and, in considerable tension, if not contradiction, a vision of "liberated" masses adjuring profit, competition, personal achievement, and any form of gratification not instantly and equally available to all. . . . Suppose millions upon millions of us cannot be persuaded that we would be happier if we freed ourselves of the achievement ethic . . . , have those seized of a higher vision the right to coerce us into conforming to it?[47]

For his success in "getting" the 1960s, the historian Laura Kalman tells us, Alexander Bickel was burned in effigy by Yale Law School students.[48]

The largest part of Bickel's ire was, however, directed at the jurisprudence of the later years of the Warren Court. Various developments—massive resistance to desegregation in the South, the complexities of desegregation efforts in the North and, most especially, the revolution in voting rights jurisprudence—made Bickel question the direction taken by the Court and increasingly convinced him that it was falling into mistake. His frustration took the form of an explicit embrace of the philosophy of Edmund Burke. He began *The Morality of Consent* by describing two traditions that "diverged in response to the impact of the French Revolution on political thought." These were the contractarian tradition associated with Locke and Rousseau, on the one hand, and the Whig tradition associated with Burke, on the other. The latter, Bickel argued, "is my own model."[49] But Bickel's Burke was also, as we shall see, a modernist.

For Bickel, the Warren Court of the mid-1960s and after lapsed into mistake precisely by losing the vague, imprecise, ambiguous, "mood"-like quality that Bickel felt was essential for legal "principles." Instead, the path chosen by the Warren Court was increasingly too clear, too determined, too given.

In *The Supreme Court and the Idea of Progress* (1970), originally delivered as the Oliver Wendell Holmes Lectures at Harvard Law School in October 1969, the leitmotif of Bickel's critique of the Warren Court was that the Court "imagine[d] the past and remember[ed] the future."[50] By this intriguing phrase, Bickel meant that the Warren Court had been thoroughly seduced by a teleological or foundational understanding of history.[51] Such an understanding of history led the Court to "imagine the past," in other words, to construct a past for itself that did not correspond to the facts.[52] At the same time, it led the Court to "remember the future," to work toward bringing into being a future already known, rather than one that could unfold on its own terms. The Court's embrace of teleological history was doing violence to, or committing mistake vis-à-vis, the manifold complexities of past, present, and future that Bickel felt could only be approached as a poetic endeavor that would yield a "mood."

What was the animating logic of the Warren Court's teleological history, according to Bickel? In the opening chapter of *The Supreme Court and the Idea of Progress,* entitled "The Heavenly City of the Twentieth Century Justices" (a riff on the title of the historian Carl Becker's influential 1932 history of the eighteenth-century philosophers, *The Heavenly City of the Eighteenth Century Philosophers*), Bickel rather contemptuously characterizes the Court's historical teleology as follows:

> The Justices of the Warren Court thus ventured to identify a goal. It was necessarily a grand one—if we had to give it a single name, that name . . . would be the Egalitarian Society. And the Justices steered by this goal . . . in the be-

> lief that progress, called history, would validate their course, and that another generation, remembering its own future, would imagine them favorably.[53]

In embracing this altogether too clear philosophy, the Warren Court was engaged in a "heedless break with the past."[54] At the same time, Bickel complained about "the rate at which the Court has wreaked itself upon . . . society . . . and the rate at which . . . society as a whole seems to be hurtling towards its future."[55] An altogether excessive number of legal "principles" was being deployed to strike down democratically generated legislation. "Principles" had to be few in number, Bickel now insisted, and had to be defined in the "narrowest possible compass."[56] They had to be "coherent, analytically warranted, principled declarations of general norms."[57] From the Burkean perspective that Bickel was increasingly coming to embrace, the Court seemed, like the French revolutionaries, perpetually to be engaging in "some luxuriant outburst of theory."[58] Indeed, the Court of *Griswold v. Connecticut* (1965), which struck down anti-contraception legislation, was not that different in its overreaching from the *Lochner* Court, which had struck down labor laws: "On a linear plane we are not so far from where we started."[59]

In general, what Bickel found to be lacking in the Warren Court's application of legal "principles" was a measure of "mood." He complained about the abandonment of "a wise suspense in forming opinions, wise reserve in expressing them, and wise tardiness in trying to realize them."[60] The Court's "first obligation" was, he argued, "to move cautiously, straining for decisions in small compass, more hesitant to deny principles held by some segments of the society than ready to affirm comprehensive ones for all, mindful of the dominant role the political institutions are allowed, and always anxious first to invent compromises and accommodations before declaring firm and unambiguous principles."[61] If law as "mood" could function as a "true lie," the Warren Court's reckless embrace of an excessively well defined philosophy as truth exposed it to the charge that it was encroaching upon the legitimate sphere of democratic politics.

In declaring legal "principles" that overturned democratic legislation, Bickel now insisted, the Court should "produce nothing wholly new and retain nothing wholly obsolete."[62] This was lifted almost verbatim from Burke's *Reflections on the Revolution in France* (1790), in which Burke had defended the diffuse common law temporality of Great Britain's constitution as follows: "Thus, . . . in what we improve, we are never wholly new; in what we retain, we are never wholly obsolete."[63] Bickel's affiliation with the Legal Process school also came to the fore, meshing perfectly with his

Burkean impulse to brake the rate of change. Nothing provided greater refuge from reckless and rapid change than a commitment to procedure, that most lawyerly part of law and one that the Legal Process school had made the very ontology of law. Procedural safeguards, Bickel argued, "were relatively well-defined by a less than usually imagined past."[64] In *The Morality of Consent,* Bickel lauded the "hard-core of procedural provisions, found chiefly in the Bill of Rights" that possessed a "relative definiteness of terms" and "definiteness of history."[65] The Warren Court had prided itself on "cutting through legal technicalities, in piercing through procedure to get to substance. But legal technicalities are the stuff of law, and piercing through a particular substance to get to procedures suitable to many substances is in fact what the task of law most often is."[66]

Even as law lost its "mood"-like quality and plunged into mistake as the Warren Court fell under the spell of an increasingly well defined historical teleology of progress, the realm of democratic politics—that is, the realm that law acted upon—came for Bickel to be possessed of a complexity, multiplicity, contradiction, accommodation, and compromise that gave rise to "mood." "Mood" was thus not just a necessary quality for law if it were to avoid mistakes; it was also a desirable quality for democratic politics.

Although Bickel had supported the result in *Brown,* as mentioned above, he had quite early on been opposed to the Warren Court's voting rights jurisprudence. This opposition intensified in his later, more conservative writings. Bickel's views of American democracy were no doubt of a piece with the views of democracy put forward by postwar American intellectuals—most prominently at Yale—who celebrated America's pluralist, messy, group-based democracy and contrasted it favorably to other more logically ordered political systems.[67] However, like James Kent, Joseph Story, Christopher Tiedeman, and a range of other American common law thinkers, Bickel also subscribed to the view that suffrage was only a very small part of American democracy, and not even the most important part of it. In 1970, Bickel wrote:

> The Madisonian model of a multiplicity of factions vying against each other and checking each other still more nearly fits our system. . . . It is perfectly clear as well that, aside from the judges, many other elites that are not immediately and not directly controlled by the electoral process wield power in American government. . . . Elections are the tip of the iceberg; the bulk of the political process is below. The jockeying, the bargaining, the trading, the threatening and the promising, the checking and the balancing, the spurring and the vetoing are continuous.[68]

Majoritarianism of the Warren Court variety, Bickel conceded, "was heady stuff," precisely the kind of seductive theoretical will to truth he was suspicious of. But it was, paradoxically, "heady stuff" that led by virtue of its excessive clarity only to a rationalistic aridity, an unaesthetic deintoxication or disenchantment of the public sphere. "It is, in truth, a tide flowing with the swiftness of a slogan—whether popular sovereignty, as in the past, or one man, one vote, as in the Warren Court's formulation. The tide is apt to sweep over all institutions, seeking its level everywhere."[69] Like the French revolutionaries, who had divided France into départements of equal size, heedlessly cutting through regions of differing size, history, and intrinsic meaning, the voting rights jurisprudence of the Court drove toward "a certain symmetry in [the] deployment of the majoritarian principle and of a concept of centralized and pervasive law."[70]

In Bickel's view, "the Court's majoritarianism [was] ill-conceived. . . . [E]galitarianism [was] a worthy ideal but not in all circumstances a self-evident virtue, and centralized, unmitigatedly legalitarian government [bore] the seed of tyranny."[71] American democracy should be left in (what Bickel took to be) its Madisonian state, a diverse conglomeration of different power groups of varying size, playing off one another, jockeying for influence in a system essentially incapable of reduction to mathematical principles such as "one man, one vote." If this were not allowed, and if the Court's symmetrical "one man, one vote" principle were applied rigorously and across the board, Bickel argued that American democracy would experience what he called a loss of "intensity." Bickel's hope was to stay the hand of the Court or, failing that, that America would nevertheless revert to a diverse, asymmetrical democracy of groups rather than individuals, groups working simultaneously in a manner possessed "of intensities that no ballot can register."[72]

A Burkean concern for continuity with the institutions of the past, in Bickel's hands, thus comes to be sublimated into a concern for preserving "intensities" that—like the "mood"-like vagueness of legal "principles"—defies theoretical determination or measurement ("intensities that no ballot can register"). Thus, the reason for respecting existing democratic arrangements was not a concern for continuity with the past as such as much as it was a concern for preserving institutions that, in their variety, complexity, and multiplicity, gave rise to a diffuse sense of "intensity," which I would argue is a "mood"-like quality.[73] Like law, then, democratic politics could also be possessed of a salutary measure of vagueness, imprecision, ambiguity, and "mood."

Bickel was not without his own faith in the direction of history: he hoped or believed that the world in which both law and democratic politics were "mood"-like lay just beyond the horizon. Society would choose vagueness over clarity. In his view, the Warren Court's mistake of "remembering the future" was being shown up by widespread resistance to the Court's schemes. In the voting rights context, Bickel believed that Americans would end up rejecting the "one man, one vote" principle and revert to the more "intense" model he preferred:

> These are all indications that the society of the rather near future may be forming beyond the horizon on which the Warren Court's gaze was fixed, that it may be taking on shapes the Court did not perceive and its law cannot accommodate; that, in sum, the society may not be conforming to the Warren Court's vision.[74]

In 1970, Bickel wrote: "What the Brown opinion ultimately envisioned seems for the moment unattainable, and is becoming unwanted."[75] School desegregation efforts were running into resistance from those who wanted a spontaneous group autonomy, rather than the theoretical equality imposed by the Warren Court. According to Bickel, "[m]uch Negro opinion is now . . . more intent on group autonomy than on individual equality, or at any rate, realistically, on the equality of autonomous groups first."[76]

To be sure, Bickel's contemporaries dismissed his critiques as those of a conservative increasingly opposed to the egalitarian trend of the Warren Court decisions.[77] It is also clear that Bickel was plainly wrong with respect to some of his predictions. I am more interested, however, in reading Bickel from the perspective of (his understanding of) law's mistakes.

As we have seen, for Bickel, for law to function as a "true lie," it had to possess a measure of vagueness, ambiguity, and imprecision, a "mood"-like quality in its origins and application. Law's mistake—exemplified by the egalitarian philosophy of the Warren Court—was an espousal of too much clarity, too much definition, too evident a line of movement. When this happened, law could act against a sphere of democratic politics that could also possess the same vague, imprecise, ambiguous "mood"-like quality that law should have had.

For Bickel, then, in their ideal state, both law *and* democratic politics would possess a measure of vagueness, imprecision, and ambiguity. Both would possess the quality of a "mood." In this ideal world, law's task of judging democratic politics would be rendered more difficult. If a vague, imprecise, and blurry law is both to enable and to check an equally vague, imprecise, and blurry democratic politics, we are left with a kind of "white on white" quality, where the contrast and distinction necessary to be able to judge when a mistake is being made and to act on that mistake recede. In a world in which vagueness, imprecision, ambiguity, "mood," and "intensity" have become virtues possessed by both law and democratic politics, the task of policing the separate spheres of law and politics verges on the impossible.

Conclusion

In a mid-twentieth-century America acutely aware of both the impossibility of foundations and the need for foundations, torn in different directions by the unfolding of the Civil Rights struggle, Alexander Bickel strove to offer an account of law's place in political democracy. Law had to function as a "true lie," he argued, and to do so, it must emerge from—and function as—"mood." This could only happen through a valorization of vagueness, imprecision, ambiguity, and blurriness. When law lost these qualities—something Bickel saw in the operations of the later years of the Warren Court—law fell into mistake. What I have tried to show through this reading of Bickel is that conventional depictions of mid-twentieth-century politico-legal thought as mired in the most arid of proceduralisms offer us an impoverished picture of the period. Mid-twentieth-century legal thinkers forged a path through the dilemmas created by the imperatives of accepting and resisting the implications of Holmesian thought, of exposing law to the acid bath of history and of seeking to contain the consequences of that exposure. Some, like Bickel, turned to older common law ideas in order to forge this path, but put such older ideas to distinctly modernist uses.

At the very minimum, Bickel's valorization of law's vagueness, ambiguity, and imprecision—and his sense that law fell into mistake when it became too clear—is a paradoxical and novel way of thinking mistake. We are often (if not always) wont to judge mistakes from a perspective—mathematical, scientific, moral—that claims certainty, clarity, and definition for itself. We tend not to accuse things of being wrong because they are too *clear.*

Bickel's aesthetic investment in law as "mood"—and his sense that law would fall into mistake when it became too clear—challenges us. To begin with, it constitutes a complete reversal of critiques of the common law going all the way back to Bentham. But it raises other, more serious questions. How does one know when a "mood" has been created or disrupted? How does one argue with or contest a "mood"? If Bickel valorizes "mood"-like imprecision over more pressing questions of justice, who pays the price when law functions as "mood"? Perhaps in some cases, law's mistakes—the voting rights jurisprudence of the Warren Court in Bickel's eyes—might justify an abandoning of "mood" and might themselves become, with the passage of time, the producers of "mood," albeit this time a "mood" tilted toward equality rather than inequality? My interest here has not been to solve these essentially unresolvable questions, but to highlight one among the many ways mid-twentieth-century legal thinkers came up with for resolving the law-politics dilemma in modern America and to reveal, in so doing, the nonintuitive notion of law's mistakes as they identified them. If my account suggests a rethinking of conventional accounts of the jurisprudence of the post–World War II decades, it points as well to the productive—if sometimes also politically unsavory—uses of vagueness, imprecision, ambiguity, and "mood." Bickel does not retreat into, or hide behind, these qualities. He places them front and center. In his hands, they constitute a place from which to judge, a ground from which to name law's mistakes.

NOTES

Professor of Law and Dean's Distinguished Scholar, University of Miami School of Law. I can be reached at kparker@law.miami.edu. I would like to thank Charlton Copeland, Tracy Devine Guzmán, Patrick Gudridge, Hendrik Hartog, Renisa Mawani, and Christopher Tomlins; audiences at Amherst College, the University of California at Berkeley, and the Triangle Legal History Workshop in North Carolina; and the two outside readers for the University of Massachusetts Press. This essay was revised while I was a fellow at the National Humanities Center, Research Triangle Park, North Carolina. Adam Weiss provided assistance in cite-checking.

1. John Hart Ely, *Democracy and Distrust: A Theory of Judicial Review* (Cambridge: Harvard University Press, 1980), 71.
2. For an account of common law thought in the nineteenth century, see Kunal M. Parker, *Common Law, History, and Democracy in America, 1790–1900: Legal Thought before Modernism* (New York: Cambridge University Press, 2011).
3. 198 U.S. 45 (1905).
4. See generally Edward A. Purcell Jr., *The Crisis of Democratic Theory: Scientific Naturalism and the Problem of Value* (Louisville: University Press of Kentucky, 1973).
5. Henry Hart and Albert Sacks, *The Legal Process* (manuscript, Harvard University, 1958), 3–4, emphasis added. Later published as *The Legal Process: Basic Problems in the Making and Application of Law* (New York: Foundation Press, 1994).
6. Morton J. Horwitz, *The Transformation of American Law, 1870–1960* (New York: Oxford University Press, 1992), 255.

7. 347 U.S. 483 (1954).
8. Alexander M. Bickel, *The Morality of Consent* (New Haven: Yale University Press, 1975), 77.
9. Alexander M. Bickel, *The Least Dangerous Branch: The Supreme Court at the Bar of Politics,* 2nd ed. (New Haven: Yale University Press, 1986), 69.
10. Ibid., 25.
11. Ibid.
12. Ibid., 25–26.
13. In the seventeenth century, Sir Edward Coke, Chief Justice of the Court of Common Pleas, argued that common law judges' careful study of the law made the common law "an artificiall perfection of reason." Sir Edward Coke, *The First Part of the Institutes of the Laws of England: or a Commentary upon Littleton,* 2 vols. (New York: Garland, 1979), vol. I, L.2, c.6, sec. 138.
14. I discuss this extensively in Parker, *Common Law, History, and Democracy in America,* esp. ch. 2.
15. Bickel, *Least Dangerous Branch,* 26.
16. Ibid., 131.
17. Ibid., 244.
18. Sir William Blackstone, *Commentaries on the Laws of England,* 2nd. ed. (Oxford: Clarendon Press, 1766), I, 70.
19. Joseph H. Beale, *A Selection of Cases on the Conflict of Laws* (Cambridge: Harvard Law Review Association, 1902), III, 502.
20. Bickel, *Least Dangerous Branch,* 109.
21. Ibid., 109–10.
22. Alexander M. Bickel, *Politics and the Warren Court* (New York: Harper and Row, 1965), 261.
23. Alpheus T. Mason, "Politics: Science or Art?" *Southwestern Social Science Quarterly* 16 (December 1935): 10, quoted in Purcell, *Crisis of Democratic Theory,* 109.
24. Bickel, *Least Dangerous Branch,* 110.
25. Justice Benjamin Cardozo had also arrived at a similar conclusion when he described the process through which judges arrived at principles: "History or custom or social utility or some compelling sentiment of justice or sometimes perhaps a semi-intuitive apprehension of the pervading spirit of our law, must come to the rescue of the anxious judge, and tell him where to go." Benjamin Cardozo, *The Nature of the Judicial Process* (New Haven: Yale University Press, 1921), 43.
26. Bickel, *Least Dangerous Branch,* 199.
27. Ibid., 236.
28. *Daniel Reeves, Inc. v. Anderson,* 43 F.2d 679, 682 (2d. Cir. 1930).
29. Felix Frankfurter, *Of Law and Men,* ed. Philip Elman (New York: Harcourt, Brace and Co., 1956), 19.
30. Ibid., 31, 39 (emphasis added).
31. Bickel, *Least Dangerous Branch,* 237, quoting D. Macdonald, "The Triumph of the Fact: An American Tragedy," *The Anchor Review,* vol. 2 (New York: Doubleday, 1957), 113, 124.
32. Ken I. Kersch, "Constitutive Stores about the Common Law in Modern American Conservatism," in *NOMOS: American Conservatism,* ed. Sanford Levinson and Joel Parker (New York University Press, forthcoming) (on file with author).
33. Charles E. Lindblom, "The Science of Muddling Through," *Public Administration Review* 19 (Spring 1959).
34. Bickel, *Least Dangerous Branch,* 25.
35. Ibid., 26.
36. Ibid., 155.

37. Ibid., 69.
38. Ibid., 176 (reference to the *Garner* case).
39. Ibid., 71 (emphasis added).
40. Ibid., 45.
41. Ibid., 71.
42. Ibid., 45.
43. Ibid., 237–38.
44. Ibid., 192.
45. Robert H. Bork, "Alexander M. Bickel, Political Philosopher," *1975 Supreme Court Review* 419 (1975): 419.
46. Bickel, *Morality of Consent,* 140, quoting Jason Epstein, *The Great Conspiracy Trial* (New York: Random House, 1970), 310.
47. Bickel, *Morality of Consent,* 140–41.
48. Laura Kalman, *Yale Law School and the Sixties: Revolt and Reverberations* (Chapel Hill: University of North Carolina Press, 2005), 2.
49. Bickel, *Morality of Consent,* 3. Bickel's Burkeanism should be associated with the revival of Burkeanism in the post–World War II period. See, for example, Russell Kirk, "Prescription, Authority, and Ordered Freedom," in *What Is Conservatism,* ed. Frank S. Meyer (New York: Holt, Rinehart and Winston, 1964), 37.
50. Alexander M. Bickel, *The Supreme Court and the Idea of Progress,* 2nd ed. (New Haven: Yale University Press, 1978), 13.
51. This phrase was taken from Lewis B. Namier, *Conflicts: Studies in Contemporary History* (London: Macmillan, 1942), 70.
52. By the time of *The Supreme Court and the Idea of Progress,* Bickel was even accusing his heroes, Brandeis and Frankfurter, of "imagining the past." He put it thus: "But Brandeis and Frankfurter, while democrats and pragmatists, were also moralists and reformers. They tried valiantly to avoid getting caught in the old medieval enterprise, and to find the necessary revealed truths by the method of reason elsewhere than in themselves. They sought the truths they needed in the past. Like the eighteenth century philosophers, they soon saw, however, that the past had to be imagined if it was to be of any use." Bickel, *Supreme Court and the Idea of Progress,* 23–24.
53. Ibid., 13–14.
54. Ibid., 87.
55. Ibid., 100.
56. Ibid., 95.
57. Ibid., 96.
58. Bickel, *Morality of Consent,* 24.
59. 381 U.S. 479 (1965); Bickel, *Supreme Court and the Idea of Progress,* 41.
60. Bickel, *Supreme Court and the Idea of Progress,* 31.
61. Bickel, *Morality of Consent,* 26.
62. Ibid.
63. Edmund Burke, *Reflections on the Revolution in France* in *Two Classics of the French Revolution* (New York: Anchor Books, 1989), 45–46. On Burke's common law sensibilities, see J. G. A. Pocock, "Burke and the Ancient Constitution: A Problem in the History of Ideas," in *Politics, Language and Time: Essays on Political Thought and History* (New York: Atheneum, 1971).
64. Bickel, *Supreme Court and the Idea of Progress,* 32.
65. Bickel, *Morality of Consent,* 29, quoting Felix Frankfurter, *Law and Politics,* ed. Edward F. Prichard Jr. and Archibald MacLeish (New York: Harcourt, Brace and Co., 1939), 10, 12.
66. Bickel, *Morality of Consent,* 121.

67. For an account, see Richard M. Merelman, *Pluralism at Yale: The Culture of Political Science in America* (Madison: University of Wisconsin Press, 2003).

68. Bickel, *Supreme Court and the Idea of Progress*, 83. I discuss common lawyers' opposition to the expansion of suffrage in Parker, *Common Law, History, and Democracy in America*.

69. Bickel, *Supreme Court and the Idea of Progress*, 111 (emphasis added).

70. Ibid., 112.

71. Ibid., 115.

72. Ibid., 116–17.

73. The value of democratic variation, complexity, and flux, and of resistance to uniform specification by law, is also evident in Bickel's terse characterization of *Roe v. Wade*: "On January 22, 1973, the Supreme Court, paying formal tribute to Holmes' 1905 [*Lochner*] dissent but violating its spirit, undertook to settle the abortion issue. In place of the various state abortion statutes in controversy and in flux, the Supreme Court prescribed a virtually uniform statute of its own." Bickel, *Morality of Consent*, 27.

74. Bickel, *Supreme Court and the Idea of Progress*, 117.

75. Ibid., 150.

76. Ibid., 139.

77. See, for example, Gerald Gunther, "The Subtle Vices of the 'Passive Virtues': A Comment on Principle and Expediency in Judicial Review," 64 *Columbia Law Review* 1 (1964); J. Skelly Wright, "Professor Bickel, the Scholarly Tradition, and the Supreme Court," 84 *Harvard Law Review* 769 (1971).

3

"Mistake" in American Criminal Law

Jordan M. Steiker

What counts as "mistake" in American criminal law? Over the past half century, the answer to that question has been relatively simple—when the constable (or the prosecutor) blunders. Our system for reviewing criminal convictions focuses almost exclusively on "error" related to the investigation and prosecution of crime. Police misconduct of many varieties (coercive interrogations, inappropriate identification procedures [lineups], faulty searches, and so on) sometimes requires reversal of guilty verdicts. Prosecutorial misconduct of significant but fewer varieties (failure to disclose exculpatory evidence, discriminatory use of peremptory challenges, overzealous or inflammatory argument at trial, and so forth) likewise can require reversal in some cases. Conspicuously absent is any attention to the "results" flowing from criminal convictions. We do not scrutinize punitive sentences for excessive harshness or meaningfully police conditions of confinement; nor do we regulate the increasingly restrictive opportunities for parole or clemency. We have a strong sense of what it means to be wrongly *convicted* (via defective procedures) but virtually no sense of what it means to be fairly convicted but wrongly or excessively punished. Partly as a result of this procedural frame of justice, we have what has become the most punitive criminal justice system in the world—incarcerating a disproportionate share of the world's inmates, for longer periods (relative to the rest of the world, and especially to our Western democratic "peers"), often in abject conditions. Our criminal justice system thus sits oddly on two extreme poles: we have a seemingly unparalleled regard for the *procedural* rights of persons charged with crime accompanied by an equally outlying disregard for the *substantive* rights of criminal offenders.

This essay will briefly document the enormous and puzzling divide in

American criminal justice reflected in its heightened concern for procedural regularity and its relative indifference to substantive results. It will then turn to possible explanations for this divergence, including aspects of the American constitutional framework, culture, and politics. The essay will conclude with some observations about the significance and consequences of the largely procedural conception of "mistake" in American criminal law.

American Proceduralism

Beginning in the late 1950s, the U.S. Supreme Court transformed American criminal justice by recognizing extensive federal procedural protections in state criminal adjudication. Prior to the Warren Court's efforts, state criminal justice systems were essentially unregulated by federal law. States monitored police and prosecutors via their own, often minimalist, statutory, common law, and constitutional rules, resulting in a wide range of rights and remedial structures throughout the country. State prisoners could challenge their convictions on direct review to the U.S. Supreme Court and collaterally in the lower federal courts via federal habeas corpus. But these fora were essentially limited to enforcing the Fourteenth Amendment's general guarantee of "due process," and such appeals rarely led to the identification of error in the state processes. Only extreme malfunctions in the state systems—such as the infamous mob-dominated trials of the early twentieth century—were likely to receive federal judicial attention.[1] Indeed, throughout the South, state criminal investigations and trials were notoriously deficient in safeguarding the rights of criminal defendants, particularly African Americans. Police often resorted to physical coercion (in many cases amounting to torture) to obtain confessions from suspects; defendants often faced serious punishments without adequate representation; despite post-Reconstruction decisions prohibiting the exclusion of African Americans from jury service, juries consisted almost entirely of white men. State criminal proceedings were extremely truncated by modern-day standards, with investigation, identification of the suspect, and trial (culminating in guilty verdict) occurring in a matter of days or weeks, rather than months or years, even in capital cases.

The growing discomfort with such summary criminal processes, which had earned their derisive sobriquet "legal lynchings," led the Court to rethink the role of federal constitutional law in state criminal adjudication. In the fifteen or so years spanning the late 1950s to the early 1970s, the

Court held that many of the specific procedural protections enumerated in the Bill of Rights were essential to achieve the fundamental fairness required by the Due Process Clause of the Fourteenth Amendment. In dozens of decisions, the Court "incorporated" such rights and applied them to state proceedings, resulting in the reversal of scores of state criminal convictions and sentences. The developing body of law made clear that the chief "mistakes" policed by the federal law in state criminal adjudication concerned the procedures leading up to arrest, trial, and conviction. In the early 1950s, fewer than six hundred state criminal inmates a year sought relief in federal habeas corpus claiming violations of federal right; by the early 1990s, that number had climbed to twelve thousand.[2] Federal law now regulated virtually all aspects of state criminal cases, with constitutional limits on searches, interrogations, informant testimony, prosecutorial disclosure of exculpatory evidence, bail, jury selection, counsel, and so forth.

The Court's highly visible regulation permeated popular culture, as police dramas on television depicted offenders receiving their *Miranda* warnings and police sergeants castigating officers on the beat for conducting illegal searches (which would lead to the inadmissibility of evidence at trial in light of the "exclusionary rule" now applicable to the states). In fact, a new genre of "backlash" films, such as *Dirty Harry* and *Death Wish* chastised the courts and the law enforcement establishment for their excessive concern for defendants' procedural rights—suggesting that rogue police or private vigilantes were a needed antidote to ensure that violent offenders were apprehended, punished, and incapacitated. Politicians, too, criticized the Court for its excessive solicitude of the rights of criminal defendants, especially in light of the rising rates of violent crime and growing sense of social disorder that emerged during the same era.

Notwithstanding the popular and political backlash, federal constitutional regulation of state criminal procedures has become a permanent feature of American law and practice. Police, prosecutors, defense lawyers, trial judges, and appeals courts spend significant resources determining whether investigations and trials comport with a long litany of constitutional (as well as state statutory) rules. For better or worse, American criminal justice seems, especially to outsiders, excessively and obsessively focused on whether the procedures of our adversarial system are observed. And although such rules are tempered with exceptions and limits on relief, they give a strong impression that criminal justice in the United States is subject to law and legal constraint—that the rights of criminal defendants are worthy of attention, time, and money, and that the cost of enforcing such rules is a price we must accept if we wish to punish.

American Punitiveness and the Absence of Substantive Regulation

The extensive legal regulation of criminal procedure is matched by an almost equally odd indifference to the extent of punishment. It is a familiar story that the United States has become a remarkable outlier in its rates of incarceration and the severity of its criminal sentences (including the retention of the death penalty in a majority of states). Criminologists, sociologists, and law scholars have offered a variety of explanations for the punitive turn over the past forty years, referencing such phenomena as the politics of crime, the war on drugs, the decline in civil commitments, and skepticism (from both the left and right) about the rehabilitative capacity of prisons. Less discussed and less noticed is the absence of any meaningful regulation of American punishment. Whereas criminal defendants can invoke numerous procedural guarantees as reasons to set aside sentences and convictions, they have virtually no substantive grounds for challenging the length of their sentences or the conditions of their confinement. Over the past four decades, the Supreme Court has rejected numerous proportionality challenges to criminal sentences, even as applied to nonviolent offenders. In the context of drugs, the Court summarily reversed a lower court decision that had found a forty-year sentence disproportionate as applied to an offender convicted of possessing (with intent to distribute) nine ounces of marijuana.[3] The Court subsequently upheld a life-without-possibility-of-parole sentence (LWOP) as applied to an offender convicted of possessing a large quantity of cocaine.[4] In the recidivist context, the Court recently upheld a twenty-five-year-to-life sentence as applied to an offender who had attempted to steal three golf clubs.[5] Although the Court has imposed minimal proportionality constraints in the context of the death penalty (exempting juveniles,[6] persons with intellectual disabilities,[7] and offenders convicted of rape[8]) and juvenile offenders (rejecting LWOP as applied to juveniles convicted of nonhomicidal offenses[9] and requiring "individualized" sentencing before imposing LWOP on juveniles convicted of homicide[10]), the Court's jurisprudence as a whole reflects considerable skepticism about constitutionally imposed proportionality limits. Some members of the Court have suggested that the Court should abandon proportionality review outside of the death penalty,[11] and supporters of such review can point to no case in the modern era finding a noncapital, non-LWOP sentence to be constitutionally excessive.

In short, the overwhelming majority of American inmates have no basis for arguing that their punishment is excessive or that the interests of the inmate and the community would be better served by less restrictive alternatives to incarceration. In addition, opportunities for probation and parole have declined significantly in recent years, with many states (and the federal government) abandoning parole entirely; as a result, many inmates will serve their full sentences irrespective of evidence that they no longer constitute a danger or can contribute productively to their families and communities if released from custody. Clemency, too, has dwindled both in its frequency and scope. In prior eras, executive officials would consider a wide range of justifications for commuting sentences, including unequal treatment, rehabilitation, other changed circumstances, or excessiveness. Today, many governors and pardon boards view their clemency power as little more than auxiliary to the courts—policing procedural error, and rejecting other grounds for relief if it is apparent that the applicant "received a fair trial."

In addition, both political actors and courts have been notoriously hostile to claims of deprivation relating to conditions of confinement. Prisoners have little opportunity to challenge their exposure to violence, medical neglect, restrictive housing (such as solitary confinement), denial of rehabilitative programs, substandard diet, and other harsh terms of imprisonment. Popular culture accepts as a given that inmates will be subjected to rape and violence at the hands of other prisoners, and, despite limited federal efforts to monitor sexual assault in federal and state facilities,[12] victimization rates remain remarkably high. Indeed, reports of a significant decline in violent crime throughout the United States over the past decade should take account of the possibility that some of that drop reflects merely the *shift* of such crime from free society to inside the walls of prisons and jails, where offenses short of homicide are often under-reported. The Prison Litigation Reform Act (1996) has severely undercut any judicial efforts to improve prison conditions via litigation, imposing onerous requirements for federal judicial intervention (exhaustion of administrative remedies, filing fees, physical injury requirement, and so forth). Prisoners essentially have to accept the brutality of their punishment, and claims of mistaken imposition of unlawful deprivation are largely unwelcome and rarely vindicated.

The Illustrative Case of the American Death Penalty

The American death penalty captures the enormous gulf between procedure and substance and the limited conception of "mistake" in American criminal justice. As support for the death penalty waned in the 1960s, opponents embarked on a strategy to have the Court invalidate the punishment. Although several states had repealed their capital statutes in the early 1960s, it was apparent that national abolition could be achieved only through constitutional decree. The legal strategy was twofold: demonstrate that the prevailing system of administering the death penalty had become excessively arbitrary given the remarkable decline in capital sentencing and executions (especially in light of the breadth of death eligibility within state statutes), and urge the Court to recognize that the increasingly rare recourse to the death penalty reflected widespread societal rejection of the punishment. The strategy produced a monumental victory in Furman v. Georgia,[13] when the Court declared the prevailing administration of the death penalty "cruel and unusual" punishment in violation of the Eighth Amendment. The result was supported by five justices, each writing separately about the defects of the status quo. Only two justices—Brennan and Marshall—agreed with the substantive claim that the death penalty as a punishment was constitutionally infirm and could not be administered in a constitutional fashion. The remaining justices focused primarily on the absence of procedural safeguards to ensure that the penalty was administered in a fair manner and targeted only the truly "worst" offenders.

When states reacted to Furman with new capital statutes, the Court reaffirmed the largely procedural frame of the decision. The Court regarded the new safeguards in the post-Furman statutes (enumeration of aggravating factors, bifurcated proceedings, mandatory appellate review, and so forth) as vastly preferable to the prior regime in which jurors were afforded unbridled discretion to choose life versus death. The Court did not demand any demonstration that the distribution of capital sentences was in fact less arbitrary and more principled than the prior distribution. Moreover, a decade later, in McCleskey v. Kemp,[14] when sophisticated empirical research indicated that racial discrimination continued to influence outcomes in capital cases, the Court rejected the claim that the Constitution demands any threshold level of reliability or nondiscrimination. The Court's constitutionalization of death penalty law, captured by the principle that "death is different," requires heightened procedural protections in capital cases, but the states (and thus ultimately the Court) have no power over the actual results in capital sentencing. Hence, the only "mistakes" addressable by the Court relate to the failure of states to implement procedural protections. The logical extreme of this position was subsequently reflected in Herrera v. Collins,[15] in which the Court refused to embrace the proposition that the Constitution prohibits the execution of an innocent person. Herrera offered "new evidence" of his innocence a few years after his conviction and capital sentence (including the alleged confession of the "true" killer). The state courts refused to entertain any such evidence because it was offered more than thirty days after trial. The Court, in rejecting Herrera's claim, insisted that federal courts traditionally entertain only claims of "constitutional violation," and not simply claims of factual error regarding the accuracy of the conviction. As a constitutional matter, a claimed "mistake" must go to the procedures used to secure the conviction, and the issue of actual innocence is irrelevant. The Court ultimately did not decide whether the Constitution forbids the execution of a demonstrably innocent person, and has yet definitively to do so. Overall, though, Herrera illustrates the Court's position that the judicial role with respect to the death penalty is largely confined to ensuring adequate procedures.

Moreover, the Court has resisted efforts to protect condemned inmates from increasingly harsh terms of confinement or potentially painful executions. Over the past two decades, most death penalty jurisdictions have made solitary confinement the norm on death row, requiring inmates to endure years or even decades without human contact. Such confinement, which traditionally was triggered in response to poor behavior on the part of an inmate ("administrative segregation"), has now become part of the routine punishment of a death sentence, leading some critics to argue that the death penalty now entails "two" punishments—long-term psychological deprivation followed by an execution. In addition, inmates challenging execution methods have had little success in the courts. In the late nineteenth century, the Court upheld the transition from hanging to electrocution,[16] and subsequently refused relief to an inmate whose botched electrocution led him to challenge further efforts to consummate his execution (the prospect of which was termed "death by installments").[17] The Court, declaring that "[a]ccidents happen for which no man is to blame,"[18] held that the Constitution is not violated where there is no purpose to inflict unnecessary pain. That decision foreshadowed the Court's most recent decision upholding Kentucky's lethal injection protocol,[19] which was challenged on the grounds that it had insufficient safeguards against the possibility of unnecessary pain on the part of the condemned. Overall, the Court minimally polices states' choices regarding the execution process, and its "death-is-different" jurisprudence reserves scrutiny almost exclusively for the procedures culminating in a conviction and sentence, rather than the post-trial circumstances leading to an execution.

Mistake as Procedural Error Rather than Substantive Violation: Causes?

What accounts for the American fixation on procedure and indifference to substance? Part of the answer might relate to the American inheritance of its common law, adversarial system. Such a system views criminal adjudication as a form of "contest," in which the state is obligated to provide fair rules and an impartial arbiter. The adversarial system lends itself to clear enumeration of procedural safeguards, many of which (the right against self-incrimination, for example) do not fit comfortably in civil inquisitorial systems. The American adversarial system highlights the unique and powerful role of lay jurors, and the valorization of that role tends to discourage judicial overrides of jury verdicts on substantive grounds; rather, judges are expected to police the inputs of the decision (enforcing complicated rules of evidence, appropriate forms of examination, cross-examination, and argument before the jury), but rarely to police outcomes.

Our Constitution, too, elevates procedure over substance. Much of the Bill of Rights focuses on protections against police and prosecutorial overreaching, including the guarantee against unreasonable searches and seizures (and accompanying requirements for warrants), the prohibitions against double jeopardy and self-incrimination, the right to a grand jury in certain cases, the right to a speedy and public trial, the right to confront witnesses, and the right to counsel. Only the Eighth Amendment offers a substantive limit—its prohibition against "cruel and unusual punishment"—but even that limit appears to permit "cruel" punishments that are widely administered and therefore not "unusual." In his recent, posthumously published book lamenting the excessive punitiveness of American criminal justice,[20] Bill Stuntz pointedly contrasts the sorts of procedural protections secured by the American Constitution with the robust, libertarian constraints embraced at roughly the same time in France's Declaration of the Rights of Man and of the Citizen, including the pronouncement that "[t]he law ought to establish only penalties that are strictly and obviously necessary." Nothing comparable exists in the American criminal justice system, and it is telling to reflect on how such a principle might be applied to our current regime of capital punishment, LWOP sentences, mandatory-minimum sentences for nonviolent offenses (including drug possession), harsh recidivist provisions, and current conditions of confinement. Moreover, our court-centered culture contributes to the view that whatever our Constitution does not regulate is not properly subject to regulation. As indicated above, political actors increasingly understand their role as limited to reinforcing judicial limits in criminal adjudication; if no such limits extend to the appropriateness or severity of punishment in particular cases, the political branches step aside.

The absence of meaningful substantive constraints on punishment might thus be attributable in part to our common law and constitutional traditions, rooted in an adversarial conception of justice. This explanation is not entirely satisfactory. First, though the adversarial structure leans strongly toward procedural protections, it does not preclude substantive limits. Our common law peer countries are significantly less punitive in their range of punishments and have a variety of formal and informal checks on the severity of punishment. Second, though the federal Constitution secures numerous procedural protections, the failure of the Supreme Court to embrace substantive limits appears more contingent than the argument from constitutional text would suggest. Both the Cruel and Unusual Punishments Clause and the Due Process Clause provide ample room for more vigorous substantive protection; indeed, at various points in our constitutional history the Court has read the Due Process Clause to safeguard numerous substantive rights outside of the criminal context, including rights of privacy, bodily integrity, and economic liberty. Moreover, the focus on *federal* constitutional limits seems inapt, given the relatively recent focus on federal constitutional limits as the primary constraint on state criminal processes. All fifty states have their own constitutions, and state constitutions are subject to frequent revision. Some state constitutions afford greater substantive protections than the federal Constitution (for example, Louisiana prohibited forcibly medicating a death-sentenced inmate to render him competent for execution under state constitutional provisions barring cruel and unusual punishment and protecting privacy, even though the federal Constitution had not been so construed),[21] but by and large even state constitutions are quite limited in their substantive protections. Given that state constitutions are of more recent vintage, are not tied to the federal constitutional text, and are also procedurally rather than substantively focused, there are likely forces other than path dependence traceable to the federal Constitution that account for the limited substantive protections common to both federal and state constitutions.

A cultural explanation for our enforcement of procedural rather than substantive justice would highlight various aspects of American individualism, including notions of personal rather than communal responsibility, a pervasive commitment to markets and competition, and skepticism about claims of equality. As a culture, the United States has been resistant to claims that individuals do not bear full responsibility for criminal activity. Our robust embrace of retributivism, and the belief that offenders deserve punishment in some meaningful proportion to the harm they cause, contrasts with theories that locate responsibility in, and allocate blame to, other social and institutional actors, including the government. Albert Camus famously argued that every society in some sense produces the criminality it then seeks to punish—reflecting a belief that deprivation and inequality can undermine the full assignment of blame to individual criminal offenders.[22] The absence of widespread belief in collective responsibility for crime might contribute to the institutional reluctance to treat particular impositions of punishment as excessive or mistaken. Similarly, the belief in markets and competition as best allocating resources resonates with our model of criminal adjudication, in which the adversarial process generates "just" outcomes by virtue of the process itself. Along these lines, it is likely not coincidental that the United States is an outlier not only in its harsh punishments but also in its levels of inequality and minimalist safety net. A heightened belief in individual responsibility facilitates toleration of disparities in the distribution of wealth and toleration in both the severity and distribution of punishment.

This sort of cultural account has weaknesses as well. While it is true that the United States has long lacked significant substantive constraints on punishment, the status of the United States as an outlier in the severity of its punishments is of relatively recent vintage. For much of our history, the United States was on the other end of the spectrum—in its reform (and, in some states, early abolition) of capital punishment, in its early embrace of penitentiaries, and in its recognition of rehabilitation as the primary goal of punishment. Indeed, in his observations of American criminal justice in the nineteenth century, de Tocqueville argued that American respect for the individual accounted for its relative *mildness* in punishment. The fact that the American embrace of procedural protections and its imposition of harsh criminal sanctions are both relatively new and not reflective of long-standing trends or practices suggests that claims of deep-seated cultural determinism are problematic.

A third possibility is that the connection between heightened procedural protections and harsh, arbitrary punishments is actually *causal*—that the growth of severe punishments and limited substantive safeguards was in part a response to the excessive solicitude of the Warren Court for the rights of criminal defendants. Stuntz makes a version of this argument and claims that the turn toward highly punitive sanctions was prompted in part by the Warren Court revolution, which, among other things, denied local control over criminal justice issues. Increased procedural safeguards generated a political backlash, especially as they coincided with increases in violent crime (which themselves were partly the product of diminished local democratic control).[23] Others have argued more straightforwardly that the Warren Court simply opened a space for the politics of crime. Politicians seized on the increased insecurity (attributable to rising crime and judicial protection of criminal defendants) and viewed criminal justice policy as a newly available source of political power—a form of political entrepreneurship. President Nixon famously regarded crime as a wedge issue that, together with busing and other explicitly racial or racially coded issues, could provide inroads for the Republican Party in the previously "solid" Democratic South. The politicization of crime continued at local and national levels for several decades, playing a prominent role in the elections of presidents Reagan and George Bush Sr.

These causal, political accounts of the connection between American procedural reform and substantive harshness have some power, but they face some difficulties as well. In reviewing Stuntz's thesis, Stephen Shulhofer argues that the timeline of criminal justice reforms simply does not fit the causal claim.[24] Federal drug mandatories predated the Warren Court revolution. And the harshest drug law and punitive policies were embraced well after the Warren Court revolution had run its course. American punitiveness, Schulhofer insists, could just as easily be attributable to the crack epidemic and the convergence between the left and the right about the inadequacies of rehabilitation as an attainable criminal justice goal. Perhaps most tellingly, Schulhofer argues that a similar set of punitive policies emerged in Thatcher's Britain at about the same time as they emerged in the United States, despite no comparable embrace in Britain of expansive procedural protections.[25]

Schulhofer's reference to the broad skepticism (among liberals and conservatives) regarding rehabilitation points to an additional explanation for procedural but not substantive protection. It is obvious that procedural safeguards reflect a distrust of unchecked governmental power—the fear that the state will overreach in its efforts to convict defendants. Less obvious—but perhaps no less true—is that our recent gravitation toward harsh, unreviewable punishments also reflects distrust of government.[26] The adoption of mandatory-minimum sentences, the withdrawal of probationary and parole options, and the retention of the death penalty all stem in part from fear that bureaucratic government officials will make poor choices and will exercise excessive leniency if afforded discretion. Thus, though a familiar refrain for death penalty opponents is to highlight the perceived hypocrisy of entrusting the government with the power over life and death at a time when there is widespread distrust regarding the government's ability to manage more mundane tasks (mail service, tax collection, road maintenance), the retention of the death penalty and the broader efforts to curb governmental discretion with respect to punishment manifest profoundly *anti*-governmental views. In this sense, procedural checks and the withdrawal of substantive safeguards might be regarded as a united populist front against inept or potentially dishonest governmental actors.

Mistake as Procedural Error Rather than Substantive Violation: Significance?

Our current approach in American criminal law, in which defendants have a vast reservoir of procedural rights and virtually no substantive protections against excessive punishment, has important consequences. The high visibility of procedural regulation induces a false or at least exaggerated belief in the general fairness and reliability of the criminal justice system. The media portrays criminal adjudication as an aggressive battle between prosecutors and high-powered defense lawyers armed with a staggering array of procedural cards, in which manifestly guilty offenders are frequently cut loose because of hypertechnical, judicially imposed rules of police and prosecutorial behavior. The highly visible procedural safeguards mask the reality of underenforced norms of procedural fairness. The growth of punitive penalties—accompanied by broad deference in their application—substantially undercuts the value of procedural rights. The availability of harsh sentences induces criminal defendants to accept plea bargains, as the discounted penalty is of greater value than the (often remote) prospect that enforcement of procedural rights will produce an acquittal at trial. Indeed, harsh penalties will induce criminal defendants not simply to waive procedural safeguards but to accept punishment despite innocence, given the reasonable fear that factual innocence will not always prevail and the extraordinary pressures defense attorneys face to settle cases rather than to proceed to trial.

But just as the absence of substantive protection can often frustrate procedural norms, procedural norms can in some cases counterbalance substantive deregulation. This possibility is most evident in the prevailing regulation of the American death penalty. As noted above, the Court's decisions have largely afforded procedural protections and eschewed substantive guarantees; the ultimate decision whether to retain or abolish capital punishment remains with the states, and the Court has not enforced any requirements regarding the distribution of the death penalty (apart from a few narrow proportionality protections for discrete classes of offenders, such as juveniles and offenders with intellectual disabilities). During the first two decades of this course of regulation, the highly visible procedural safeguards coupled with the absence of any significant substantive limitations created precisely the sort of legitimation problems described above, in which the actors both within and outside the system were likely to view the death penalty as "fair enough" despite the reality that its imposition continued to be arbitrary and discriminatory.[27] Now, though, the toll of several decades of procedural regulation has become more apparent. Even though the actual procedural rights recognized by the Court are relatively minimal, their implementation and enforcement put enormous financial strains on states' capital systems.[28] Those burdens, in turn, have led several states to repeal the death penalty and many others to reduce their recourse to the punishment. Death sentencing has dropped nationwide by more than 65 percent over the past two decades or so, and that drop reflects in part the unanticipated consequences of long-term procedural regulation. Procedural safeguards have in effect placed substantive limits on the practical application of capital punishment in the United States.[29]

The procedural path to substantive restriction entails other dimensions. By recognizing and enforcing only procedural rights, the Court has influenced discourse and assumed an agenda-setting function. Much of the public debate surrounding the death penalty tracks the Court's largely procedural framework, and noninstrumental arguments, such as those focusing on human dignity and the appropriate relation between citizen and state, have largely dropped out of view. This dynamic is evident outside the death penalty context as well, where the absence of any meaningful review of harsh sentencing practices has contributed to the absence of such debate in public and political arenas.[30]

Indeed, the decision of courts to forgo substantive review of punishment is motivated in part by its sense of institutional competence. Courts worry about the absence of manageable standards for determining what counts as excessive punishment, so they focus on procedural safeguards in the administration of criminal penalties. The problem, though, is that the subtlety of the "institutional competence" argument is often lost on other institutions, and nonjudicial actors often regard the absence of constitutionally crafted protective doctrines as a reason for eschewing the need for substantive protections altogether. By not recognizing the possibility of "mistake" in the severity of punishments, or in their application to particular offenders, courts inadvertently communicate that punishments cannot be "wrong" along these dimensions.

The concept of "mistake" appears in numerous legal contexts, often referring to various types of cognitive error committed by legal actors. For example, complicated bodies of doctrine distinguish between mistakes of "law" and "fact" for the purpose of determining the enforceability of contracts or the imposition of criminal liability. This paper looks at "mistake" from a different, nontechnical perspective—as a category addressing what the law seeks to correct. In American criminal practice, procedural regularity, rather than substantive justice, has become the overriding focus, and that focus has serious consequences. Courts spend extraordinary time reviewing the propriety of police investigations and the fairness of trials, and virtually no time on the appropriateness of ultimate punishments. These efforts contribute to the popular perception that the legitimacy of punishment rests on whether particular "rules" are followed prior to its imposition. At the same time, courts, executive officials, and the wider public appear increasingly uninterested in whether the amount or type of punishment imposed in a particular case is justified in light of the nature of the offense and offender.

As argued above, the valorization of process has both contributed to, and is reflected in, the remarkable inattention to the current American experiment with harsh sentencing practices and staggering rates of incarceration. Although some actors within and outside of the criminal justice system have highlighted the consequences of these policies for offenders and their communities, the legal system has virtually no vocabulary (much less doctrine) for addressing these developments. The United States, once known primarily for its solicitude for the rights of the accused, is now regarded as distinctive in its punitiveness toward the convicted. Perhaps part of the solution going forward is a rethinking of how and when the criminal justice system makes "mistakes."

NOTES

1. See, for example, *Moore v. Dempsey*, 261 U.S. 86 (1923).

2. In *Brown v. Allen*, 344 U.S. 443, 536–37 (1953), Justice Jackson decried the "haystack" of petitions—541—filed by state prisoners in 1951; by 1990, that figure was around 12,000. L. Ralph Mecham, "Annual Report of the Director of the Administrative Office of the United States Courts" 191 (Admin Office U.S. Courts 1991) (1990 figures).

3. *Hutto v. Davis*, 454 U.S. 370 (1982).

4. *Harmelin v. Michigan*, 501 U.S. 957 (1991).

5. 538 U.S. 11 (2003).

6. *Roper v. Simmons*, 543 U.S. 551 (2005).

7. *Atkins v. Virginia*, 536 U.S. 304 (2002).

8. *Coker v. Georgia*, 433 U.S. 584 (1977); *Kennedy v. Louisiana*, 554 U.S. 407 (2008).

9. *Graham v. Florida*, 560 U.S. 48 (2010).

10. *Miller v. Alabama*, 132 S, Ct, 2455 (2012).

11. Harmelin, 501 U.S. at 996 (Scalia, J., joined by C. J. Rehnquist).

12. Prison Rape Elimination Act of 2003.

13. 408 U.S. 238 (1972).

14. 481 U.S. 279 (1987).

15. 506 U.S. 390 (1993).

16. In re Kemmler, 136 U.S. 436 (1890).

17. *Francis v. Resweber*, 329 U.S. 459 (1947).

18. Ibid.

19. *Baze v. Rees*, 553 U.S. 35 (2008).

20. William Stuntz, *The Collapse of American Criminal Justice* (Cambridge: Harvard University Press, 2011), 76.

21. *Perry v. Louisiana*, 498 U.S. 38 (1990).

22. Albert Camus, "Reflections on the Guillotine," in *Reflexions sur la peine Capitale*, ed. Arthur Koestler and Albert Camus (Paris: Calmann-Levy, 1957).

23. Stuntz, *Collapse of American Criminal Justice*, n. 20, at 236–43.

24. Stephen Schulhofer, "Criminal Justice, Local Democracy, and Constitutional Rights," *Michigan Law Review* 111 (2013): 1045, 1076.

25. Ibid., at 1078.

26. David Garland, *Peculiar Institution: America's Death Penalty in an Age of Abolition* (Cambridge: Harvard University Press, 2010).

27. Carol S. Steiker and Jordan M. Steiker, "Sober Second Thoughts: Reflections on Two Decades of Constitutional Regulation of Capital Punishment," *Harvard Law Review* 109 (1995): 357.

28. Carol S. Steiker and Jordan Steiker, "Entrenchment and/or Destabilization? Reflections on (Another) Two Decades of Constitutional Regulation of Capital Punishment," *Journal of Law and Inequality* 30 (2012): 211.

29. Ibid., at 235.

30. Carol S. Steiker and Jordan M. Steiker, "Capital Punishment: A Century of Discontinuous Debate," *Journal of Criminal Law and Criminology* 100 (2010): 643.

4

The Ghosts in the "Machinery of Death"

The Rhetoric of Mistake in Lethal Injection Reform

Jody Lyneé Madeira

> One might think that in the United States, where technology exists to send astronauts to the moon with perfection, we should be able to shoot people to the hereafter with similar precision.
>
> —Marian Borg and Michael Radelet, "On Botched Executions"

Introduction

"To err is human"—that old saw has graced everything from refrigerator magnets to Internet memes. As pedestrian as that phrase has become, it contains a pearl of truth: the potential for mistake is inherent in human activity. Such errors have been particularly evident in the context of lethal injection, which has become haunted by mistake as evidenced by inmate pain and suffering, witness discomfort, lengthy execution attempts, or full-blown failures such as the Oklahoma execution of Clayton Lockett on April 29, 2014. In a rare move, many courts, legislatures, and departments of correction have initiated reforms; however, rapid innovation also intensifies organizational stress, increasing the likelihood of the very mistakes that reforms purportedly reduce. Regardless of execution method, the fact that we have capital punishment on the books means that we must acknowledge the possibility of fallibility and mistake, and engage with their consequences and ethical implications. As Jesse Wegman asserted in a *New York Times* blog one month after the Lockett execution, "[T]he death penalty is, like all punishments, debated, litigated, and carried out by imperfect human beings in an inescapably political environment. Governments choose how to kill their citizens not through a logical or even rational process, but in response to the conflicting priorities of multiple constituencies."[1]

Yet, the secrecy that frequently pervades lethal injection reform is at odds with democratic principles; though the state executes in the name of "the people," it is now increasingly impossible for citizens to learn what their state is doing. This opaqueness is dangerous to inmates and to citizens alike; it is our democratic right and privilege to decide what should be done about current lethal injection quandaries to determine where we want to draw the line, and what measures and outcomes are acceptable.

Moreover, though lethal injection reform aims to reduce mistakes, it is inadvertently creating an institutional environment in which mistakes thrive. This happens in two ways. First, legislatures, courts, and other sources such as the public and media exert pressure to modify protocols and pharmaceuticals. This pressure and the awareness that institutional actions are under intense scrutiny heightens stress, which in turn increases the risk of mistake—effectively dooming a world they are trying to save. And because legislatures often delegate the authority to design and implement these changes to the director of corrections or prison warden, reform directives could imply that these projects should or could be completed while the department is still carrying out scheduled executions. Second, corporations and countries that oppose capital punishment have enacted export and distribution controls to ensure that they are not inadvertently supplying lethal injection drugs. But these measures have the direct consequence of forcing states to innovate with new products and technologies in order to carry out scheduled executions, thereby further increasing the risk of mistake. Of course, these actors might only be trying to distance themselves from a practice they find objectionable. This distance, however, also has an important strategic effect: it creates mistakes, and more frequent mistakes make a stronger case for abolition. Either way, because constricted supplies increases the likelihood of error, these actors are also complicit in creating an institutional culture of mistake.

Lethal injection reform is a case study of how organizations can best manage mistake. There is a scholarly literature directly relevant to this analysis that has not yet been tapped: scholarship on organizational deviance, or "dark side" studies. For organizations to manage mistake effectively, four key factors must be present: (1) agreement on appropriate objectives; (2) efforts to reach objectives led by people who have demonstrated good judgment and judgmental confidence (recognized by self and others); (3) respect for expertise from internal and external sources; and (4) effective and utilized feedback mechanisms. A healthy organizational culture recognizes that, although mistake may be inevitable, its risk can be minimized. Acknowledgment of mistake becomes a marker of professionalism, and recognition, reporting, and redesign its hallmarks.

In capital punishment, it is difficult to create this culture, and the current system is likely to increase mistake. There is no agreement on objectives, even among departments of correction ("Corrections") and courts; should the end result be death, or is it a quick death, or one with minimal pain? Larger disagreements on objectives between death penalty advocates and opponents have closed down pharmaceutical markets, and there is close scrutiny (or as close as secrecy legislation allows) of protocols and drugs. The process is so politicized that there is little deference to expertise; proponents view protocol objections as efforts to end capital punishment, not reform lethal injection, and opponents see those involved in executions as inherently suspect participants in an innately undignified process. The existence and efficacy of feedback mechanisms is unknown. Evidence exists that there is little real commitment to minimizing errors. Those in charge of executions view the ultimate goal as killing a condemned inmate. To them, criticism and challenges are inevitable, and most "glitches" are molehills made into mountains, and the condemned is easily dehumanized. Even if execution team members perceive their job as designing executions that are as quick and painless as possible, they are not given the necessary tools for this project, often do not possess professional expertise and training, and do not command deference and respect.

In Part I, this chapter will describe how lethal injection, once touted as the most humane of all execution methods, became so controversial, and the cultural, legal, and market pressures that have forced states and Corrections to reform protocols. Part II will briefly survey "dark side" organizational studies, in which mistake and other forms of organizational deviance are not dysfunctional or abnormal but implicit in normal organizational practices. Organizational deviance is enabled and reinforced by social and cultural practices, psychological factors, organizational norms and structures, and overlaps with technology and technological innovation. In Part III, this "dark side" approach is applied to lethal injection reform, focusing on three key areas: execution technologies and executioners' traditional culture of innovation; processes of protocol development and reform; and reactions to mistakes. This chapter concludes by urging new reforms within organizational culture, such as feedback mechanisms and transparency that reduce opportunities for organizational deviance, use expertise effectively, and facilitate urgently needed systems of information gathering and exchange.

I. Into the Crucible of Lethal Injection Reform

A Brief History of Current Lethal Injection Reforms

Lethal injection has been the most common execution method for approximately forty years, since its adoption in 1977 in Oklahoma. Oklahoma legislators Bill Wiseman,[2] who wanted to make execution more humane,[3] and Bill Dawson, who worried about the cost of fixing the state's electric chair, sought help in creating a lethal injection protocol. After the Oklahoma Medical Association refused to help, Wiseman sought out state medical examiner Dr. Jay Chapman.[4] Chapman initially asserted that he had no experience in this context, but he eventually proposed an intravenous three-drug cocktail of sodium thiopental, pancuronium bromide, and potassium chloride that was also approved by the anesthesiologist Dr. Stanley Deutsch.[5] Although the Oklahoma state assembly's reception of the new lethal injection method was lukewarm and "tentative," it nonetheless quickly adopted it. Other states rapidly followed suit, with many copying Oklahoma's lethal injection statute.[6] As the trial court in *Baze v. Rees* asserted, "there is scant evidence that ensuing States' adoption of lethal injection was supported by any additional medical or scientific studies. . . . [T]he various States simply fell in line relying solely on Oklahoma's protocol."[7] By 2009, all death penalty states had switched to lethal injection, with most using the same three-drug protocol.[8]

For years, inmates challenged the constitutionality of lethal injection, to no avail. Then, in 2005, the Supreme Court ruled in *Hill v. McDonough*[9] that inmates could challenge the constitutionality of a form of execution (here, lethal injection) as violating the Eighth Amendment under 42 U.S.C. § 1983, even though they had already sought habeas relief. Three years later, the Supreme Court upheld Kentucky's three-drug lethal injection protocol in *Baze vs. Reese*.[10] Under the *Baze* standard, to prove an Eighth Amendment violation inmates had to show that a state's lethal injection protocol presented a " 'substantial' or 'objectively intolerable' risk of serious harm," and propose an alternative procedure that was "feasible, readily implemented, and in fact significantly reduces a substantial risk of severe pain."[11] Since *Baze*, state courts have been largely indifferent to lethal injection claims.[12] Even so, challenges have skyrocketed since 2008, and inmates' claims are both "prolific and variable."[13] Moreover, *Baze* may now have only limited precedential value, since litigated issues have "only remote or nonexistent parallels" to *Baze* issues, and some questions are "no longer viable."[14] Yet, *Baze* and its standards were reaffirmed when the U.S. Supreme Court affirmed the constitutionality of midazolam as part of a three-drug lethal injection cocktail in *Glossip v. Gross*, where Justice Alito, writing for the majority, noted that Oklahoma had recently reformed its protocol and repeated *Baze*'s contention that federal courts should not "embroil [themselves] in ongoing scientific controversies beyond their expertise."[15]

Indeed, unforeseen events since *Baze* have wreaked havoc on states' abilities to procure lethal injection drugs. There has been much speculation that the three-drug cocktail upheld in *Baze* risked administering too little anesthetic; in that scenario, paralyzed but conscious inmates would endure enormous but invisible suffering from the potassium chloride injection. But political forces and their market consequences, not judicial intervention, have brought lethal injection to its knees. Currently, states are faced with dwindling, exhausted, or expired supplies, restrictions on drug importation, and manufacturers' efforts to prevent their products from being used in lethal injection protocols. Political matters such as foreign export controls and manufacturer opposition have pushed states away from a position of certainty. Public relations factors have also influenced reform; though courts and experts have suggested a single massive barbiturate dose (often, pentobarbital) in lieu of a three-drug cocktail, most officials have long been resistant. In the late 1970s, Dr. Ralph Gray, head of Texas correctional medicine, "was afraid of a hue and cry" and rejected this formulation because "people would think we are treating people the same way that we're treating animals."[16]

Although some novel solutions have been proposed, including funding drug production in state laboratories,[17] states have increasingly relied on two problematic sources: compounding pharmacies and foreign manufacturers. Compounding pharmacies are not regulated by the Food and Drug Administration (FDA) as are commercial manufacturers, but instead are regulated "rather permissively by the states."[18] Yet, compounding pharmacies have troubled histories; in October 2012, a Massachusetts compounding pharmacy produced a contaminated steroid that killed sixty-four people and made hundreds ill, and a subsequent FDA inspection uncovered still other problems.[19] Indeed, when South Dakota switched to a one-drug protocol in October 2012, it obtained its pentobarbital from a compounding pharmacy; after the executed inmate snored and remained open-eyed throughout his execution, an investigation revealed that the product contained a fungus.[20]

Proposed federal legislation and potential regulation by state legislatures and pharmacy boards could increase oversight of compounding pharmacies. Reforms could require public disclosure of what drugs compounding pharmacies manufacture and purchaser identities, and could even prohibit lethal pharmaceutical production.[21] Such steps toward transparency would be a bright light in a tunnel otherwise dimmed by state secrecy efforts. After *Baze,* inmates' attorneys sought to obtain information about lethal injection drugs and providers through discovery requests and Freedom of Information Act (FOIA) requests.[22] Some states attempted to thwart these tactics by passing secrecy legislation protecting lethal injection protocols and suppliers' and participants' identities.[23] These attorneys responded by suing corrections departments, claiming this legislation violated their condemned clients' rights to due process and eviscerated their ability to bring Eighth Amendment claims.[24]

State access to foreign-manufactured lethal injection drugs has also been difficult. In 2010, a campaign by the London anti–death penalty organization Reprieve persuaded U.K. pharmaceutical companies,[25] and European states and corporations unpleasantly aware of their connections to American capital punishment, with dramatic market repercussions. Sodium thiopental was manufactured in the United States by Hospira, Inc., until 2009, when it became too difficult to obtain an active ingredient.[26] When Hospira attempted to begin production in Italy, authorities "threatened legal action,"[27] prompting Hospira to cease production in January 2011.[28] Thereafter, states began to import the drug from other European sources, and the FDA allowed this importation under its enforcement discretion so that the foreign-sourced thiopental did not have to undergo normal approval processes.[29]

After states began to import foreign-sourced thiopental, some groups began to question where these drugs came from. In 2010, the Drug Enforcement Agency (DEA) investigated and ultimately asked many states to surrender their thiopental supplies.[30] In July of 2011, a group of death row inmates in Arizona, California, and Tennessee sued the FDA in *Beaty v. Food and Drug Administration* over the importation of unapproved thiopental, alleging it had unlawfully allowed shipments of a "misbranded," "adulterated," and unapproved drug to enter the United States, contrary to long-standing agency policies.[31] Both the federal district court and the U.S. Court of Appeals for the DC Circuit (in *Cook v. Food and Drug Administration*)[32] agreed and granted the plaintiffs a permanent injection barring the FDA from permitting entry of foreign-sourced thiopental that was misbranded or otherwise violated regulations.[33]

After *Baze,* the three-drug protocol began to fall out of judicial favor even as drugs became harder to find. In *State v. Rivera,* an Ohio judge invalidated the state's three-drug protocol because it likely caused pain, and recommended a single barbiturate injection,[34] prompting Ohio to move to a single-drug protocol using thiopental. Other states followed suit, proving once again that "for over a century, states have closely followed the execution strategies of others states."[35] After *Beaty* and *Cook,* states also began to amend protocols to replace thiopental with pentobarbital or other drugs.

Currently, at least fifteen states have switched to protocols using pentobarbital, manufactured in Europe. England placed export controls on thiopental in November 2010 following the Reprieve campaign and quickly did so for similar drugs, spurring other countries to enact similar bans. These efforts culminated in a European Union (EU) export ban on capital punishment drugs under the EU Torture Regulation.[36] Manufacturers currently require purchasers to obtain the drug through one wholesaler and to sign forms stating that they are not a prison and will not sell the drug.[37] State attempts to replace pentobarbital with propofol and phenobarbital have triggered additional European export bans and manufacturer opposition, such as those from German corporation Fresenius Kabi.[38]

Pharmaceutical corporations' objections imply that they regard the death penalty as unethical and inhumane. Danish pharmaceutical corporation Lundbeck asserted that it "adamantly opposes the distressing misuse of our product in capital punishment,"[39] and "it contradicts everything we are in business to do—provide therapies that improve people's lives."[40] London-based phenobarbital manufacturer Hikma Pharmaceuticals stated that it "strongly objects to the use of any of its products in capital punishment," since the company "aims to improve lives."[41] New Jersey–based Par

Pharmaceuticals alleged that the use of its Brevital in lethal injection was "inconsistent with its medical indications," and contradicted its corporate mission of "help[ing] improve the quality of life."[42] Manufacturer resistance has even spread beyond pharmaceutical companies; after an article in the *New England Journal of Medicine* revealed that North Carolina had used one of its Bispectral Index monitors in the execution of Willie Brown Jr. in April 2006, Aspect Medical Systems announced that it "does not support the use of BIS technology in conjunction with lethal injections,"[43] and that this use was "inconsistent with Aspect's mission to improve patient's [*sic*] lives by helping healthcare professionals deliver the best possible patient care."[44]

This accords with professional medical associations' efforts to remove doctors and other medical professionals from execution chambers, with the American Medical Association (AMA) and others[45] passing ethical guidelines barring members from participating.[46] These groups cite the Hippocratic Oath and other ethical standards, as well as the fact that medical professionals are sworn to preserve, not take, life, and the possibility that execution participation could undermine other patients' trust.[47]

The Sociology of Mistake and the "Dark Side" of Organizations

In describing how the Corrections culture and lethal injection reform cultivate mistake, this chapter will assess these phenomena from the perspective of "dark side" organizational studies, which has analyzed mistake, misconduct, disaster, and misfortune. This approach posits institutional cultures, structures, and norms that direct actors toward certain goals, identify particular goal-achieving strategies, and normalize as rational decisions made in pursuit of these ends (even if others outside the organization may perceive these same decisions as deviant).[48] This perspective contradicts rational theories of organizational decision-making, which construct institutional actors as amoral decision makers whose deplored "actions are motivated by rational calculation of costs and opportunities."[49] From the rational standpoint, decisions to violate "laws, rules, or administrative regulations" appear amoral, intentional, and calculated because these violations entail punishment that will presumably motivate decision makers to consider negative consequences before choosing to violate. Whereas organizational actors in the rational approach know that they are making deviant decisions, in the "dark side" approach actors do not regard their decisions as deviant because these choices comport with organizational culture and align with preferred organizational goals.

Because mistake is not the result of chance but is inherent within systems, it is particularly likely to occur under conditions that strain organizational systems and actors. Several characteristics are related to organizational deviance, including environmental uncertainty (difficulty predicting future circumstances); task complexity; organizational and work site control; scarce resources; inefficient or inappropriate institutional relationships, structures, or practices; too little information; risk levels; technologies; regulatory environments; organizational power structures or hierarchies; and suboptimal organizational learning or habit-following.[50] The "extreme rule-mindedness" of bureaucratic institutions can distract actors from considering and adopting the most appropriate behaviors. Crucially, mistake, misconduct, and disaster are not only "socially defined in relation to the norms of some particular group" but "defined only in retrospect, when outcomes are known."[51] For example, institutional actors can "neglect information that contradicts their conviction that a technological system is safe," and normalization of deviance can occur when certain organizational structures or priorities "neutralize signals of danger."[52]

Mistakes[53] are always "unwitting or unintended."[54] In negotiating unexpected events, organizations and employees can "neutralize and normalize" certain mistakes, constructing them as routine. We judge a mistake's seriousness "by the outcome," and one that "causes death is usually the most drastic."[55] Therefore, our knowledge of mistake comes from "research in the fields where mistakes cost people their money or their lives: medicine and the military, aviation and Wall Street."[56] Mistakes are slippery because they can "occur with the best information and the best intentions or through carelessness and lack of knowledge."[57]

Misconduct, in contrast, consists of intentional acts or omissions that "violate internal rules, laws, or administrative regulations on behalf of organizational goals."[58] Here, employees can be "socialized into" misconduct when it is customary to violate rules in pursuit of goals. In mistake, risk and uncertainty are associated with tasks, but in misconduct, they are associated with cognition, decision, and reaction.[59] Often, the question is at what point organizational environments, structures, and norms produce mistake as opposed to misconduct, as the line between these categories can be thin. Both mistake and misconduct often precede disaster, defined as a "routine nonconformity that significantly departs from normative experience . . . a physical, cultural, and emotional event incurring social loss" that is often "large-scale, unusually costly, unusually public, unusually unexpected, or some combination."[60] Disasters are often preceded by "long incubation periods, typified by rule violations, discrepant events that accumulated unnoticed, and cultural beliefs about hazards that together prevented intervention."[61]

In addition, there is another category of unfortunate events: misfortune, or "bad luck."[62] According to Paget, misfortune, "like an accident or an act of nature, does not bear the mark of the human hand."[63] In pure misfortune, all rules are followed and there is no organizational or individual "deviance" per se, but something untoward and unexpected nonetheless occurs. In contrast, unwitting mistake occurs "when we have to act so quickly, or under so much pressure, that we can't stop to take thought."[64] The distinction between the two is based on the absence or presence of human agency. Included within misfortune are all truly unpredictable incidents, whereas organizational deviance comprises mistake. The trick is identifying the boundaries of deviation and distinguishing mistake from misconduct, necessitating that we stand in an actor's shoes. Misfortune is hardly the type of action that we connect with Corrections decision-making; although Corrections faces stressors such as execution dates and political pressures, these are not the types of factors that demand an immediate, on-the-spot response (in contrast to execution emergency such as a blown vein).

Mistake is culturally understood to be both beneficial and harmful—both failure and learning experience. Indeed, a popular American creed teaches the importance of learning from one's mistakes; this tenet has been espoused by the likes of Ralph Waldo Emerson, Albert Einstein, and, more recently, reality TV's makeover genre.[65] Along these lines, James Reason defines error as "the inevitable and usually acceptable price human beings have to pay for their remarkable ability to cope with very different informational tasks quickly and, more often than not, effectively."[66] Failure is a "static concept," while other similar terms—a "learning experience, a trial, a reinvention"—imply that failure can be transformative.[67] A degree of deviance is not only inherent within human activity but necessary for scientific and social progress. Karl Popper once observed that applying the scientific method to institutions does not entail the belief that we have not made mistakes but "the greater art of accepting responsibility for them, of learning from them and applying what we learn correctively."[68] Americans have built a virtual pantheon on the interdependency of mistake, failure, and success; mistake, after all, enables failure, but also "mastery, invention and achievement"—all of which (on the "light side") entail such romantic concepts as "the power of surrender, the propulsion of the 'near win,' the critical role of play in achieving innovation, and the importance of grit and creative practice."[69]

But admonitions to learn from mistakes may fall on deaf ears, as no one is in an especial hurry either to make or own up to a mistake, and Americans believe that "mistakes mean you are stupid."[70] Tugend emphasizes "the inherent tension between what we're told—that we must make mistakes in order to learn, how all great leaders and inventors have embraced them—and the reality that we often get punished for making mistakes and therefore try to avoid them—or cover them up—as much as possible."[71] One consequence of coupling mistake and stupidity is that mistakes becomes shameful or connote punishment, not learning opportunities that engender growth. Yet, "[b]eing wrong is a distinct experience of being" and "is different from the experience of being blameworthy and at fault."[72] Therein lies the importance of the "honest mistake," which "disclaims blame" but also introduces "the possibility of being both mistaken and unblameworthy."[73]

One example of how an institution distinguishes mistake from other deviations and holds perpetrators accountable involves how internists—young doctors-in-training—are socialized into a particular culture of mistake and mistake construction. Internists also "learn by practice," and "mistakes are fateful and . . . repetition on living or valuable material is necessary to learn the skills."[74] Here, mistake—"an unanticipated negative consequence of a medical intervention"—was simultaneously inevitable and a bogeyman to be feared.[75] Internists managed mistake through several strategies: (a) not constructing a problem as an error (characterizing medicine as a "gray area," repressing or forgetting, and redefining a mistake as a nonmistake); (b) externalizing blame onto bureaucracy, colleagues, or patients; and (c) contextualizing an error as within the bounds of appropriate clinical judgment at that time. A constructive culture in which doctors do not believe it is necessary to disclose errors and do not consider repercussions can obscure mistakes from the public and "raise . . . questions about the social accountability of doctors."[76] Significantly, subsequent publications document changes in the medical culture of mistake construction within the past decade that prioritize extensive organizational follow-up, willingness to readily acknowledge and discuss mistakes with patients, and filing state incident reports.[77] This new willingness to acknowledge error has also resulted in product redesign, use of checklists, and changing norms of power and hierarchy to encourage colleagues to raise concerns about errors in progress.[78]

Deconstructing the dark side of lethal injection innovation is not just a story of Corrections departments, officials, and execution team members; it is also a story of "unruly" technology.[79] Although technology is often publicly portrayed as "mechanical rule-following behavior" and "autonomous and 'internally' unproblematic," Wynne argues that it is actually a "form of large-scale, 'real-time' experiment."[80] Technology is closely associated with the construction of misfortune. Before an incident, experts communicate publicly that all is under control, "rigorously checked, and maintained by careful inspection"; afterward, they assert that there is no such thing as "zero risk" and that they cannot be accountable for "inevitable uncertainties."[81]

Acceptable bounds of failure are "made up under negotiation from experience."[82] Those who use technology "continual[ly] invent . . . and negotiate new rules and relationships" beyond those designers intended, "develop[ing] the technology in unanticipated ways."[83] Thus, technological use and adaptation is an "ever-accumulating practical 'craft' tradition."[84] This adaptation or "differentiation" or technology allows it to "correspond with the variety of social and physical worlds in which it is enacted."[85] There may be contradictory assessments of which rules should apply to a given situation, and "illegitimate extension of technological rules and practices into the unsafe or irresponsible is never clearly definable."[86] Because technological uses are adaptive and in flux, it is harder to define "safe" uses, and "it becomes more complicated to define responsibility or negligence."[87]

II. Illuminating the "Dark Side" of Lethal Injection Reform

Lethal injection reform and "botched" executions can be deconstructed as organizational deviance using the "dark side" perspective. This section first explores various definitions of "botched" executions, after which it assesses organizational deviance in lethal injection. Thereafter, this section discusses how states and Corrections departments normalize deviance, and finally explicates how clashing constructions of botched executions as mistake have forced lethal injection reforms.

Defining "Botched" Executions

In common parlance, "botched" executions occur when something goes wrong. Others, however, have defined 'botched" in more specific and specialized ways. Borg and Radelet define a "botched" execution as "involving unanticipated problems or delays that caused, at least arguably, agony for the prisoner or that reflect gross incompetence of the executioner."[88] Significantly, this definition's use of "unanticipated" renders botched executions constitutionally *un*problematic under *Baze,* in which unconstitutional mistakes must pose a "serious risk" of harm. Denno uses the term to refer to executions that have "demonstrated technical, mechanical, or physical mishaps that substantially heighten the likelihood that an inmate experienced extreme pain and prolonged suffering."[89]

Like Borg and Radelet, Smith defines an execution as "botched" when an unforeseen incident occurs, but excludes *anticipated* prolonged death or suffering.[90] He also identifies "reasonably reliable indicators" of a botch—the "immediate reaction of witnesses" ("excessively angered, horrified, or shocked by watching the execution"), "significant or unusual public or media outrage" shortly after the execution, and "contemporary expressions of governmental or judicial concern."[91] Smith concludes that an execution was botched "if it was perceived to have been botched by actors in the society in which it took place"[92]—directly implicating the social construction of mistake and emphasizing who defines an unanticipated problem, how, and when. Finally, Haines focuses on the reaction to an execution and not the events occurring within it, defining "flawed" executions as those in which "public sentiments are offended by a breakdown in the 'normal' routine of convicting killers and putting them to death."[93] Flawed executions can have broader causes, and "may not be gory but can involve staff and inmate behavior, or doubts about guilt or sentence 'fit.'"[94] Note that all of these definitions *retrospectively* identify executions as mistakes.

Lethal Injection as Organizational Deviance

This section will discuss how mistake is rooted in the pragmatic uncertainty of lethal injection technologies; its social, institutional, political, and cultural positions; institutional pressures; and the difficulty of acquiring and exchanging information and resources.

Capital punishment involves various layers of deviance. The road to execution begins with a murder for which an inmate is accused, tried, and condemned; all subsequent proceedings flow from this initial misconduct or alleged misconduct. Other examples of inmate deviance testify to other misconduct or character flaws, such as poor veins from drug use or obesity. These factors are often connected to execution flaws, rendering inmates complicit in their own botched executions.

As in other institutions, deviance is also inherent within Corrections structures and norms. The Supreme Court conceded as much in *Baze* by selecting a standard—"substantial risk of serious harm"—that confirms it is constitutionally permissible not to eliminate all risk. While the same can be said for the "untoward, readily avoidable risk" standard favored by justices Ginsburg and Souter, that standard has a much lower foreseeability threshold for deviance ("untoward" vs. "substantial" risk) and does not focus on the resulting harm's severity.

Much of lethal injection's deviance stems from its uncertainty. The analogous context of medical work is described as "error-ridden activity because it is inexact, uncertain, and practiced on the human body."[95] In execution work, as in medical work, there is a "process of discovery and response, of risked action and error."[96] Both execution work and medical work are simultaneously craft and action, "a field of expertise, a technical occupation, an applied science, or a profession" as well as "a practice, a praxis, and, in the latter sense, an activity of knowledge and ignorance, of expertise and error, of improvisation, artistry, failure, and ineptitude."[97]

Another source of deviance is the political, social, and cultural conditions in which lethal injections take place. Corrections' own legitimacy rests upon its ability to negotiate flawed executions effectively, either by successfully normalizing such incidents or by taking steps to reduce them. In executing an inmate, Corrections must fulfill several complementary and contradictory obligations owed to several parties, and prioritize some above others. Corrections owes the state and inmate a duty to carry out the execution efficiently with a minimum of delay and drama, as well as an obligation to allow public officials, journalists, and likely victims' family members to witness the event. It also owes a constitutional duty both to the state and inmate to execute humanely in accordance with the Eighth Amendment. The authority and trust reposited in Corrections, and therefore its social legitimacy, depend upon its fulfillment of these responsibilities, even under uncertain conditions. Currently, Corrections faces a double bind: it loses political and bureaucratic capital and incenses pro–death penalty family members if it does not execute, but becomes tainted with allegations of ethical or moral illegitimacy if it does.

Current conditions in lethal injection reform are ripe for organizational deviance. Many Corrections departments are under intense pressure to revise lethal injection environments and protocols in terms of everything from physical environment to execution team members, from medical monitoring to lethal drugs. Under public and political scrutiny, Corrections must comply with tight deadlines such as protocol revision time limits and execution dates, and overcome scarce resources as drug supplies become exhausted and as regulation of foreign-sourced drugs and compounding pharmacies imposes new constraints. These stressors have trapped Corrections in contests of efficiency vs. effectiveness and compliance vs. humaneness, and created powerful incentives for the rapid diffusion of untested technologies. These considerations help to decouple mistake from blameworthiness and fault *before* a flawed execution, when Corrections officials make decisions in increasingly constrained and non-optimal conditions—choices they are unlikely to see as deviant but as necessary to carry out Corrections missions under adverse conditions. Yet, if the execution is botched, blame and fault likely reattach to state and Corrections officials.

Finally, even if Corrections acknowledges an execution as deviant, accumulating knowledge about deviant executions is also problematic. Corrections acquires immediate feedback from experiences in its own lethal injection chamber and gleans secondary knowledge from other states' efforts. Flaws—misfortunes or mistakes—can be recognized as they occur. Critically, in executions, death defines success, not failure. A mistake becomes a death that occurs in an inappropriate manner—where the inmate does not appear to peacefully go to sleep, where the procedure takes an inordinate amount of time, or where some other untoward event occurs—or, most markedly, where death *fails* to occur at all. One signal of deviance is Corrections' decision to close the curtains or blinds separating witnesses from the lethal injection chamber, preventing those in attendance from viewing how a problem unfolds and is resolved. A flawed execution most often prompts the state to step in and effect cessation—of witnessing, of a particular execution, or of all executions through moratoriums or abolition. Moreover, the very fact that Corrections voluntarily or involuntarily initiates lethal injection reform means that problems have been identified and constructed as mistakes. To search for new lethal injection drugs and administration methods implies that previous ones were faulty or suboptimal, and thus to admit that lethal injection itself entails risk.

Normalizing Deviance in Lethal Injection Reform

What implications do the environmental, social, and institutional contexts of lethal injection reform have within "dark side" organizational theory? To use Reason's terminology, currently states and Corrections most often construct each flawed execution as an isolated and unpredictable misfortune, and respond accordingly. Cumulatively, however, these patterns of "botched" executions constitute mistake or misconduct and demand a more appropriate and far-reaching response.

Corrections has long benefited from a presumption of good faith, social legitimacy, and safety. As have executioners throughout the centuries, Corrections officials have frequently tinkered with lethal technology, such as by changing the structure of gallows, rope length and type, and the balance of counterweights. Institutional norms have thus permitted and even mandated latent experimentation. Indeed, in her dissent in *Glossip,* Justice Sotomayor noted that "the procedural flaws that marred the Lockett execution created the conditions for an unintended (and grotesque) experiment on midazolam's efficacy."[98] Notably, this encouragement of innovation—usually a positive, proactive, "light side" characteristic—acquires more ominous tones when the target of innovation is accomplishing another's death. Corrections has long explored execution methods through a "learning-by-doing" process, and may interpret each botched execution as a unique event instead of a patterned consequence of haphazard lethal injection reform.

From the Corrections perspective, lethal injection reform is likely perceived as no different than past modifications to other execution methods such as hanging or electrocution. Lethal injection innovation does not violate organizational norms or rules, but reflects attempts to comply with them, further illustrating how "light side" institutional characteristics such as innovation can acquire "dark side" propensities. Corrections norms and institutional culture have rendered such innovation normal or acceptable, although outsiders likely regard it as deviant (because of objections to capital punishment, the higher risk of botched executions, or ethical imperatives). Now this culture of innovation has become mandatory in states in which legislatures and courts have initiated lethal injection reform. Corrections are now being forced to construct botched executions as *preventable* mistakes, not arbitrary misfortunes, and instructed to systematically learn from them. But, as before lethal injection reform, decisions will continue to be made on the basis of imperfect knowledge.[99]

Because many lethal injection reforms are unprecedented and untested, technical problems become anticipated, routine occurrences. Proceeding with executions in the face of so many unknowns implies that these risks are acceptable. Acquiring more information can alter the calculus of risk acceptability; however, Corrections are most likely to regard botched executions as discrete misfortunes and not as patterned mistakes that could expose organizational actions as deviant: "If flawed executions occur only rarely (or [are] . . . believed to be infrequent events) and if correctional authorities respond skillfully, they are likely to pose no threat to the death penalty itself. They will instead be interpreted as unfortunate errors which can be prevented through further experience or technological improvements."[100] Of course, as more and more executions are botched, it becomes much harder to ignore patterned deviance, and more difficult to argue that flawed executions are unforeseeable misfortune or even mistake and not misconduct. At some tipping point, this position will become untenable. Then, to the extent that botched executions are seen as the predictable result of defective protocols, untested drugs, and untrained personnel, an intent akin to the "deliberate indifference" standard of prison abuse cases might be imputed to the state.[101]

How Constructions of Deviance Compel Change

Of course, other institutions and actors besides the state and Corrections—the public, the media, courts, and market actors—also construct problematic executions as deviant. This begs the question of what factors distinguish misfortune, mistake, and misconduct across the spectrum of interested institutions. Is it the degree of pain that an inmate appears to experience, as measured by physical or verbal behaviors? Or the time it takes for the inmate to die? Or the fact that death occurs at all? And how does the construction of mistake differ with the identity of the constructing party? To answer these questions, we can examine how various institutions—anti–death penalty organizations, corporations and foreign countries, federal and state courts, and media—construct lethal injection as mistake.

Anti–Death Penalty Organizations

Anti–death penalty organizations and individuals construct capital punishment negatively as mistake or even misconduct, and are quick to use individual executions to strengthen this stance. While states and Corrections are aware of anti–death penalty constructions, they also know that these characterizations are not binding upon official policy until they gain political or judicial traction, producing moratoria or abolition. Until then, however, anti–death penalty constructions likely have limited efficacy: "Though unpredictable physiological reactions and mechanical glitches may make technical flaws more intractable, it is often difficult for activists to arouse much public indignation over. . . . the suffering of persons who cared little about the pain they inflicted on their victims and victims' families."[102] Anti–death penalty efforts, however, have helped to make journalists see "flaws in the process as newsworthy."[103] And this publicity generates public pressure, which in turn can prompt a governmental response.

Countries and Corporations

Market actors such as other countries and corporations also construct executions—and the death penalty—as something unethical or immoral and counter to therapeutic medical treatment. As discussed in Part I, manufacturers of pharmaceuticals and medical technology object to the use of their products in lethal injections as nonindicated and counter to product design and manufacturer mission, and condemn capital punishment. This language is thick with implications of immorality; manufacturers term lethal injection a "distressing misuse" that they "strongly object" to and refuse to be "complicit" in. This illustrates that constructions of mistake can take on distinct and different affective traits.

More important, controls that corporations and countries have put into place force states to innovate with new products and technologies in order to carry out scheduled executions, heightening the likelihood of mistake. Perhaps these parties were trying to distance themselves from capital punishment; perhaps they intended to create chaos, strengthening the case for abolition. Regardless of their reasons, they are equally complicit in creating an institutional culture of mistake by constricting supplies and compelling states to rapidly innovate and procure drugs from other less reliable sources such as compounding pharmacies. This raises the important question of who is really interested in reducing mistake and under what conditions, and how we should understand the moral complicity of market actors, although it is beyond the scope of this chapter to fully address the deep moral problem of mistake embedded in institutional choice.

Courts

Courts also construct problematic executions in certain ways. After Willie Francis survived his 1946 Louisiana electrocution despite receiving two jolts, the Supreme Court characterized the execution as a misfortune and not a mistake: "Accidents happen for which no man is to blame. . . . [L]aws cannot prevent accidents."[104] Characterizing an execution flaw as a misfortune sets it apart as both unactionable and unhelpful as a model for future conduct. Courts come closest to categorizing an execution as a mistake or misconduct when ordering states to reform lethal injection protocols deemed unconstitutional, forcing states and Corrections to evaluate their protocols in a principled manner and learn from their own and others' mistakes. Only unconstitutional errors, however, spur change, and many reviews are far from principled. In addition, reform measures can effect change but can also further strain already mistake-prone environments. Ironically, then, taking steps to eradicate mistake by making executions more humane and efficient can intensify pressure, increasing risk while attempting to reduce it. Another complicating factor is that, whatever courts direct, "the legal system and the corrections bureaucracy are different cultures."[105] As Judge Fogel observed after his experience in the Morales case, "Institutions have their own customs, perspectives, and ways of initiating or resisting change. . . . [W]e have to be mindful of such institutional differences if we expect our orders to have their intended effect."

Federal and state courts utilize unique standards and terminologies for mistake, based on its constitutional significance. Courts distinguish an "innocent misadventure" or an "isolated mishap" or failure[106]—events that are misfortunes—from a "substantial" or "objectively intolerable" risk of harm—events that are unconstitutional mistakes.[107] Judicial constructions of mistake under a constitutional standard are effectively biased toward misfortune rather than mistake. For one thing, courts seem comfortable conceding that errors and imperfections are inherent. Judges acknowledge that "[s]ome risk of pain is inherent in any method of execution—no matter how humane—if only from the prospect of error in following the required procedure," and that "despite conscious efforts . . . the process will never advance to a level of scientific precision."[108] For another, courts usually garb Corrections in a presumption of good faith, and recognize the high threshold that inmates face in establishing "a serious risk of substantial harm" or "objectively intolerable risk" under *Baze*—a threshold that the Fifth Circuit deemed "almost impossible" without "intentional malevolence."[109]

Although mistakes are constructed as learning experiences that can be redressed through inmate litigation, judicial standards constrain which errors become unconstitutional and therefore instructive. Courts require inmates to produce evidence of actual errors that occurred under the same or similar conditions in which they will be executed, and these errors must have occurred at certain points during the execution process (postinjection, not preinjection). Since "anecdotal" evidence of mistake is insufficient, inmates must give detailed descriptions of past executions; courts have criticized the insufficiency of evidence when inmates lack details of how executions actually went wrong in that particular state (for example, presenting an expert testifying from experience with executions in another state).[110] Courts routinely note that they will not consider the "risk of accident," but instead scrutinize the constitutionality of a state's written protocol; one court tautologically stated, "The only risk in the Virginia protocol occurs if a mistake or accident happens."[111]

Moreover, even if a problem indisputably occurs, it must have an untoward effect on the inmate to be actionable; a problematic execution does not necessarily constitute "serious pain and unconstitutional punishment."[112] Even where executioners had injected a second round of potassium chloride in past executions, suggesting mistake, the court stated that the plaintiff inmate could not prevail because he did not show that these previously executed inmates were conscious before the second injection.[113] Pain must rise to a "serious" level; in one case, the court found that suffering was "short-lived" because it lasted three minutes.[114] And this effect must occur at the right time, usually after the injection has begun. Following Rommel Broom's failed execution in Ohio, the court found that the state's two-hour attempt to site the IV was not a mistake within the execution procedure, but a "failing . . . in the preparatory stages": "[W]e cannot hold that establishing the IV access is part of the punishment of execution. For us to find that attempting to establish IV catheters constitutes the execution attempt would place the state in an untenable position."[115]

Federal and state courts have also all but ruled out entire sources of error as "mistakes." Exchanging one drug for another (vecuronium bromide for pancuronium bromide, or pentobarbital for sodium thiopental) is not unconstitutional,[116] nor does it matter if drugs are used in an "off-label" manner.[117] Problematic insertions of IVs and catheters are not unconstitutional but are deemed "common" problems in medical treatment.[118] Similarly, it is unproblematic that states delegate authority to choose and change protocols to Corrections officials or wardens.[119] Courts evince more concern when a protocol is improperly adopted,[120] when inmates are given insufficient time to review a protocol,[121] when records are improperly kept,[122] or when a state deviates from its protocol, as in this judicial quip: "It is the policy of the State of Ohio that the State follows its written execution protocol, except when it does not. This is nonsense."[123] Finally, some courts are concerned about secrecy, and usually find it "troubling" when inmates do not have timely notice of a protocol.[124]

Media

Predictably, the judiciary and the media construct mistake very differently. The media, in contrast, have considerable freedom to label an execution "botched" or a problematic lethal injection a "mistake" or "error," but their willingness to do so has fluctuated over time.

Based on a content analysis of newspaper coverage of botched executions from 1890 to 2010, Sarat et al. have observed that early-twentieth-century news coverage did not construct such events as injustices but rather as misfortunes, helping to "neutralize the abolitionist potential" of these events.[125] The authors observe that this coverage utilized a "'recuperative' narrative: a storyline that offers justifications and reasoned explanations for the gruesome spectacles it meticulously describes" so as to "reassure readers that capital punishment is both humane and just."[126] The botched execution as misfortune is an "important hallmark" of this narrative.[127]

Common coverage themes include portraying the execution as a misfortune that was unforeseeable and unpreventable; discussing a unique or freakish characteristic of the inmate as if to pass blame to him; and offering a recuperative explanation (claiming all rules were followed, the inmate died quickly or did not suffer pain or was otherwise unaffected by the occurrence, identifying alternative explanations for inmate sounds or movements). Stories may even rehabilitate an executioner overseeing a botched execution from a bungler to a hero.[128]

Newspapers began to report on patterns of botched executions in the 1970s and 1980s, often counterposing the shortcomings of electrocution to the peace of lethal injection, blaming nameless "authorities" for flaws.[129] Yet this openness to link "particular botched executions [to] . . . a problematic technology" was undermined by the quest for objectivity and the balanced reporting technique, where journalists quoted opposing sources and suppressed their own voices.[130] After electrocution was discontinued in favor of lethal injection, newspaper accounts "attribute[d] more significance to botches," treated the new method as a "subject of genuine controversy," and identified problems with the three-drug protocol.[131] Today, Sarat et al. conclude, flawed executions remain newsworthy, although accounts of botches as "unavoidable misfortunes rather than as symptoms of injustice . . . have not offered readers a "deeper witnessing" of the execution scene and, in turn, of capital punishment itself."[132]

Media coverage frequently draws parallels between botched lethal injections, establishing patterns of mistakes such as difficulties finding vein access.[133] Moreover, sources often assert that mistake is inherent within lethal injection, usually by quoting academic experts such as Austin Sarat and Deborah Denno.[134] Media sources recognize many of the same categories of execution errors as courts, such as human error, problematic veins, protocol deviations, execution team incompetence, and drug errors (that is, inaccurately calculated dosages, full dosages not administered, improper drug mixing, improperly timed drug administration). But they categorize them as mistakes, not misfortunes. Media sources rely primarily on "symptoms" of mistake, the most important of which is pain and suffering communicated through inmate behaviors or sounds; others include time spent trying to locate intravenous access, how long it takes an inmate to die once injection(s) begin, and execution procedure delays.

Much media coverage follows and is substantively determined by the unique facts of infamously flawed executions. News coverage of flawed lethal injections skyrocketed in 2014 from a yearly average of approximately 100 articles from 2010 to 2013 to approximately 1300 articles per year in 2014, as shown by "document distribution" graphs compiled by databases such as Factiva. Searching "lethal injection, botched" in *Time* for examples results in forty-one total hits, only eleven of which come from years prior to 2014, and none of which come from 2011 or 2012.

A content analysis of the landslide of media coverage of Oklahoma's botched execution of Clayton Lockett on April 29, 2014, evinced a host of trends and patterns. The most common theme was condemning the execution as inhumane and problematic—in essence, constructing it as a significant mistake or even misconduct. Media sources labeled it "controversial," frequently mentioned that it "raised questions" or "renewed debates" over specific lethal injection protocols, lethal injection, or the death penalty itself; and observed that there would be both an Oklahoma investigation and Department of Justice review of all state execution protocols. Media also commented on the ethics of Oklahoma's decision to carry out the execution despite the high potential for mistake, and the broader ethical implications of secrecy. As Samuel Rodriguez noted in a *Time* article with respect to Governor Mary Fallin's willingness to proceed, "Oklahoma's decision to move forward with this execution showed an insufficient concern for human life. Beforehand, legal and medical experts warned that the experimental execution protocol and the secrecy surrounding it could lead to disastrous consequences. Oklahoma ignored these concerns."[135] Media sources speculated on the impact that the Lockett execution would have upon the timing and procedures of future executions. Some remarked that this mistake reverberated beyond America's borders to international circles. But in a countertrend, media sources observed that many members of the public were not unduly troubled by Lockett's suffering.[136]

A recent development in execution coverage is the "journalist chronology," in which media witnesses record an execution through a time-series of developments. This technique inserts the journalist into the story, but as an "objective" witness who supposedly documents what happens, as it happens. The chronology diminishes distance both between the journalist and her readers and between readers and the execution, situating readers within the execution as a lived event and temporal experience. These chronologies are more comprehensive, including not only what measures the state takes and how the inmate reacts but also witness behaviors (such as witnesses exchanging shocked glances or crying),[137] and goings-on before and after the curtain opens. These narratives are also naturally antiredemptive, in that these chronologies end with the uneasy taint of witnessing a flawed and perhaps inhumane death. Although there were journalist chronologies of the 2005 execution of Stanley "Tookie" Williams, this coverage genre becomes more popular from 2011 on. Chronologies covered the 2011 Troy Davis execution, and chronologies were especially popular for the Rommel Broom and Clayton Lockett executions.[138] In a novel twist, Associated Press reporter Bailey Elise McBride tweeted about Lockett's execution immediately afterward, based on information from prison authorities and from a colleague who had witnessed the execution.

Thus, states and Corrections now find themselves in a very different environment than when they only had to worry about nonbinding anti–death penalty characterizations of deviance. Powerful parties—courts, corporations, and the media—not only construct problematic executions as mistakes or misconduct, but their characterizations are often dramatically at odds with those of states and Corrections assertions of misfortune. Unlike anti–death penalty adherents, these more influential institutional constructions can force states and Corrections to take action. Analogized to the children's game of thumb wrestling, states and Corrections always emerged victorious against anti–death penalty adherents because they were the bigger, stronger party. Now, however, states and Corrections find themselves under the thumbs of courts, market forces, and media and public opinion and are almost situated as underdogs or victims. Judicial, political, and market forces cumulatively compel one construction of flawed executions as tainted by unconstitutionality and immorality, as mistake and perhaps misconduct.

III. Particular Issues in the Dark Side of Litigation Reform

With a more comprehensive understanding of how "dark side" organizational studies research can be applied to lethal injection, we can now explore in more detail three interdependent areas that have proven particularly thorny for states and Corrections departments to negotiate: technological innovation and implementation, protocol design and reform, and responding to egregious botches (managing organizational deviance).

The Travails of Technology

A discussion of Corrections' culture of mistake and mistake construction would be incomplete without considering the relationship between Corrections officials and lethal technologies. Here, technology primarily refers to pharmaceuticals, drug administration techniques, execution chamber design, equipment and furnishings, and consciousness monitoring methods, but also implicates team training and evaluation strategies and record-keeping methods.

Corrections employees and execution team members are not amoral decision makers who decide to violate rules in pursuit of organizational goals. Corrections officials usually have wide discretion to set their own rules and procedures, and perhaps even to choose pharmaceuticals, even if they cannot change the execution method. Like medical sites, Corrections is a "'closed world' with its own rules of . . . decisionmaking."[139] They operate under uncertain conditions and "learn by doing," with vague instructions or little to no guidance on how to create and implement lethal injection reforms. Thus, lethal injection technology is a "form of large-scale, 'real-time' experiment."[140] And there are no perfect conditions of lethal technological implementation. States do not appear discomfited by this laxness; states have only recently adopted written protocols. These written protocols also attempt to erect (or reinforce) a culture of distance; they "never use the word 'kill'" and "often adopt the passive voice and maintain a narrow focus on a fractured set of minute actions."[141]

There is currently much pressure to adapt therapeutic technologies to lethal injection, given current market constraints—corporate disgust for lethal injection and ensuing scarce resources, an urgent need to comply with schedules, few comparable research contexts to guide technological implementation, changing circumstances of application as different inmates are executed, and contests over secrecy versus public disclosure of lethal technologies. Indeed, Justice Sotomayor addressed the devastating collective impact of these factors in her dissent in Glossip:

> Nor certainly, should these rapidly changing circumstances give us any greater confidence that the execution methods ultimately selected will be sufficiently humane to satisfy the Eighth Amendment. Quite the contrary. The execution protocols States hurriedly devise as they scramble to locate new and untested drugs . . . are all the more likely to be cruel and unusual—presumably, these drugs would have been the States' first choice were they in fact more effective. . . . Courts' review of execution methods should be more, not less, searching when States are engaged in what is effect human experimentation.[142]

Yet, we should prioritize effectiveness (attaining desired outcomes of executing expediently and minimizing pain and harm) over efficiency (executing quickly and cheaply). This will assist in reducing mistake; efficiency norms are coupled with "optimism and success-oriented strategies" and do not prioritize "error detection and error correction," which require more pessimistic attitudes.[143] Lethal injection adaptation is remarkably like the stages of medical innovation adoption (as distinct from FDA drug approval processes). Execution methods are hailed as more humane, and are adopted and implemented before being closely evaluated. They are evaluated through use, only to become criticized and modified after botched executions reveal their limitations. Moreover, execution is a context that, like emergency medicine, seems incompatible with empirical research; imagine an institutional review board application for a controlled study to determine the lethal efficacy of various drugs on human subjects. Corrections departments lack the academic affiliations or professional incentives to make rigorous research commitments; a commitment to scientific goals and comparative research might even oppose the Corrections mission of killing an inmate as quickly as possible without cruel and unusual punishment. Moreover, perhaps human death as a phenomenon undergoes "a particular degradation when subjected to radical, untested interventions."[144]

Corrections actors have a well-defined relationship to technology and technological innovation, and have historically "tinkered" with other lethal technologies such as the gallows, noose, electric chair, gas chamber, and lethal injection apparatus and chemicals. Executioners throughout history have described execution as a "craft" or an "art," developed a lethal corpus of knowledge, and attributed botched hangings to the work of "amateurs."[145] Bumbling executioners earn a dark but dubious footnote in history; Jack Ketch is still infamous as a notoriously incompetent medieval axeman.[146] It makes us uneasy when we find out that our own executioners are incompetent or of less than stellar character, as when an execution team leader who was "responsible for the custody of sodium thiopental" is later disciplined for "smuggling illegal drugs into the prison."[147] Witness the rise and fall of Fred Leuchter, who had no background in medicine, engineering, or science and yet provided dozens of states with advice and products to execute condemned inmates. His company, Fred Al. Leuchter Associates, Inc., was the only commercial provider of execution equipment and training in the United States, providing technology such as gallows, electric chairs, gas chambers, and even lethal injection machines, and was used by at least twenty-seven states.[148] After his court testimony was repeatedly discredited,[149] Leuchter's career in lethal technology finally ended in 1990 when he was criminally charged in Massachusetts for holding himself out as an engineer without a license; thereafter, states began to deny his contracts for lack of qualifications.[150]

Adapting therapeutic pharmaceuticals to lethal injection clearly contradicts their intended use; manufacturers have publicly condemned these actions and in some cases taken radical steps to prevent Corrections departments from obtaining their products. But however grisly these adaptive processes, this lethal innovation fits into larger patterns of technological use. Like other technologies, lethal drugs are both objects and artifacts; they have both "a determinate physical essence that has consequences . . . [and are] embedded in [a] social context within which [they have] meaning."[151] There is little doubt that lethal drugs are risky technologies, and that states and Corrections are "both victims of political shifts in regulatory policy . . . and powerful actors that shape it."[152] Therefore, Corrections has the power to determine not only what is a "mistake" and what counts as risk in the first place, but to adapt new technologies with little intervention from others. And yet they have thus far failed to do so successfully, building an image of a bumbling bureaucracy and stoking public frustration.

> Finally, as in other contexts of technological innovation, it is difficult to define what technological uses are "safe," to establish the boundaries of negligence, and to distinguish legitimate from illegitimate technological extension. Some commentators go further than asserting that lethal injection reform is misconduct if shoddily handled, and argue that it is actually illegal research or experimentation that violates bioethics standards and/or state law. Earlier, in the nineteenth and twentieth centuries, electrocution, gas, and lethal in-

jection experiments were conducted on animals, and there are even records of physicians witnessing an inmate's gas chamber execution in order to see what happened.[153] Philpott speculates that such activities could violate the federal "Common Rule," barring any unapproved "systematic investigation, including research, development, testing and evaluation, designed to develop or contribute to generalizable knowledge."[154] Federal research guidelines require IRB approval and management and participants' voluntary informed consent, and provide special protections for prisoners as research subjects. Many states also restrict research on prisoners to therapeutic studies.

Shah argues that several states are violating state law prohibitions against research by measuring the effects of and experimenting with lethal injection protocols and drugs, gathering information to improve future executions, and even mandating review of medical literature, legal opinions, and other jurisdictions' protocols and experience.[155] The current impetus toward lethal injection reform will only compel further research efforts: "[S]tates will be conducting practice runs of executions, changing drug amounts, instituting new procedures, and then gathering data about the success of these new procedures to be published and reviewed by courts in their states." South Dakota has recently enacted legislation stating that execution by lethal injection "may not be construed to be the practice of medicine," as if to exempt "learning-by-doing" from the category of medical research.[156] Nor do lethal injection reform efforts constitute rigorous or reliable research; "there is no evidentiary basis to suggest that they might improve lethal injection for other inmates and they are not being tested in a controlled, rigorous fashion," and such research may be unethical if one considers that the population of death row inmates may have been unfairly selected.[157]

Protocol Design and Reform

Lethal injection protocol design and reform are projects largely consigned to Corrections, regardless of whether a state has a lethal injection statute and regardless of its interpretation.[158] The federal government assigns protocol design to the Federal Bureau of Prisons.[159] Here, too, the original Oklahoma three-drug protocol has long exerted tremendous influence; federal officials preparing for Timothy McVeigh's 2001 execution attended four state lethal injections and adopted the same cocktail.[160] It was only after 2007 that state legislatures began to reevaluate who should make these determinations, although statutes differ as to whether they cede control to the legislature or to the director of Corrections or prison warden (as in South Dakota).[161] Botches can prompt critical reevaluation;

following Clayton Lockett's April 29, 2014, execution in Oklahoma, Corrections director Robert Patton stated that, while the prison warden held "all responsibility and decision-making" in the current protocol, these matters should rest on "upper management and ultimately on the Director of Corrections."[162]

The consensus is that whoever is in charge is failing. According to one commentator, "The adoption of lethal injection protocols throughout the United States can best be described as a cascade of misinformation whereby authorities in one jurisdiction copied, sometimes verbatim, the procedures in another. . . . [T]he protocols were adopted without independent research or consultation with qualified experts."[163] Conducting a nationwide study of lethal injection protocols, Denno found that many were "far too vague to allow for adequate assessment," and "often revealed striking errors and a shocking level of ignorance about the procedure."

States' adventures in lethal injection, including reform, have been what Associated Press reporter Ron Word terms a "learning exercise."[164] And they are still learning; nearly thirty-seven years after Oklahoma adopted lethal injection, it still has not refined this execution method. Following Clayton Lockett's execution in Oklahoma on April 29, 2014, Corrections director Robert Patton announced his intention to actively investigate other options, and to "explore best practices from other states and ensure the Oklahoma protocol adopts proven standards."[165] One wonders whether such practices exist; no state has found a "magic bullet," and few relevant analogues exist. Nor have states been enthusiastic or quick to learn from veterinary sources; the American Veterinary Medicine Association prohibited paralytics in animal euthanasia years before states began to stop using these drugs and has for many years used a safer procedure with readily available pharmaceuticals.[166]

A recent past riddled with flawed lethal injections calls into question states' ability to learn from and apply new information, even if helpful resources could be identified. Case law documents instances in which states do not follow good learning practices, such as educating staff on potential lethal injection errors and following good record-keeping practices. In *Morales*, Judge Fogel found "critical deficiencies" in the protocol, including "inconsistent and unreliable screening of execution team members"; "lack of meaningful training, supervision, and oversight of the execution team" (including members' ignorance about the drugs used, "risks or potential problems associated with the procedure," and improper past reactions to botched executions); "inconsistent and unreliable record-keeping"; and "inadequate lighting, overcrowded conditions, and poorly designed facilities."[167] One execution team member, a registered nurse responsible for mixing and preparing sodium thiopental, testified, "We don't have training, really."[168]

And team members in one state may not even make needed improvements from one execution to the next. The California execution team failed to "set an intravenous line" during Stanley "Tookie" Williams's 2005 execution, and state counsel assured Judge Fogel at the evidentiary hearing that this error "was a lesson well learned, one that will never occur again."[169] Yet, Judge Fogel observed, it did not "take steps sufficient to ensure that a similar or worse problem would not occur" in the next execution or incorporate it into plans for Morales's scheduled execution.[170] Such findings prompted Judge Fogel to comment, "Given that the state is taking a human life, the pervasive lack of professionalism . . . at the very least is deeply disturbing."[171]

Moreover, when states do use medical expertise, the quality of these sources is either unknown or of questionable competence. In 2013, Arkansas announced a switch to phenobarbital, on the basis that "several death-row inmates mentioned in a lawsuit that it might be an available drug"; a state Corrections spokesperson said only that it had "consulted medical sources" before making the decision.[172] Moreover, some medical experts have been of dubious quality. In *Taylor v. Crawford,* the Eighth Circuit described how "Dr. Doe I," a surgeon, was in charge of mixing chemicals and IV insertion but did not record the dose actually administered to the inmate, was unconcerned about how his dyslexia affected chemical mixing, had discretion to modify chemical doses at will based on medical judgment (and thus to reduce dosages), and monitored the inmate's anesthetic depth by observing the inmate's face through an observation window "partially obstructed by blinds," with the inmate facing away from the window.[173] In addition, Dr. Doe I had been sued for malpractice more than twenty times and reprimanded by the state board for concealing malpractice suits from the hospital where he practiced.[174] The district court barred Dr. Doe I from future participation.[175]

In addition, past state reviews of protocols or reform measures have not been thorough, comprehensive, or rigorous. Optimal procedures would include a "thorough" protocol review, including the manner of drug injection, consciousness checks, quality of record-keeping, and perhaps consultation with "independent experts" and "other jurisdictions" and "undertaken with an openness to the idea of making significant improvements."[176] Yet an Ohio review of a botched execution culminated in a "two-and-a-half page report."[177] A review commission initiated by the Florida governor after the botched execution of Angel Diaz issued its final report only four months after Diaz's execution.[178] In another hearing ordered by the Florida Supreme Court, Corrections officials explained how they ensured that an inmate's death was "humane and dignified"; a *Washington Post* reporter commented on participants' "farcical discussion of minutia" that ignored drug selection but focused instead on the use of a "shake and shout" versus "trapezoid pinch" consciousness check and on making the gurney more comfortable.[179] After District Court judge Fogel ordered California to conduct a "thorough review" of its lethal injection protocol in *Morales,* the state met at the governor's office for one and a half hours.[180] Attendees had made only minor protocol revisions, "reducing the initial dosage of sodium thiopental and adding a second intravenous line that would provide a continuing flow of that drug," and "no further review of the protocol took place."[181] As a result, Judge Fogel conducted his own evidentiary hearing, which lasted several days.[182]

Nor is information readily forthcoming on how states and the federal government select and revise protocols, given state secrecy. Corrections personnel control secrecy during the execution by closing the blinds or curtains, controlling visual access to the death chamber, or by removing witnesses altogether. Conducting nationwide studies of lethal injection protocols in 2001 and 2005, Denno found that states "typically withheld more information than in the past."[183] Fewer than one-third of states with complete protocols in 2001 had them in 2005; nearly four times as many states asserted that their protocols were confidential; two states said that they had no protocols; and one state gave no information.[184] Thus, half of states using lethal injection "did not allow any evaluation of their protocols, either because the information is confidential or nonexistent."[185] One newspaper article asserted that "states have revealed little, if any, information about how they go about picking drugs."[186] States maintain that they have compelling reasons for concealing the identities of involved persons, including encouraging companies and medical professionals to assist with executions and curbing threats to prison officials and prisons from anti–death penalty individuals or groups.

Judicial rulings and secrecy legislation have furthered states' efforts to render confidential protocol information or participant identities. When Pennsylvania switched to compounded drugs for lethal injection, it took two federal court orders to disclose the drug source as well as a class action lawsuit challenging the protocol's constitutionality. At first, Pennsylvania refused to reveal the drug supplier, lest it face public pressure to cease providing drugs for lethal injection.[187] And many states have gone further and passed lethal injection secrecy legislation—often when they begin to implement new protocols or obtain drugs from new sources. When Georgia proposed to use compounded drugs in 2013, it passed the Lethal Injection Secrecy Act, which rendered "a confidential state secret" the identities of an individual or entity that "manufacturers, supplies, compounds, or prescribes the drugs, medical supplies, or medical equipment."[188] Louisiana protects those who "participate or perform ancillary functions . . . either directly or indirectly";[189] Arizona keeps secret the identity of executioners and persons ancillarily involved;[190] Oklahoma protects the identities of execution participants and suppliers of drugs, medical supplies, or medical equipment, but not the execution drug(s);[191] and Missouri's secrecy statute protects execution team members and renders the protocol a "closed record" except for that section describing "the administration of lethal gas or lethal chemicals."[192] Arkansas passed a bill in February 2013 authorizing the director of Correction to develop execution procedures that are not subject to the state's Administrative Procedure Act or Freedom of Information Act.[193] South Dakota passed a bill in February 2013 protecting the identities of any "person or entity supplying or administering the intravenous injection substance or substances."[194] In April 2013, Tennessee expanded its current law protecting the identity of persons involved in the execution to include entities as well as state employees, contractors, and volunteers.[195]

Nor have most state courts been quick to overturn secrecy measures. The Georgia Supreme Court recently upheld the state's Lethal Injection Secrecy Act in May 2014 in *Owens v. Hill*,[196] holding that the inmate could not show how keeping lethal injection drugs secret could lead to cruel and unusual punishment. Although Hill had argued that compounding pharmacies' products could be contaminated, the court ruled that this was not a concern where the inmate "will never have the opportunity to suffer the negative medical effects from infection or allergic reactions from a possibly non-sterile drug," even though certain contaminants could cause a precipitous blood pressure drop and death: "[S]uch a side effect . . . is certainly not a worry in an execution." The court noted that such measures "avoi[ded] the risk of harassment or some other form of retaliation . . . as well as simply offering those willing to participate whatever comfort or peace that anonymity might offer," and that without confidentiality "there is a significant risk that persons and entities necessary to the execution would become unwilling to participate."[197] This has, in fact, happened; after Texas announced in late 2013 that it had purchased pentobarbital from the Woodlands Compounding Pharmacy, the compounding pharmacy demanded that the drugs be returned, stating that it had been promised secrecy.[198]

The Oklahoma execution of Clayton Lockett provides a compelling case study of the struggle over secrecy measures. On March 21, 2014, Oklahoma revealed a new lethal injection protocol giving Corrections discretion to choose among five different drug combinations; Corrections would tell the inmate which combination it would use. Attorneys for inmates Clayton Lockett and Charles Warner challenged the secrecy statute. On March 26, 2014, an Oklahoma district court declared the statute unconstitutional because it prohibited inmates' right of judicial access; the Oklahoma Supreme Court initially granted a stay, but then ruled in favor of Corrections, finding that it was sufficient that inmates knew what drugs would be used and that inmates need not know who supplied them.[199] Justice Taylor, concurring in the judgment, wrote that

> from the very beginning this so called "civil" litigation has been frivolous and a complete waste of time and resources of the Supreme Court of Oklahoma. . . . [If the prisoners] were being executed in the electric chair, they would have no right to know whether OG&E or PSO were providing the electricity; if they were being hanged, they would have no right to know whether it be by cotton or nylon rope; or if they were being executed by firing squad, they would have no right to know whether it be by Winchester or Remington ammunition.[200]

Thereafter, Clayton Lockett was executed in an infamously botched execution in which Lockett "convulsed violently during the execution and tried to lift his head after a doctor declared him unconscious," dying of an apparent heart attack forty-three minutes after the execution commenced.[201] The incident garnered public horror, and a rare comment from President Obama that the execution was "deeply troubling."[202] Following Lockett's execution, the Justice Department announced that it was currently reviewing the federal Bureau of Prisons execution protocol, and would "expand its review to include a survey of state-level protocols and related policy issues."[203]

But in a handful of states, secrecy is under attack. State justice departments have begun to get involved; offices of the attorney general in Delaware and Texas ordered state Corrections departments to respond to access requests for information on lethal injection protocols, drugs, purchases, and inventories.[204] In Texas, an official stated that keeping suppliers' identity secret to prevent "harassment and harm" was not a sufficient reason.[205] In May 2013, an ACLU challenge to Colorado's secrecy practices garnered a district court order mandating the release of a redacted protocol; the supplier's identity was redacted, with the judge reasoning that the need to protect the pharmacy's business and employees "far outweighs" public disclosure.[206] A federal judge ruled in June 2013 that the Louisiana Department of Corrections had to publicly disclose its protocol, inventory, drugs, and expiration dates.[207] Alabama's legislature recently rejected a bill masking the names of companies and individuals involved in the production of lethal injection drugs.[208] In Louisiana, a lethal injection secrecy bill under consideration was withdrawn on June 3, 2014.[209]

How States and Corrections Departments Respond to Mistake

President John F. Kennedy once stated, "[S]uccess has many fathers, but failure is an orphan"; perhaps, however, "failure is an orphan until we give it a narrative."[210] What, then, is the narrative of failure in the execution context?

As previously discussed, misfortune, mistake, and misconduct are constructed according to particular cultures, norms, and motivations. Prior to an event, institutional actors can define situations and justify choices using organization logic so that they appear "acceptable and nondeviant"; afterward, they may retrospectively explain deviance by aligning their behavior with norms and nondeviant expectations.[211] This, in turn, changes the culture of mistake construction. For instance, after electrocution became the dominant execution method, it became "conventional wisdom" that although an electrocution death was "instantaneous," it appeared "particularly dramatic and painful"; this "common sense" observation attempted to take the sting out of the spectacle, neutralizing visual indices of pain and suffering and malfunctioning equipment as accurate indications of a botched execution.[212] Here, however, an execution method touted as peaceful and humane is under attack; in lethal injection, signs of pain and suffering have put the sting back into the spectacle, with dramatic results.

Although there is scarce data on whether states initiate disciplinary proceedings and changes to team composition after flawed executions, there appear to be very few negative consequences for states, Corrections, and employees. Corrections departments are usually left to their own devices to negotiate and remedy risks. Execution team members are most often anonymous, and are unlikely to be held accountable beyond internal Corrections measures. As Bienen argues, "Even in the most extreme situation of a completely botched and tortuous execution, the failure to follow the protocols would not result in liability for state actors."[213] While the usual penalty for "professional incompetence" is usually for a state employee to be fired, in some states lethal injection protocols are "exempt from review under administrative procedures acts."[214] Presumably, state investigations could fire or reassign officials and team members, but these proceedings largely result in new procedures, not personnel shake-ups (and such changes probably would not be effective solutions). It is not as if a flawed execution is likely to violate legislative or judicial standards; though courts and legislatures may initiate lethal injection reform, they tend to be "hands-off" in recommending specific protocol or pharmaceutical changes. Moreover, states and Corrections usually construct flawed executions as either unproblematic or misfortunes for which blame and responsibility cannot be affixed. The state certainly takes a reputational "hit" and could be sued by the executed inmate's family, although such suits are very infrequent.[215]

Glimpses into how states and Corrections departments react to a flawed execution are usually restricted to spokespersons' remarks, most of which deny that the inmate was affected and/or claim that the botch was an isolated misfortune and not the latest in a series of mistakes. Erratic glimpses illustrate, however, that these institutions are risk averse and seek to evade responsibility for flawed executions. In federal district court testimony in *Taylor v. Crawford,* a physician attending Missouri executions testified that the director of Corrections had instructed him to "keep [the director] looking good . . . so [the director] does not have to go out and explain why we made a mistake or we may have a problem or why it didn't go smoothly."[216] Similarly, the Lockett execution was unusual in that the state and its Corrections Department failed to circle the wagons. After blame for the botch was imputed to Oklahoma execution team members, a spokesperson for the Oklahoma Corrections Professionals, a statewide association representing corrections employees, countered, "Everything was done according to state law and protocol. . . . The Department of Corrections didn't have anything to do with the state deciding it would use some experimental cocktail of drugs."[217] The spokesperson also complained that "[t]he agency has been left to deal with this crisis on its own while the governor and Legislature bury their heads in the sand."[218]

Smith identifies four common government responses to botched executions: implementing minor reforms (establishing investigative commissions, "increased standardisation of methodologies or implements, mandating increased executioner expertise, or general pledges to do better"), making executions more private (restricting press and public ability to witness executions), adopting or inventing "new and improved" execution methods, and abolition.[219] But of course there are other possible reactions, evinced in remarks following a lethal debacle: asserting that mistakes are inevitable, focusing on the execution's lethal end result, asserting that the incident was an unforeseeable misfortune that did not affect the inmate, attributing flaws to human error, and blaming inmates.

One strategy is to acknowledge that there is an inherent potential for mistake; one member of California's execution team testified that "shit does happen" when executions are conducted.[220] Attorney General Bob Butterworth even celebrated risky execution technology. After twelve-inch flames erupted from Medina's head during his execution in the state's electric chair, christened "Old Sparky," Butterworth remarked, "People who wish to commit murder, they'd better not do it in the state of Florida because we may have a problem with our electric chair."[221] Another related strategy is to refocus from the execution's flaws to its optimal end result: the inmate's death. The warden of St. Quentin responded to a deposition question on what would qualify as a successful execution by describing it as one where "the inmate ends up dead at the end of the process."[222]

Most often, Corrections personnel assert that a botched execution was an unforeseeable misfortune rather than a mistake, or fail to characterize the occurrence at all—a strategy that can deincentivize states to learn from and make changes following flawed executions. Although media sources may pronounce an execution "botched," if they portray the incident as an aberration and minimize or deny its effect on the inmate, this will reassure the public.[223] In the 1977 execution of Jimmy Lee Gray in Mississippi's gas chamber, witnesses watched as Gray appeared to be gasping and in contortions when witnesses were escorted out of the observation room; the state corrections commissioner stated that these behaviors were "reflexive actions" but admitted there "was a need to 'refine the process' of execution."[224] After Alabama's electric chair malfunctioned during John Louis Evans III's execution in 1983, smoke and flames burst from the chair and it took three tries before Evans was dead; Prison Commissioner Fred Smith stated that Evans had died immediately after the first attempt and that "apparent signs of life were merely palpitations of the heart."[225]

Only rarely do Corrections or the state attribute flaws to human error. In the 1990 execution of Jesse Joseph Tafero and the 1989 execution of Horace F. Dunkins, the errors were using a synthetic sponge instead of a natural sea sponge to conduct the current, and a reversed electric chair cable connection, respectively.[226] In Stephen McCoy's 1989 lethal injection in Texas, McCoy "gagged, coughed violently, and underwent bodily contortions"; afterward, the Texas attorney general "suggested that perhaps the required dose of chemicals had been underestimated."[227]

Prisoner and prison worker behavior can also lead to problems. In John Spenkelenk's 1979 electrocution in Florida, there were allegations that Spenkelenk had been "brutalized" before the execution; a state investigation later found no physical abuse, but uncovered evidence that Spenkelenk had been "taunted verbally," there had been a "loud exchange" between the inmate and prison workers before he was placed in the chair, many people were in the chamber, and the inmate was not afforded a chance to speak.[228] Afterward, "prison officials stated that executions would go more smoothly once the routine became better established."[229]

Finally, one can assign blame or agency for botched executions to inmates. Inmates have been blamed for many flaws, from not being good electricity conductors to being difficult to execute because they were freakish or junkies.[230] At other times, an inmate's poor veins (often attributed to a history of drug abuse) or obesity have made it hard for technicians to find a vein in which to site the IV catheter. Most recently, in the Oklahoma execution of Clayton Lockett on April 29, 2014, media witnesses reported that the director of Corrections stated that the execution was stopped because of a "vein failure in which the chemicals did not make it into the offender."[231] These incidents are unlikely to earn public sympathy, however; following the 2000 execution of Bennie Demps, who in his last words complained that he was "butchered" when officials searched for a suitable vein for thirty-three minutes, public "anger was directed more at Demps than at the death penalty."[232] Thus, Smith concludes that "[t]he reasonably efficient execution method of lethal injection has given the abolitionist who would rely on the horror of botched executions a particularly difficult row to hoe."[233]

Conclusion: Toward Transparency

We know, more so than ever after the Lockett execution in April of 2014, that mistakes are inherent, and perhaps now endemic, within lethal injection. Thus, we must decide at what point mistakes become routine or foreseeable enough—and reform efforts loose enough—that mistake becomes misconduct. Is a learning curve acceptable; if so, how steep can it be? If not, what is the proper remedy—a moratorium, abolition, or a return to a previous method, such as electrocution? These determinations, however, requires transparency—an ideal in short supply for condemned inmates and citizens alike. Moreover, some states are now classifying such information as being beyond state administrative procedure acts and therefore outside the scope of public review and debate. Even in states without such regulations, there is a dearth of forums for public notice and comment on execution protocols.

As in other contexts impacted by opacity and politics (such as financial market reforms), to reduce the high risk of botched lethal injections, we must change current institutional cultures that influence how and when executions are constructed as misfortune or mistake, and what the consequences of mistake should be. Such cultural change is certainly possible; it has occurred on a grander scale than lethal injection reform. Over the past decade, the health care industry has succeeded in drastically changing its culture of mistake construction, resulting in dramatic reductions in medical error, changes in power/hierarchy structures, product redesign, and willingness to openly confront and acknowledge mistakes. Within this proposed cultural shift, a prime focus should be not on assigning blame and responsibility but on creating practices that are easy, predictable, effective, and efficient. Another key task within changing the culture of mistake is acknowledging and working through the deep moral problem of mistake embedded in institutional choice. Courts, legislatures, corporations, and countries all attempt to direct reform efforts, albeit in different ways and to achieve different ends (designing safe and effective practices and communicating moral objection, respectively). Yet, all efforts, regardless of their agents' motivation, increase the risk of mistake.

Several changes can help with this cultural shift. First, lethal injection reform should either be the province of state legislators (with input from Corrections officials) or, if left within the Corrections departments, should be subject to state administrative procedure acts that mandate public notice and commentary. Such a step will enhance transparency for inmate legal challenges as well as for public notice and comment.

Second, states and the federal government should create a clearinghouse through which to share experiences and information. This requires a move away from secrecy toward transparency, most notably by repealing secrecy statutes. It also requires cultivating a respect for expertise, from both internal and external authorities. In order for such systematic data gathering and exchange to be useful, however, states must commit to detailed record-keeping; thus, participants should collectively determine what information should be collected and reported, as well as the standards for some categories of information (such as postmortem toxicology reports). As Shah remarks:

> [T]o determine whether lethal injection is constitutional, it will take a systematic, careful analysis of the risks involved in lethal injection—the type of determination that states have not attempted to make to date, and that they may lack the expertise or objectivity to undertake. This investigation cannot involve prisoners without some attention to the ethical issues involved to minimize risks and the possibility of exploitation. In addition, it will also require democratic deliberation about these risks and a societal determination about the acceptability risks and uncertainty involved.[234]

This, then, is how law and lawmakers, both legislative and judicial, inmates and those outside prison walls, can and must influence mistake. Legal actors can help to provide informed guidance on what are appropriate objectives, and how they can be reached; provide more space for and legitimize specialists and expertise, and accumulate, publish, and act on the basis of their knowledge; delegate decision-making authority to appropriate individuals; and mandate feedback mechanisms, including those that reach beyond organizational boundaries. Law can effect cultural change, for better or for worse.

The few lights in the darkness of lethal injection reform, such as Judge Fogel's orders in *Morales,* demonstrate how far short of professionalism other efforts fall. But cultural change requires a spark—an incentive. Admittedly, this spark is rather fragile in lethal injection reform, threatening to die out between botches. Thus, we cannot allow society and its institutions—including the media, executives, legislatures, courts, and Corrections—to become complacent about botched executions, and must actively prevent execution mistakes from becoming yet another banal evil. The idea that mistakes are inevitable in human endeavor can easily lead to the conclusion that they are routine, anticipated, and therefore somehow acceptable. But facing the truth does not excuse prevention efforts; it compels them. We must continue to give mistakes immediacy, perceiving them as targets to be reduced and, if possible, eliminated, like workplace accidents. Although there is likely no such thing as a "perfect" execution method, we cannot construct the debate over lethal injection reform as undecidable or unfixable as we have social debates over abortion and gun control. That is yet another reason why the public must demand a place at the table in deliberations over lethal injection reform, and why legislatures must give them a seat. As U.S. district judge Gaitan, who oversaw *Taylor v. Crawford*, remarked, "[W]e should strive to make public as many details of the execution as possible, so that the condemned can know what to expect and the public can know what the state is doing. . . . [W]e cannot expect the public's standards [of decency] to evolve if the public is unaware of what procedures are actually performed upon the condemned."[235]

NOTES

Epigraph: Marian J. Borg and Michael L. Radelet, "On Botched Executions," in *Capital Punishment: Strategies for Abolition*, ed. Peter Hodgkinson and William A. Schabas (Cambridge: Cambridge University Press, 2004), 143.

1. Jesse Wegman, "There Is No Such Thing as a 'Clean' Execution," *Taking Note*, Editorial Page Editor's blog, *New York Times*, June 5, 2014, http://takingnote.blogs.nytimes.com.
2. This fact is mentioned in *Furman v. Georgia*, 408 U.S. 238 (1972).
3. Scott Thompson, "Oklahoma Man Who Developed Lethal Injection Recipe Lived with Regret," *News on 6*, May 1, 2014, www.newson6.com.
4. "A New Test for Evaluating Eighth Amendment Challenges to Lethal Injections," *Harvard Law Review* 120(5) (2007): 1310.
5. Ibid.
6. Deborah W. Denno, "Lethal Injection Chaos Post-*Baze*," *Georgetown Law Journal* 102 (2014): 1341.
7. Ibid., citing *Baze vs. Rees*, 2005 WL 5797977, at *2 (Ky. Cir. Ct. July 8, 2005).
8. Ibid.
9. 547 U.S. 573 (2005).
10. 553 U.S. 356 (2008).
11. Justices Thomas and Scalia proposed an alternate standard, that an execution method would violate the Eighth Amendment only if deliberately designed to inflict pain. Justices Gensburg and Stevens argued for a standard of "an untoward, readily avoidable risk of inflicting severe and unnecessary pain," and Justice Breyer applied the "significant risk of unnecessary suffering" standard to Kentucky's protocol. *Baze*, 553 U.S. at 1556, 1566, 1567.
12. "A New Test for Evaluating Eighth Amendment Challenges to Lethal Injections," 1306; Denno, "Lethal Injection Chaos Post-*Baze*," 1349.
13. Denno, "Lethal Injection Chaos Post-*Baze*," 1346, 1335.
14. Ibid., 1346.
15. Quoting *Glossip*, 576 U.S. at ___ (2015) (p. 6 of slip opinion).
16. Ty Alper, "Anesthetizing the Public Conscience: Lethal Injection and Animal Euthanasia," *Fordham Urban Law Journal* 35 (June 2008): 817.
17. See Mark Berman, "Missouri Attorney General Wants the State to Produce Its Own Lethal Injection Drugs," *Washington Post*, May 29, 2014, www.washingtonpost.com.

18. Denno, "Lethal Injection Chaos Post-*Baze*," 1336.
19. Ibid., 1337.
20. Ibid., 1376.
21. Ibid., 1337–38.
22. Kimberly Newberry, "Secrecy in Lethal Injection: How the Oklahoma Courts Are Supporting a Deadly Double Standard," *Jurist*, June 1, 2014, http://jurist.org.
23. Ibid.
24. Ibid.
25. Ibid.
26. *Cook v. Food and Drug Administration*, 733 F.3d 1 (D.C. Cir. 2013) (hereinafter "*Cook v. FDA*").
27. Ibid.
28. Hospira, "Statement from Hospira Regarding Its Halt of Production of Pentothal," press release, January 21, 2011; letter from Hospira to Ohio Department of Rehabilitation and Corrections, March 31, 2010, both www.deathpenaltyinfo.org.
29. Nicholas Meyers, "*Cook v. FDA* and the Importation and Release of Lethal Injection Drugs," *Journal of Law and the Biosciences* (May 2014): 1–2; first published online at http://jlb.oxfordjournals.org/.
30. Newberry, "Secrecy in Lethal Injection."
31. *Beaty v. Food and Drug Administration*, 858 F. Supp.2d 30 (D.D.C. 2012); Meyers, "*Cook v. FDA* and the Importation and Release of Lethal Injection Drugs," 2 (citing *Beaty v. FDA*, 858 F. Supp.2d at 43).
32. *Beaty* and *Cook* are the same case; over the course of the litigation, Beaty had been executed and Cook was named successor plaintiff.
33. Ibid. at 43, *Cook v. FDA*, 733 F.3d at 3.
34. Denno, "Lethal Injection Chaos Post-*Baze*," 1354–55.
35. Ibid., 1357.
36. Sean Philpott, "Execution by Lethal Injection: Illegal Research?" *Hastings Center Report*, March–April 2014, 12.
37. Meyers, "*Cook v. FDA* and the Importation and Release of Lethal Injection Drugs," 4.
38. Ibid.
39. Lundbeck, "Lundbeck Overhauls Pentobarbital Distribution Program to Restrict Misuse," press release, January 7, 2011, www.deathpenaltyinfo.org.
40. Lundbeck, letter to Gary C. Mohr, Director, Ohio Department of Rehabilitation and Correction, January 26, 2011, www.deathpenaltyinfo.org.
41. Hikma Pharmaceuticals, "Hikma Pharmaceuticals Strongly Objects to the Use of Its Products in Capital Punishment," press release, May 5, 2014, www.deathpenaltyinfo.org.
42. Par Pharmaceutical, "Par Pharmaceutical Statement on Brevital Sodium," press release, May 27, 2014, http://pr.parpharm.com.
43. Aspect Medical Systems, "Aspect Medical Systems Comments on Prospective Article in June 15, 2006 *New England Journal of Medicine*," press release, June 15, 2006, http://phx.corporate-ir.net.
44. Ibid.
45. Other organizations include the American Society of Anesthesiologists (which adopted the AMA's Code of Ethics stance in 2001) and the American Nurses' Association. Deborah W. Denno, "The Lethal Injection Quandary: How Medicine Has Dismantled the Death Penalty," *Fordham Law Review* 76 (2007): 80.
46. American Medical Association, "Opinion 2.06—Capital Punishment," *AMA Code of Medical Ethics*, www.ama-assn.org.
47. Kenneth Baum, "To Comfort Always: Physician Participation in Executions," *New York University Journal of Legislation and Public Policy* 5 (2001): 47.

48. Diane Vaughan, "Rational Choice, Situated Action, and the Social Control of Organizations," *Law and Society Review* 32 (1998): 32.
49. Ibid., 23.
50. Diane Vaughan, "The Dark Side of Organizations: Mistake, Misconduct, and Disaster," *Annual Review of Sociology* 25 (1999): 275.
51. Ibid., 283.
52. Ibid., 296.
53. Ibid., 284.
54. Marianne A. Paget, *The Unity of Mistakes* (Philadelphia: Temple University Press), 12.
55. Alina Tugend, *Better by Mistake: The Unexpected Benefits of Being Wrong* (New York: Riverhead Books / Penguin, 2011), 12.
56. Joseph T. Hallinan, *Why We Make Mistakes: How We Look without Seeing, Forget Things in Seconds, and Are All Pretty Sure We Are Way above Average* (New York: Broadway Books, 2009), 5.
57. Tugend, *Better by Mistake,* 12.
58. Vaughan, "The Dark Side of Organizations," 288.
59. Ibid., 291.
60. Ibid., 292.
61. Ibid., 294.
62. *Merriam-Webster Online,* s.v. "misfortune," www.merriam-webster.com.
63. Paget, *The Unity of Mistakes,* 12.
64. Charles Baxter, "Dysfunctional Narratives, or 'Mistakes Were Made,'" *Ploughshares* 20(2/3) (1994): 74.
65. Tugend, *Better by Mistake,* 2, 38.
66. Ibid., 40.
67. Sarah Lewis, *The Rise: Creativity, the Gift of Failure, and the Search for Mastery* (New York: Simon and Schuster, 2014), 12.
68. Martin Landau and Donald Chisholm, "The Arrogance of Optimism: Notes on Failure-Avoidance Management," *Journal of Contingencies and Crisis Management* 3(2) (1995): 77.
69. Lewis, *The Rise,* 11.
70. Carol Tavris and Elliot Aronson, *Mistakes Were Made (But Not by Me): Why We Justify Foolish Beliefs, Bad Decisions, and Hurtful Acts* (New York: Harvest/Harcourt, 2007), 230.
71. Tugend, *Better by Mistake,* 2.
72. Paget, *The Unity of Mistake,* 4.
73. Ibid., 12.
74. Everett C. Hughes, "Mistakes at Work," *Canadian Journal of Economics and Political Science* 17(3) (1951): 300, 321.
75. Terry Mizrahi, "Managing Medical Mistakes: Ideology, Insularity and Accountability among Internists in Training," *Social Science and Medicine* 19(2) (1984): 135.
76. Ibid., 142–43.
77. Tugend, *Better by Mistake,* 108.
78. Ibid., 115–30.
79. Brian Wynne, "Unruly Technology: Practical Rules, Impractical Discourses, and Public Understanding," *Social Studies of Science* 18 (1988).
80. Ibid., 149.
81. Ibid.
82. Ibid., 151.
83. Ibid., 152.

84. Ibid., 154.
85. Ibid.
86. Ibid.
87. Ibid., 156.
88. Borg and Radelet, "On Botched Executions," 143.
89. Deborah W. Denno, "Getting to Death: Are Executions Constitutional?" *Iowa Law Review* 82 (1997): 338 n. 10.
90. Stephen Eliot Smith, "Going through All These Things Twice: A Brief History of Botched Injections," *Otago Law Review* 12(4) (2012): 779.
91. Ibid.
92. Ibid.
93. Herb Haines, "Flawed Executions: The Anti-Death Penalty Movement and the Politics of Capital Punishment," *Social Problems* 39(2) (May 1992): 125.
94. Ibid.
95. Vaughan, "The Dark Side of Organizations," 286.
96. Paget, *The Unity of Mistakes,* 17.
97. Ibid., 147.
98. Quoting *Glossip,* 576 U.S. at ___ (Sotomayor, J., dissenting) (p. 19 of dissent).
99. For discussion in a comparable context, see Eileen Munro, "Avoidable and Unavoidable Mistakes in Child Protection Work," *British Journal of Social Work* 26(6) (1996).
100. Haines, "Flawed Executions, 127.
101. The "deliberate indifference" standard is found in prison abuse cases such as *Hudson v. McMillian,* 503 U.S. 1 (1992); "A New Test for Evaluating Eighth Amendment Challenges to Lethal Injections," 1318.
102. Haines, "Flawed Executions, 135.
103. Ibid., 132.
104. Smith, "Going through All These Things Twice," 820, citing *Louisiana ex rel Francis v. Resweber,* 329 U.S. 459, 464 (1947).
105. Jeremy Fogel, "In the Eye of the Storm: A Judge's Experience in Lethal-Injection Litigation," *Fordham Urban Law Journal* 35 (2008): 748.
106. *Baze,* 553 U.S. at 1531; *Dickens v. Brewer,* 631 F.3d 1139, 1147–48 (9th Cir. 2011); *Lopez v. Brewer,* 680 F.3d 1068, 1075 (9th Cir. 2012); *Emmett v. Johnson,* 532 F.3d 291, 296–97 (4th Cir 2008).
107. *Baze,* 553 U.S. at 1556.
108. *West v. Schofield,* 380 S.W.3d 105, 113 (Tenn. Ct. App. 2012); *Emmett v. Johnson,* 511 F.Supp.2d 634, 643 (E.D. Va. 2007).
109. *Raby v. Livingston,* 600 F.3d 552, 561 (5th Circuit 2010).
110. *Rhoades v. Reinke,* 830 F.Supp.2d 1046, 1065 (D. Iowa 2011); *People v. Davis,* 49 Cal.4th 539, 628–29) (CA 2009); *Arthur v. Thomas,* 674 F.3d 1257, 1262 (11th Cir. 2012).
111. *Walker v. Johnson,* 448 F.Supp.2d 719, 723 (E.D. Va. 2006); *Taylor v. Crawford,* 487 F.3d 1072, 1080 (8th Cir. 2007); *Nooner v. Norris,* 594 F.3d 592, 602 (8th Cir. 2010); *Raby,* 600 F.3d at 561.
112. *Rhoades,* 830 F.Supp.2d at 1065.
113. *Walker,* 448 F.Supp.2d at 723. For a contrasting perspective, consult *Harbison v. Little,* 571 F.3d 531, 537–38 (6th Cir. 2009) (stating that the district court had found a risk of unnecessary pain from executioners' inability to identify problems associated with IV insertion).
114. *DeYoung v. Owens,* 646 F.3d 1319, 1326 (11th Cir. 2011).
115. *State v. Broom,* 2012 WL 504504 (Ct. App. Oh. 2012) at *6.

116. *Ferguson v. Warden, Florida State Prison*, 493 Fed.Appx. 22, 24 (11 Cir. 2012); *DeYoung*, 646 F.3d at 1324–25; *Powell v. Thomas*, 641 F.3d 1255, 1257 (11th Cir. 2011).

117. *Valle v. State*, 70 So.3d 530, 542 (FL 2011).

118. *Lopez*, 680 F.3d at 1074; *Raby*, 600 F.3d at 558–61 (upholding Texas lethal injection protocol where evidence of problems with inserting IVs); *Cooey v. Strickland*, 589 F.3d 210, 217–18, 224, 233–34 (6th Cir. 2009) (upholding Ohio protocol despite evidence of problems inserting IV); *Emmett*, 532 F.3d 303, 306–8 (4th Cir. 2008) (upholding Virginia protocol despite problems with IV lines).

119. *Hill v. Owens*, 738 S.E2d 56, 63 (GA 2013).

120. *Evans v. State*, 396 Md. 256, 340) (Ct. App. Md. 2006); *Sims v. Department of Corrections and Rehabilitation*, 216 Cal.App.4th 1059, 1074 (Ct. App. CA 2013).

121. *Oken v. Sizer*, 321 F.Supp.2d 658, 664 (D. Md. 2006).

122. *Morales v. Tilton*, 465 F.Supp.2d 972, 979 (N.D. Cal. 2006).

123. *Cooey v. Kasich*, 801 F.Supp.2d 623, 624 (S.D. OH 2011).

124. *Lopez*, 680 F.3d at 1075; *Oken v. Sizer*, 321 F.Supp.2d at 664. For a contrasting perspective, consult *Sepulvado v. Jindal*, 729 F.3d 413, 420 (5th Cir. 2013) ("There is no violation of the Due Process Clause from the uncertainty that Louisiana has imposed on Sepulvado by withholding the details of its execution protocol. Perhaps the state's secrecy masks 'a substantial risk of serious harm,' but it does not create one.")

125. Austin Sarat et al., *Gruesome Spectacles: Botched Executions and America's Death Penalty* (Stanford: Stanford University Press, 2014), 149–50.

126. Ibid., 154–55.

127. Ibid., 155.

128. Ibid., 158–59.

129. Ibid., 167–68.

130. Ibid., 168.

131. Ibid., 173, 174.

132. Ibid., 175.

133. Ben Crair, "Cruel but Not Unusual: How Oklahoma Botched Clayton Lockett's Execution," *New Republic*, April 30, 2014, www.newrepublic.com (drawing parallels between Diaz, Clark, and Broom executions).

134. See, for example, Austin Sarat et al., "Lethal Injection Leads to the Most Botched Executions," *Daily Beast*, April 30, 2014, www.thedailybeast.com; Greg Mitchell, "How Lethal Injections Became the Go-To Method For Executions in America," *Nation*, May 9, 2014, www.thenation.com.

135. Samuel Rodriguez, "Botched Oklahoma Execution Should Prompt Moral Outcry among Evangelicals," *Time*, May 5, 2014, http://time.com.

136. Matt Pearce, "In Victim's Oklahoma Town, No Tears for Inmate in Botched Execution," *Los Angeles Times*, May 5, 2014, www.latimes.com; Scott Martelle, "Opinion: Oklahoma Is Investigating Itself over Botched Execution? Please," *Los Angeles Times*, April 30, 2014, www.latimes.com.

137. Ziva Branstetter, "Eyewitness Account: A Minute-by-Minute Look at What Happened during Clayton Lockett's Execution," *Tulsa World*, May 1, 2014, www.tulsaworld.com.

138. See, for example, Adam Housley, "Reporter's Notebook: Inside the Execution Chamber," *Fox News*, December 13, 2005, www.foxnews.com; Rhonda Cook, Greg Bluestein, and Joann Merrigan, "'He Blinked His Eyes Rapidly, Squeezed Them Tight and the Curtains Closed': Eye-witness Accounts of Troy Davis's Execution—By Reporters Who Watched Him Die," *London Daily Mail*, September 22, 2011, www.dailymail.co.uk; Mark Berman, "A Reporter's Grim Account from a Botched Execution," *Washington*

Post, April 30, 2014, www.washingtonpost.com; Page Williams, "Witnesses to a Botched Execution," *New Yorker,* April 30, 2014, www.newyorker.com.

139. Jeanne Guillemin, "Experiment and Illusion in Reproductive Medicine," *Human Nature* 5(1) (1994): 16.

140. Wynne, "Unruly Technology," 149.

141. Leigh B. Bienen, "Anomalies: Ritual and Language in Lethal Injection Regulations," *Fordham Urban Law Journal* 35 (2008): 857.

142. Quoting *Glossip,* 576 U.S. at ___ (Sotomayor, J., dissenting) (p. 29 of dissent).

143. Landau and Chisholm, "The Arrogance of Optimism," 68, 70, 71.

144. Guillemin, "Experiment and Illusion in Reproductive Medicine," 19.

145. Sarat et al., *Gruesome Spectacles,* 39, 45.

146. Smith, "Going through All These Things Twice," 797.

147. Morales, 465 F.Supp.2d at 979.

148. Deborah W. Denno, "Is Electrocution an Unconstitutional Method of Execution? The Engineering of Death over the Century," *William & Mary Law Review* (35) (1994): 551, 626, 627 n. 496.

149. Deborah E. Lipstadt, *Denying the Holocaust: The Growing Assault on Truth and Memory* (New York: Penguin Books, 2012).

150. Errol Morris, "Mr. Death: Transcript," errolmorris.com, May 12, 1999, http://errolmorris.com; "Expert on Execution Denied State Contract," *Chicago Tribune,* August 18, 1990, http://articles.chicagotribune.com.

151. Vaughan, "The Dark Side of Organizations," 279.

152. Ibid., 293.

153. Sarat et al., *Gruesome Spectacles,* 62–63, 92, 100.

154. Philpott, "Execution by Lethal Injection," 11; S. K. Shah, "How Lethal Injection Reform Constitutes Impermissible Research on Prisoners," *American Criminal Law Review* 45 (2008), 1108.

155. See generally, Shah, "How Lethal Injection Reform Constitutes Impermissible Research on Prisoners."

156. Ibid., 1142, 1132.

157. Ibid., 1137–38.

158. Denno, "Lethal Injection Chaos Post-*Baze,*" 1356.

159. 28 C.F.R. § 26.3(a)(4) (2014).

160. Kevin Johnson, "Federal Warden Prepares for 'Unnatural' Job," *USA Today,* May 8, 2001, 4A.

161. S.D. Codified Laws § 23A-27A-32 (2014).

162. Letter from Robert Patton to Hon. Mary Fallin, May 1, 2014, www.theguardian.com.

163. Berkeley Death Penalty Clinic, "*Baze v. Rees* Q & A 13, What evidence supports the assertion that lethal injection protocols are developed by people who lack the necessary qualifications and skills to devise them?" www.law.berkeley.edu.

164. Liliana Segura, "Florida's Gruesome Execution Theater," *Washington Post,* March 19, 2014, www.washingtonpost.com.

165. Letter from Oklahoma Department of Corrections director Robert Patton to Governor Mary Fallin, *Guardian,* May 1, 2014, www.theguardian.com.

166. Alper, "Anesthetizing the Public Conscience," 821.

167. *Morales,* 465 F. Supp.2d at 979–80.

168. Ibid., 979.

169. Ibid.

170. Ibid.

171. Ibid., 980.

172. Jeannie Nuss, "Arkansas Turns to Different Lethal Injection Drug," Associated Press, April 19, 2013, http://news.yahoo.com.

173. *Taylor*, 487 F.3d at 1075.

174. Jeremy Kohler, "Behind the Mask of the Execution Doctor," *St. Louis Post-Dispatch*, July 30, 2006, A1.

175. *Taylor*, 487 F.3d at 1078.

176. *Morales*, 465 F. Supp.2d at 983.

177. Denno, "The Lethal Injection Quandary," 119.

178. Ibid.

179. Segura, "Florida's Gruesome Execution Theater."

180. Fogel, "In the Eye of the Storm," 745–46.

181. Ibid.

182. Ibid.

183. Denno, "The Lethal Injection Chaos Post-*Baze*," 1377.

184. Ibid., 1379.

185. Ibid.

186. Nuss, "Arkansas Turns to Different Lethal Injection Drug."

187. Denno, "The Lethal Injection Chaos Post-*Baze*," 1377.

188. Georgia Code § 42-5-36(d) (2014).

189. LSA-R.S. 15:570(G) (2014).

190. AZ Rev. Stat. 13-757(C) (2014).

191. 22 Okl.St.Ann. 1015(B) (2014).

192. Mo.Rev.Stat. § 546.720(2).

193. Arkansas Code § 5-4-617(f), (g) (2014).

194. S.D. Codified Laws § 23A-27A-31.2 (2014).

195. Tenn. Code Ann. § 10-7-504(h)(1) (West 2014).

196. *Owens v. Hill*, 1014 WL 2025129 (May 19, 2014).

197. Ibid. at *10.

198. Carey Gillam, "Texas Says Won't Return Execution Drugs to Pharmacy Facing Scrutiny," *Reuters*, October 7, 2013, www.reuters.com.

199. "Judge Rejects 'Secret' Oklahoma Capital Punishment Law," *BBC*, March 26, 2014, www.bbc.com; *Lockett v. Evans*, 2014 OK 34 (April 23, 2014), http://scholar.google.com.

200. *Lockett v. Evans*.

201. Associated Press, "Botched Execution 'Deeply Troubling,' Says Barack Obama," *Guardian*, www.theguardian.com.

202. Ibid.

203. Ibid.

204. Denno, "The Lethal Injection Chaos Post-*Baze*," 1380.

205. Ibid.

206. Ibid., 1381.

207. Ibid., 1380.

208. Bryan Lyman, "Death Penalty Secrecy Bill Fails," *Montgomery Advertiser*, April 4, 2014, www.montgomeryadvertiser.com.

209. Julia O'Donoghue, "Louisiana Legislator Pulls Bill to Keep Death Penalty Drugs Confidential," *New Orleans Times-Picayune*, June 3, 2014, www.nola.com.

210. Lewis, *The Rise*, 198.

211. Vaughan, "The Dark Side of Organizations," 280.

212. Smith, "Going through All These Things Twice," 819.

213. Bienen, "Anomalies," 876.

214. Ibid.

215. See, for example, *McGuire v. Mohr,* 2:14-cv-00093 (S.D.Oh. 2014).

216. Transcript of testimony of John Doe No.1 at 62, *Taylor v. Crawford,* No. 05-4173 (W.D. Mo. June 5, 2006), www.law.berkeley.edu.

217. Jacob Gershman, "Don't Blame Us for Execution Mishap, Say Oklahoma Prison Workers," *Wall Street Journal,* April 30, 2014, http://blogs.wsj.com.

218. Ibid.

219. Smith, "Going through All These Things Twice," 779.

220. Fogel, "In the Eye of the Storm," 746.

221. Smith, "Going through All These Things Twice," 821.

222. Fogel, "In the Eye of the Storm," 746.

223. See, for example, Sarat et al., *Gruesome Spectacles,* 147.

224. Haines, "Flawed Executions," 128.

225. Ibid., 127.

226. Ibid., 128.

227. Ibid.

228. Ibid., 129.

229. Ibid.

230. Sarat et al., *Gruesome Spectacles,* 148, 162–63, 169, 171.

231. Branstetter, "Eyewitness Account."

232. Smith, "Going through All These Things Twice," 824.

233. Ibid.

234. Shah, "How Lethal Injection Reform Constitutes Impermissible Research on Prisoners," 1144–45.

235. Hon. Fernando J. Gaitan Jr., "Challenges Facing Society in the Implementation of the Death Penalty," *Fordham Urban Law Journal* 35 (June 2008): 786.

5

Mistaken for Consensus

Hung Juries, the Allen Charge, and the End of Jury Deliberation

SONALI CHAKRAVARTI

The declaration of a hung jury is one of the most dramatic moments in the legal process. All of the resources and efforts invested in a trial can be perceived to have been for naught when a jury expected to reach a unanimous verdict (either guilty or not guilty) fails to do so. For the defendant, a hung jury may be celebrated as a brief reprieve—there will be another trial or pressure to plea bargain from the state, but it is significant that a jury of one's peers did not find the evidence adequately convincing. For the prosecution, the hung jury is likely felt as a waste of time and money. The judge often has a more complex perspective, as she may understand why the jury failed to reach a consensus but is still disappointed with the outcome of a mistrial (almost always cause for greater official scrutiny of the decisions of the judge). This essay examines when the hung jury should be understood as a mistake—that is, an outcome that reveals a breakdown in the procedures of the trial or undermines the tenets of the adversarial justice system. The hung jury is a sanctioned option within U.S. law so should it not be seen as an aberration, but the mixed reactions to it suggest room for interpretation about what it reveals about the jury process and the obstacles to consensus.

The hung jury is also a highly significant outcome for the judge because it results in a mistrial; to prevent such an outcome a judge may issue a version of the Allen charge, a second set of instructions a judge gives to a jury that appears to be struggling to reach unanimity. The judge may address topics such as the expense of the trial, the value of the randomness of the jury selection process, and the expectation of reasonable doubt in order to motivate the jury to reach a verdict. The Allen charge is one of the more controversial aspects of jury procedure, alternately seen as helpful or coercive depending on the context, and its illegality in twenty-three states attests to this status. An investigation into the Allen charge sharpens the question and clarifies the conditions that would hinder the possibility of a legitimate hung jury and render an entirely different type of mistake.

The conceptual armature of Jürgen Habermas's work on discourse ethics is relevant to the question of hung juries because of the ways in which jury procedure within the U.S. legal system manifests some of Habermas's central philosophical ideals, but it has not been the object of his attention. Written in a more abstract register, Habermas's defense of discourse ethics is meant to generate a means for testing the legitimacy of norms, but his work also gives insight into the conditions that would be desirable for decisions as immediate and pragmatic as jury verdicts. Using his formulations of the Ideal Speech Situation and of the lifeworld as conceptual touchstones allows for an interpretation of the legitimate hung jury as a highly significant outcome and one that can be seen as the opposite of a mistake. Through this lens, the Allen charge also comes into focus as a misguided attempt to offset a potentially erroneous outcome with a coercive intervention.

The Allen Charge

Led by Chief Justice Fuller, a unanimous decision of the Supreme Court in 1896 decided that the judge's instructions to the jury nearing a deadlock, what would come to be known as the Allen charge, were not improper. The fact that the presiding judge spoke about the purpose of the trial, the resources involved, the integrity of the jurors, and the responsibility of minority jurors to reconsider their position was found to be acceptable and even beneficial to the jury deliberation process. The model charge from the Fifth Circuit that was approved by the court reads:

> Members of the Jury:
>
> I'm going to ask that you continue your deliberations in an effort to reach agreement upon a verdict and dispose of this case; and I have a few additional comments I would like for you to consider as you do so.
>
> This is an important case. The trial has been expensive in time, effort, money and emotional strain to both the defense and the prosecution. If you should fail to agree upon a verdict, the case will be left open and may have to be tried again. Obviously, another trial would only serve to increase the

cost to both sides, and there is no reason to believe that the case can be tried again by either side any better or more exhaustively than it has been tried before you.

Any future jury must be selected in the same manner and from the same source as you were chosen, and there is no reason to believe that the case could ever be submitted to twelve men and women more conscientious, more impartial, or more competent to decide it, or that more or clearer evidence could be produced.

If a substantial majority of your number are in favor of a conviction, those of you who disagree should reconsider whether your doubt is a reasonable one since it appears to make no effective impression upon the minds of the others. On the other hand, if a majority or even a lesser number of you are in favor of an acquittal, the rest of you should ask yourselves again, and most thoughtfully, whether you should accept the weight and sufficiency of evidence which fails to convince your fellow jurors beyond a reasonable doubt.

Remember at all times that no juror is expected to give up an honest belief he or she may have as to the weight or effect of the evidence; but, after full deliberation and consideration of the evidence in the case, it is your duty to agree upon a verdict if you can do so.

You must also remember that if the evidence in the case fails to establish guilt beyond a reasonable doubt the Defendant should have your unanimous verdict of Not Guilty.

You may be as leisurely in your deliberations as the occasion may require and should take all the time which you may feel is necessary.

The tone of the charge is intriguing, and I am drawn to the controversy because of the tension between the judicious and measured language of the charge that appears to treat those in favor and not in favor of a conviction with equanimity, and the palpable feeling that the jury is being scolded for the uncooperative actions of a few. In the contemporary legal landscape, states that allow intervention by the judge in this manner offer charges similar in tone and content. While judges are not expected to read verbatim from the model charge, certain points are to be observed, in part to defend against appellate reversal, and they include asking both majority and minority jurors to listen to the opposing side's argument and ensuring that jurors know that they are not expected to "give up an honest belief."[1] Case law since the time of the Allen decision has codified some of the most controversial aspects of the charge, also known as the "dynamite charge," and it has revealed an oft-repeated set of arguments that dissenting judges use to question its validity.

Representative of their concerns, the Coleman dissent in *Thaggard v. U.S.* (1965) posits the Allen charge as a "plea from the bench for a verdict" and is an elegant appeal to interpret the Sixth Amendment right to an impartial jury to mean a jury that is free from the interference of a judge clearly invested in a unanimous verdict.[2] From Coleman's perspective, even with the acknowledgment of the responsibilities of the majority and minority jurors, the charge still creates a disproportionate demand on dissenting voters who believe they are in violation of the judge's wishes for unanimity. He is particularly aggrieved with the language used by the lower court judge who told the jury in the course of extrapolating on the Allen charge that the "case must at some time be decided." Coleman suggested that such language effaces the option of a hung jury from the set of legitimate outcomes, even though it is a protected one which is in the spirit of an adversarial system of justice that presumes the innocence of the defendant. The fact that there is a heavy burden of proof on the state for a conviction is not a frustration of the court that should be expressed by the judge and then ameliorated by the jury. Coleman's concerns capture the legal establishment's reasons for withholding support for the Allen charge, despite its claims to efficiency and fairness.[3] The argument elaborated in the rest of the paper dovetails with these concerns, yet it approaches the question of the Allen charge from the perspective of the expectations of deliberative democracy and the conceptual validity of the hung jury.[4]

My interpretation of the jury process has many affinities with Robert Burns's understanding of the trial as an idiosyncratic institution that gives rise to its own particular (and admirable) form of judgment, one that depends on the agonistic struggle of a variety of norms and linguistic practices.[5] The trial is an insular world, not appropriate for translation into other social or political models, and attempts to do so rely on the specious isolation of parts of the process or of desirable forms of reasoning. The jury, in his assessment, must be able to render a decision free of monitoring and quality control by the judge because of the complicated nature of the decision. It is not the contingency of the decision process and the relationship between particulars and the universalism of the law (though that is part of it) that marks the distinctiveness of the jury's responsibility, Burns argues, but the multilayered way in which jurors decide about narrative coherence, social norms, and legal ideals in a manner that exceeds the conventions of deductive reasoning.

An investigation into the "mistake" of a hung jury raises the question about the relationship between the judge and jury: Should the judge be understood as the "boss" of the jury insuring that they do their jobs properly? On the one hand, it is the responsibility of the judge to impart her highly specialized knowledge about trial procedure to the jury such that there are not grounds for a mistrial. There will be times when the proper procedure is counter to both the will and instinct of the jury (such as the desire to talk about the trial with family members or on social media) and they must be instructed that their willingness to follow procedure is not a matter of discretion. The judge is thus a manager with the power to punish and sanction when expectations are not met. On the other hand, the roles of judge and jury change once the jury instructions are given. At this point the judge is less like a boss than an umpire, one who does not have say in the strategy of the game, but upholds a minimum standard of integrity. While the judge may still admonish jurors for violating court procedure, deliberation occurs in a closed room. The fact that the jury has the ultimate authority to decide within the adversarial system is interpreted to mean that the jury should not be monitored, coerced, led, or criticized by the judge or counsel as it is making its decision. The jury has a right to ask the judge questions about its task, but the jurors are no longer under her watchful eye. They are expected to take their responsibility seriously, but the judge cannot tell them that their decision is wrong (Bushell's case famously established this in 1670).[6] The argument below will suggest that the Allen charge should be seen as an inappropriate switch to the boss model of judicial authority. The jury has been entrusted with a task and it is consistent with the other procedures of jury deliberation to let them manifest this trust by giving them the freedom to conduct deliberations in the best way they can. The jury that is unable to reach consensus should not be treated as if they had strayed from their responsibility and needed the supervision of a boss. Yet what if the jury deliberates for only two minutes and returns a guilty verdict? What should the judge do then? It seems plausible to say that in two minutes there would be barely enough time to poll the jury members, let alone "deliberate" about the evidence. Still, I follow Burns in his interpretation of the complex mandate of the jury, one that challenges the received view of the primacy of proceduralism in regard to the letter of the law. The jury must navigate between multiple linguistic and cognitive practices and must be given the latitude by the judge to do it in the best manner they see fit. The Allen charge interrupts the insular world of the jury by implying that sheer will power or improved deductive reasoning will allow the majority to see the viewpoint of the minority, or vice versa. Such an assumption about the deliberation process of the jury flattens it at precisely the moment when the conditions for deliberation must be expansive and move beyond inherited formulas.[7]

On the Philosophy of Jürgen Habermas

With his attention to conditions that could foster communicative rationality, Habermas, in a remarkably ambitious way, provides a way out of the impasse of cynicism and political impossibility to which critical theory has arguably succumbed. Instead of a perspective that maintains that the political and moral spheres have been irretrievably marred by ideology and the corrosive effects of both liberalism and capitalism, his conception of communicative rationality suggested a redirection of the Enlightenment project away from instrumental rationality and toward ends that are inclusive and mutually beneficial. The ability for individuals to understand each other through everyday language, even if they begin from disparate premises, allows for the possibility of relationships that are not based solely on domination and exploitation.[8] Such communicative rationality also allows for the generation of new moral norms that garner their legitimacy from a much more inclusive process than previously theorized. The legitimacy of moral and political norms should, in his framework, thus be tied to the structural and linguistic conditions of participation in their creation, rather than tradition and an imagined premise of consent based on reason.[9]

The heuristic of the Ideal Speech Situation is Habermas's potent vision of the conditions necessary to have the kind of communicative exchange in which intersubjective recognition is possible and that is capable of generating legitimate norms. It is important to note that Habermas never expected the Ideal Speech Situation to be a blueprint for existing political institutions, nor to serve, as with Rousseau's general will, as an empirical fantasy. I follow James Bohman in suggesting that Habermas is adamantly not calling for direct democracy in a new era and does not want to make the mistake that he claims Rousseau to have made—that is, confused his new model of legitimacy with a new model for political engagement.[10] It is thus the *conceptual* preconditions for legitimacy that are of the utmost concern. In placing these conditions in conversation with the jury deliberation process, I am not drawing attention to the procedural reforms that would make them more in line with the Ideal Speech Situation; yet, the concerns he raises about the conditions for deliberation and the opportunities for the distortion of such a process can be brought to bear on thinking about the hung jury.

The Ideal Speech Situation is premised on two conditions. The first condition (U) is grounded in the assumption of universalization—that is, the assumption that for a norm to be valid, *each* individual would be able to accept it without coercion through the process of a reasonable discourse about its effects and consequences.[11] A norm becomes universalized and universalizable through the fact that its consequences are acceptable to every person and that this acceptance is reached without the coercion that can be the result of vastly unequal positions of power. The fact that each person holds the right to accept independently is central to the moral force of the outcome. The demand for unanimity, with all the challenges it implies, is the proper condition for determining the validity of norms within a system of thought that places intersubjective communication at the core of its political and moral project.

In many other fora, the need for closure is so urgent that majority rule is thought to be the most pragmatic expectation for arriving at a decision. There are many political or administrative issues on which reasonable people disagree, and given this reality, the argument goes, the will of the majority (usually a compromise in itself) must suffice to render a decision and thus make it possible for a governing body to move on to other issues or take action. However, within Habermas's framework for the legitimation of moral norms, the condition that all those who are affected must agree is not a secondary concern. Rather, it is meant to be the site of contestation and should not be obscured by strategic concerns or a type of realist pessimism which suggests that majority agreement is the best outcome one can hope for. It is not correct to equate Habermas's condition of unanimity for the legitimacy of a moral norm with an argument for the strict standard of unanimity in juries. Yet, there are still affinities—there are issues, for Habermas and in the case of juries, that are too important to risk the kind of intellectual exclusion of unpopular positions that majority rule allows. It is important to note that revisability is always in the array of possibilities regarding the legitimation of norms. Forced closure could never be compatible with the normative requirements of the Ideal Speech Situation; the real and the ideal should not be collapsed. If consensus appears only asymptotically in reference to a particular proposal, this is an explicit signal of the need for further consideration. The demand that a jury reach a decision, even one of marked dissensus, is another way in which it is in tension with the Habermasian formulation that relies on the possibility of revision.

The second condition (D), known as the discursive principle, contends that all who are affected by an issue must participate in the reason-giving and argumentation that precedes a decision. Such a dialogic process, the condition holds, must also rely on language that is accessible to all and not confined to experts or technocrats. While more broadly applicable than (U), (D) still expresses a conception of normative justification in general and cannot be applied to administrative or applied decisions, despite its reliance on informal language. Habermas's emphasis on practical discourse is in distinction to the Kantian model of norm-generation through the Categorical Imperative. With his emphasis on practical discourse, it is the actual concerns and positions of participants that must be engaged and that provide the basis for legitimate outcomes, and not a preoccupation with the logical deduction that emerges from a set of principles, justified by an external standard of universalizability. Taking (D) and (U) together, Habermas presents a high standard for the legitimacy of decisions that embodies the beliefs that relativism and subjectivity will not be the tragic fate of every discussion about principles and that all individuals are able to understand their interests and communicate them in a practical manner without the expectation of philosophical language.[12] (U) and (D) provide benchmarks that do not have easy correlates within the jury system: unanimity for the legitimacy of moral norms is far removed from the reality of unanimity in practical judgment, and the requirement of (D) that all affected parties can participate in the discourse also flounders given the mandate of the jury charge and the exclusion of others impacted by the crime from the process.[13] Still, it is remarkable to note that the distilled procedures for the legitimation of moral norms resemble the basic expectations for jury deliberation in ways that are unmatched by any other political or legal institution.

On the issue of consensus and legitimacy, the Supreme Court has not found the unanimity requirement to be sacrosanct, and the debate over the relative benefits and shortcoming of a unanimous decision rule over a majority one is long-standing.[14] In *Apodaca v. Oregon* the Supreme Court found that the Oregon Court of Appeals did not have rule by unanimous verdict because it is not integral to the fair and proper functioning of a trial. While the Sixth Amendment explicitly mentions jury unanimity as concomitant with the mandate for a jury of one's peers, the Fourteenth Amendment does not insist that all aspects are necessary at the state level.[15] Further, the Court found that there was no reason to believe that racial minorities would be given worse treatment in majority-rule juries than in unanimous ones. In the majority opinion, Justice White also separated the foundation of the unanimity rule from the reasonable doubt standard that crystallized after the Constitution.

Thus the requirement of unanimity is still an open question given the discretion allowed at the state level and the higher standard maintained at the federal one. The argument for unanimity hinges on the burden that it establishes, one fitting for an adversarial system of justice that takes as a hallowed value the presumed innocence of the defendant. It has also been argued that the quality of deliberation is higher when the outcome must be unanimous.[16] All participants are formally included (even if they choose to remain quiet during discussion), and the development of arguments and counterarguments is likely to be more extensive when the entire group must be convinced, not just the majority.[17] Unanimity ensures that when there is a guilty verdict all jury members are jointly responsible for such an act, which authorizes the state to use force and confinement when it would otherwise be unable to do so. If a jury member is unconvinced by the evidence, they must prevent the guilty decision from going forward, whereas in a majority-rule system, a jury member may be able to register her doubt but then rationalize the outcome by saying that she was powerless to stop the guilty verdict.[18]

Habermas's argument about unanimity is not so much an additional valence to these other perspectives, but a restructuring of the argument to make unanimity an essential component for legitimacy in a legal-philosophical system that is grounded in procedure and acutely aware of the systemic forces of capitalism, democratic majoritarianism, and instrumental rationality (even if he does not apply the standard to these types of institutions). The Allen charge can be seen to compromise the ideals of unanimity, in spirit if not in the exact wording of the charge. Jurors can and should be dismissed for refusal to deliberate, an act that amounts to a refusal to be part of the process of reason-giving and the adjustment of one's own ideas in light of the ideas of others. This issue is particularly salient in the case of a jury that is moving toward congealed disagreement, the kind that precipitates a discussion of the Allen charge. If the majority is in favor of a guilty verdict and one or two jurors believe that not guilty is the appropriate verdict, they must, in the spirit of jury deliberation and Habermasian discursive principles, be willing to defend their position against arguments from the opposing side as well as try to convince others to share their belief.[19] For those in support, the Allen charge is an intervention specifically targeted to deter jurors from giving up on the process of deliberation.

While a refusal to deliberate or an unwillingness to consider the arguments of an opposing faction in the jury room may cause a hung jury, there may be situations in which a hung jury satisfies a deeply held belief about the fallibility of the legal process and a hope for multiple valid interpretations of an event. Such is the case in the 2001 memoir of D. Graham Burnett, a historian who served as the foreman of a jury in a homicide case in New York City.[20] The case turned on the issue of self-defense; it seemed probable that the defendant killed the victim, but the circumstances surrounding the killing, including the possibility that the defendant feared he would be raped, were critical to jury deliberation. During the trial Burnett grew increasingly alienated from the prosecution's case, particularly from the tone with which witnesses were questioned, as well as the judge's manner. Yet, he did not lean toward a not guilty verdict at the beginning of the trial, in part because of his role as foreman and his desire to facilitate discussion, and was instead drawn to the idea of a hung jury as the outcome that would best represent his uncertainty and the inconclusive evidence. He admits that he is not entirely sure why the hung jury presented itself to him as the best option, but attributes it to an academic orientation toward evidence that sees the possibility of many narratives and the necessity of ambiguity in any interpretation. To decide on one narrative (knowing that the action would precipitate sentencing or acquittal) would require from him an amount of certainty that he did not initially believe was possible based on the evidence. Nonetheless, the deliberations ended with a unanimous finding of not guilty, with leadership from Burnett. The jury provided a personalized note to the judge in addition to the decision that indicated the jurors' ambivalence toward the legal choices with which they were presented. The jury was unanimous in their decision, but less certain that the decision fit with an idealized vision of justice; their decision of not guilty did not indicate that they found the defendant entirely free from blame, just that the blame did not warrant a guilty verdict. Burnett's memoir provides an insight into yet another motivation for the hung jury, one that is consistent with the intellectual humility of academic discourse in the humanities, but one that would also be a mistake if it superseded juror responsibility to participate in deliberation about the evidence. A principled commitment to achieving a hung jury (regardless of deliberation) is just as erroneous an orientation as an excision of the option altogether.

In addition to the logic of unanimity, the condition of (D) introduces a different way of thinking about the legitimacy of consensus that can also be applied to the Allen charge. In explaining the motivation for the Ideal Speech Situation, Habermas is animated by the possibility of creating space for political deliberation that is not primarily determined by strategic calculation. The expectation of practical discourse is in part to stave off technocratic language that acts as a veil for strategic posturing and the possibility that outcomes benefiting the few can appear to be benefiting the many. The attention to the consequences of a norm and its effect on each individual also protects against provisional acceptance of an action for future strategic play. Habermas is particularly attuned to the way in which the procedural aspects of the Ideal Speech Situation could be reduced to the bartering and domination that permeate other spheres of liberal capitalism, and the demand of consensus for democratic legitimacy is a necessary antidote. The nature of jury deliberation does not encounter the long-term strategic calculations of policy debates with which Habermas is concerned, but there are incentives for jurors to act in a strategic way in order to expedite the process or increase their status in the eyes of the judge or fellow jurors. Drawing attention to the economic incentives to end deliberation with the Allen charge gives power to the majority that is extraneous to debates about the evidence. Habermas's attention to (U) and (D) thus, through its signaling of important preconditions for discourse, suggests that the Allen charge intercepts the trajectory of fair and impartial deliberation at a particularly vulnerable place—that of a moment where the jury may be wavering between strategic and nonstrategic deliberation. The Allen charge introduces an element of strategic calculation into jury deliberation at a highly sensitive time, when jurors are fatigued and potentially frustrated. Pressure for closure and a unanimous verdict can cause a default to the normal conditions of politics in which traditional dominant groups further exert their dominance.[21] Thus, thinking with Habermas about a schematic for legitimate decision-making provides fodder for thinking about the Allen charge as a misguided convention: one cannot justify, in the name of efficacy or closure, an intervention that threatens the standard of unanimity and the premise that all jurors have standing to participate in the process in a commensurate way. To do so would be to undermine one of the conditions that provides the greatest basis for legitimacy in the jury process.

The question of strategic discourse is not the only way discourse can be corrupted for juries; another type of distortion can emerge from restrictions on what is considered acceptable for deliberation. This is a topic where critics of Habermas, rather than Habermas himself, have made interventions that could be productively applied to the jury process. Iris Marion Young notably critiqued Habermas for his elevation of the impartial point of view over a lived, embodied, and affective one as the best perspective for reaching consensus. She sees potential in the conditions for communicative rationality but argues that Habermas's model "abstracts from the rhetorical dimensions of communication, that is, the evocative terms, metaphors, dramatic elements of the speaking, by which a speaker addresses himself or herself to this particular audience. When people converse in concrete speaking situation, when they give and receive reasons from one another with the aim of reaching understanding, gesture, facial expression, tone of voice, as well as evocative metaphors and dramatic emphasis, are crucial aspects of their communication."[22] The openness to metaphor and contextual understanding may be more important in the cases of dramatic lifeworld differences, described below, than Habermas allows for within the context of (D) and (U).

On the Lifeworld

In addition to the centrality of (U) and (D), the Habermasian concept of the lifeworld can be persuasively enlisted for the defense of the hung jury as a legitimate and necessary outcome that deserves protection from the intervention of the Allen charge. For Habermas, the lifeworld is the inherited world of meaning, norms, and interpretation that one gets from society and culture and that intersects with the contingencies of personality.[23] The lifeworld encompasses how one views oneself in relation to the institutions of the family, law, and the state, and it shapes intuitions about how to evaluate worth, trustworthiness, and the burden of moral action in ways that are difficult for an individual to parse. The lifeworld is one of various influences on cognitive processes, and it is difficult for an individual to know just how strong the influence is. Habermas builds upon the concept of lifeworld to make two important distinctions: the first is between lifeworld and system, where the system refers to the forces of the market that impose an instrumental rationality motivated by concerns of wealth and political domination on the inherited interpretations of the lifeworld. The second distinction, of particular relevance to the deliberative process, is between the lifeworld participants already hold and bring to the process and the one they come to agree upon with their fellow jurors. He writes:

> On the one side we have the horizon of unquestioned, intersubjectively shared, nonthematized certitudes that participants in communication have "at their backs." On the other side, participants in communication face the

communicative contents constituted within a world: objects that they perceive and manipulate, norms that they observe or violate, and lived experiences to which they have privileged access and which they can express. To the extent to which participants in communication can conceive of what they reach agreement on as something in a world, something detached from the lifeworld background from which it emerged, what is explicitly known comes to be distinguished from what is implicitly certain.[24]

Thus the lifeworld is foundationally important for the process of deliberation, but successful agreement requires the surrender from its deterministic aspects and the pull of tradition, culture, and the comfort of previously held coherent positions. The lifeworld for participants is what exists "at their back," yet as comprehensive as the lifeworld is, it does not prohibit communication in its fullest sense; they are able to detach the lifeworld and come to a shared understanding of the issue at hand. With this detachment comes the constructive project of explicitly creating new norms and being bound in a different way to fellow citizens. In the jury context, how jurors perceive the law and the criminal justice system, as well as their understanding of how bias and prejudice affect the law, is part of the background implied by the lifeworld. Yet it is their belief in the integrity of the court and of the procedures in place for jury deliberation that creates the cognitive environment that enables them to decide on the facts of the case and create a shared reality distinct from the lifeworld. This is the trajectory for consensus, but *dissensus,* the less desirable outcome for both Habermas and juries, can also be seen through the lens of lifeworld. When jurors are selected, they are asked questions to determine whether they can accept the terms of the court despite the inherited forms of knowledge and assumptions that are embedded in their lifeworlds. One cannot be assumed to have abandoned previous conceptions, as the quotation above affirms, but the possibility of agreement with others within the procedural expectations of the court must be salient. In such a situation, jurors form a shared lifeworld through immersive experience of the trial and then attempt to agree on a shared decision. They may also disagree even though they have a shared lifeworld.[25] However, given that one's lifeworld can exert a profound hold on how one understands issues such as criminality, poverty, punishment, and prejudice, it may make detachment for the sake of a shared lifeworld impossible in a given case. To put it another way, there may be cases in which differences in lifeworlds, through no fault of the court or the jurors per se, come to bear on the evidence in such a way that consensus cannot be reached.

A Conflict of Lifeworlds

It has been asserted in the secondary literature that Habermas pays inadequate attention to theorizing the conditions when conflict cannot be transcended through consensus achieved by the procedural conditions of discourse ethics.[26] Habermas reflected on civil disobedience in the context of protests against the building of a nuclear plant and the installation of cruise and Pershing missiles in Germany in 1981, and his position suggests parallels with the lifeworld differences I see as possible in juries.[27] Like the hung jury, civil disobedience is the last resort after all other legitimate (or in the case of juries, more highly desirable) actions have been exhausted; they can never become the default course of action if the functions of the institutions (that of the trial or the rule of law) are to be preserved. In his one speech on the topic, Habermas suggests that civil disobedience in the context of nuclear disarmament must be seen as essentially symbolic in its undermining of the legitimacy of a particular political will and thus neither a fundamental threat to the stability provided by law nor the instantiation of a viable alternative legal order. It is interesting to note that a symbolic interpretation of a hung jury would be highly problematic, even for those who want to protect their legitimacy. The jury must decide on one case and one case alone. No juror should use the case at hand in order to make a larger point about the criminal justice system or about the law itself (the exception of nullification notwithstanding). A jury that hangs to make a symbolic point would rankle the officers of the court and would represent just the type of mistake that proponents of the Allen charge want to avoid.

Returning to the issue of dissensus, Habermas understood civil disobedience to be the result of two different interpretations of the lifeworld. Those who opposed the creation of the nuclear plan believed that the abuse of the environment, the closed process of decision-making leading up to the policy, and the impact of the capitalist market were all systemic threats to the values of their lifeworld. Achieving a consensus with those who represented this alternate set of commitments would be akin to abandoning the foundational aspects of the protesters' own lifeworld. These are the conditions, Habermas suggests, that call for civil disobedience and should engender a legitimate challenge to particular laws through direct action: "The dissensus which gains expression in this complex 'no' aims not at this or that measure or policy; it is rooted in the rejection of a life-form—namely, that life-form which has been stylized as the normal prototype—which is tailored to the needs of a capitalism modernization process, programmed for possessive individualism, for values of material security, and for the striving of competition and production, and which rests on the repression of both fear and the experience of death."[28] In such situations, saying "no" to the law and to the ideal of consensus itself emerges for Habermas as a necessary step for the further maturation of democracy and for the moral integrity of the individual who disagrees with a certain policy. A similar impasse can emerge in the jury room, where the lifeworlds of a subset of jurors converge to reject the reasoning and interpretation offered by another subset.

The conditions of universality and respect for the moral equality of each person continue to be, for Habermas, the most important checks against coercion. White and Farr highlight moral equality as the linchpin that holds Habermas's theory of civil disobedience together.[29] Without the concept of moral equality, the mandate for consensus could lead the majority to insist upon compromise as evidence of good-faith deliberation. A genuine desire by the majority of jurors for the legitimacy that consensus would entail (and a belief in the reasonableness of their position) could inadvertently compromise the condition of the equality of each participation. Subsequently, the line between compromise and coercion becomes difficult to decipher. They write: "In our unorthodox account, this no-saying is not directly connected with the expectation of redemption through the achievement of rational consensus; rather, it is connected only to the expectation of some significant moral-political space being available that honors this value of the morally equal voice of each. Without this qualification, an appeal to compromises does not necessarily provide much improvement over situations of pure coercion: I agree not to shoot you, if you agree to hand over your wallet. The concept of a 'presumptively just compromise' may only be a rough standard, but it clearly disavows 'agreements' of this sort."[30] Thus the justness of an outcome, whether in compromise or dissensus, is fixed with regard to the treatment of each participant as a moral equal and one not expected to be subsumed by the desire for consensus. Were the normative weight on unanimity less, there would be greater latitude for compromises that activated strategic concerns or leveraged implicit hierarchies. Instead, to respect the morally equal voice of each, the possibility of legitimate dissensus as it emerges from irreconcilable lifeworlds must be recognized.

Lasse Thomassen further highlights that the ability to say "no" in

Habermas's model is a constitutive part of understanding what it means to say "yes" in the context of consensus.[31] He extrapolates that within Habermas's discursive model "one must interrogate the norms that constitute the 'moral-political space' of equality to find out if what appear as noise, silence, or even a 'yes' may in fact be 'no.'"[32] Similar to the point above regarding the need for heightened attention to deliberative coercion that masquerades as compromise, Thomassen suggests that there are oblique ways in which disagreement may be registered even under favorable discursive conditions. Habermas's careful elucidation of the ideal conditions for deliberation thereby provides reasons for even greater scrutiny of such phenomenon and for skepticism regarding interventions such as the Allen charge which suggest that "noise" can be ameliorated with repeated instructions. Instead, the noise and the silence to which Thomassen refers may be better understood as nascent markers of significant lifeworld differences when they appear during jury deliberation. These differences may be activated by the particularities of the case and the same jury on a different case may not see these differences manifest, but the Habermasian insight here is the importance of deferring an interpretation until the jury itself is ready to make one. Differences in perceptions of law enforcement, the purpose of punishment, and the relationship between poverty and crime, all stemming from the lifeworlds of jurors, can be fundamental in the interpretation of evidence in a particular case, and even the best faith attempts at deliberation cannot transcend them.[33]

The Legitimate Hung Jury

Although hung juries do not usually divide along race, it is fruitful to consider race as a factor that strongly influences one's lifeworld and could thus be significant in juries that cannot reach an agreement.[34] Judith Butler's interpretation of the Rodney King verdict provides a case study in which differences in lifeworld could have been persuasive as reasons for a hung jury. In her reflections on the case, Butler questions how a white jury would interpret the video footage of police officers beating Rodney King fifty-three times with a baton as a legitimate use of force by the officers, and she expresses her disbelief that one juror saw King as the aggressor in the situation and "in control."[35] When the jury returns a verdict of not guilty, a decision that would spark riots in Los Angeles, Butler asserts that it is not just a matter of differences in interpretation between the jurors and others who saw the incident as embedded in racist motivations and institutional legacies. She writes:

> It is not, then, a question of negotiating between what is "seen," on the one hand, and a "reading" which is imposed upon the visual evidence, on the other. In a sense, the problem is even worse: to the extent that there is a racist organization and disposition of the visible, it will work to circumscribe what qualifies as visual evidence, such that it is in some cases impossible to establish the "truth" of racist brutality through recourse to visual evidence. For when the visual is fully schematized by racism, the "visual evidence" to which one refers will always and only refute conditions based upon it; for it is possible within this racism episteme that no black person can seek recourse to the visible as the sure ground of evidence.[36]

In the language of the lifeworld, the differences between a lifeworld that perpetually (and perhaps unconsciously) sees the black male body as a source of threat and one that does not are not differences in interpretation of the evidence (or the part of discussion that relies on persuasion and reason-giving in a Habermasian system), but rather they emerge from the act of seeing itself. The lifeworld cannot be detached from agreement in the way Habermas suggests because it is constitutive of perception itself and consensus cannot be wrung from even the best of deliberative conditions. The Rodney King verdict shows how racial prejudices can deeply affect deliberation from the beginning and do so in ways that evade the formal protections that the jury system sets up. A hung jury in such a situation would perhaps have been a desirable outcome because it would have shown the presence of an alternative lifeworld in the jury room—one that interpreted the evidence differently and might have persuaded the other jurors or precipitated a mistrial. Even if such a juror were not able to persuade the others, the inability to reach consensus would have allowed for more time to be devoted to the case and would have perhaps involved the service of a more diverse group of jurors in another trial.

The language Butler employs when she asserts that a racist episteme can be fully determinative of how one interprets evidence is arguably the type of reasoning and strategic posturing that Habermas wants to mitigate with the right conditions for discourse. Taking the idea even further, if epistemes were all as rigid as Butler suggests consensus would never be possible, since the entire premise of jury deliberation would be reduced to whether there is enough demographic compatibility to achieve unanimity. Hierarchies of power and audibility are real, and formal protections of unanimity and practical discourse will not be enough. It is in situations like this where the ideals Young has laid out (such as the possibilities of metaphors and embodied affect for communication) may be more effective than the discursive principles Habermas suggests.[37] Consensus will not come from direct argumentation perhaps, but more subtle shifts in understanding the worldviews of others. Habermas's understanding of the potential for agreement despite lifeworld differences is persuasive as a way to think about juries because of the jurors' commitment to the institution of the trial, the integrity of its procedures, and the gravity that comes with their ultimate decision-making authority—all of these may be synthesized into a lifeworld and decision-making process that resonates with all. Yet Butler's sharp assessment of the proceedings of the Rodney King trial draws much-needed attention to the potential legitimacy of disagreement in the jury box and the ways formal protections of the deliberative process can be impotent in the face of injustice, bias, and coercion.

The language of *belief* in the Allen charge, as well as the suggestion that holdout jurors are not cooperating in the deliberative process, suggests that it is a matter of conscience that is preventing a juror from being convinced, and this is not always accurate or desirable. Drawing upon Habermas's understanding of the lifeworld and Butler's language of the racial episteme points to something more systematic than a discrete belief in the mind of a holdout juror. The inability to achieve consensus with other jurors may not be because an individual cannot shake a doubt that exceeds what is reasonable; it may be the result of a more comprehensive difference in how she views and interprets evidence and the pressures that motivate citizens and law enforcement.[38]

The fact that Habermas has been accused of not giving adequate attention to legitimate conflict is related to an additional critique that he fails to consider specific issues that arise in the formation of the lifeworld for marginal members of the citizenry, those who do not fit into dominant conceptions of gender or race, for example. Nancy Fraser's critique of Habermas for his lack of attention to the ways in which women's consent during deliberation is misunderstood and misconstrued in both the public and private spheres is meant to point to the fragility of the deliberative space from the perspective of women, despite the fact that they are necessary for the "universalization" Habermas desires.[39] Fraser writes that the consent women give, in sexual situations and others, can be willfully and violently misread, such that an agentic act becomes a passive one (for example, when "no" is interpreted to mean "yes"), and her critique can be broadened to include the dangers of formal proceduralism obscuring the dynamics of power within jury deliberation. Fraser's critique suggests that racial minority jurors who also make up the minority on the jury decision are even more vulnerable to having their perspectives obscured in light of the desire for consensus. The very fact that each juror must register an opinion, not just give tacit consent or remain neutral, is a worthy protection against the problems of traditionally marginalized voiced within Habermas's model.

Furthermore, Fraser's concern about the incorporation of the perspective of women within the Ideal Speech Situation also centers on the distinction Habermas draws between the system and lifeworld with concerns of the material world and the labor of the household falling under the rubric of system. Fraser suggests that for traditionally marginalized groups such a distinction is incongruous, and their relationship to labor is the basis for lifeworld, not an oppositional force within it. Following from this, we can surmise that the way the lifeworld influences decisions in the context of a jury may not always follow the stark demarcation that Habermas would like. The interlocking concerns of system and lifeworld, especially in the case of certain groups, can become salient in jury deliberation and be a factor in divergent lifeworlds. Recognition of the validity of such an impasse is also a constructive response to the reality that power relations in society can be replicated within the jury room and require a heightened degree of protection to maintain the conditions of deliberation.

One might counter that the Allen charge is merely restating expectations that were given in the original jury charge. If the language of the charge suggests the need for consideration of the strategic values of expediency and the expectation that the jury follow certain procedures for deliberation and these guidelines are coercive, this is a problem with the original charge itself, and broader reforms should be made to the jury system. The Allen charge, the argument might go, is only a reminder at a critical time of the accepted responsibilities of the jury. If it encourages further debate toward the end of consensus, this is a net gain. If not, the jury is not worse off than when they approached the judge or were otherwise perceived to be on the cusp of deadlock. Yet, what Habermas's theory reveals is the need to protect the conditions of deliberation at each stage, particularly against the corruption of the goals of the process and in the service of the equal respect that is granted to each participant. The fact that there are obstacles toward achieving the Habermasian ideals of unanimity and equal participation does not mean they are irrelevant or in need of replacement. Rather, his philosophical defense of discourse ethics alongside his understanding of the reality of lifeworld differences provides a way to understand the significance of the hung jury (and the error of the Allen charge). It is interesting to note that in simulated jury studies, majority jurors were more likely to exercise influence in the jury room after an Allen charge and were emboldened to assert the veracity of their position. Even though all jurors were equally advised to reconsider their positions, the intervention of the judge through the Allen charge fortified the majority position and gave the majority the impression that had the support of the judge in moving to consensus.[40] This was especially true when the case hinged on issues of values and judgments, rather than technical concerns. Specifically, Smith and Kassin found that normative pressures from the majority predominated in juries that were discussing questions of values and personal standards, whereas information influence was more important in juries that decided on issues of fact.[41] Their research found that juries "in cases that involve community and moral standards (e.g. those that involve obscenity, abortion, police brutality, euthanasia or political dissent)" may be more susceptible to the influence of the Allen charge.[42] While Habermas would be hopeful that consensus could be achieved even in these types of cases through fair and impartial deliberation (and in even broader situations of norm legitimation than is generally sought through jury decisions), I have argued that cases that fail to reach consensus may sometimes be grounded in these types of lifeworld differences, not on a willful failure to deliberate or an incompetence regarding the evidence (though the confidentiality of jury deliberation makes it hard to know). Thus the Allen charge empowers majority jurors to exert further normative influence in precisely the types of cases that are likely to activate different understandings of the lifeworld. The Rodney King case did not turn on the issue of an Allen charge, but I invoke it to show how fragile lifeworld positions in the jury might be when there is an overwhelming alternative (especially a prejudiced one). Juries that have reached an impasse are not the cases that should have their deliberation hastened for the sake of efficiency; these are the cases likely to be manifestations of a legitimate hung jury and not the mistake.

The controversy over the Allen charge can be seen as the dueling dangers of two types of mistakes. The first is the mistake of a coercive action by the court that upsets the delicate balance of the jury deliberation process for the sake of a unanimous verdict. The second mistake in question is that of the hung jury. The hung jury results in a mistrial and prolongs the criminal justice process such that it may extend to another trial or plea-bargaining. From the perspective of efficiency, a hung jury is suboptimal and arguably a "mistake" precipitated by the actions of the judge or attorneys. A hung jury can also be seen as a mistake if jurors refuse to partake in the work of argument, interpretation, and persuasion on the questions of evidence and the burden of proof. This is not the case in juries that are divided because of substantial lifeworld differences that make shared interpretation of the evidence impossible. Jurors in cases like these cannot step away from their lifeworld interpretation in order to achieve consensus. To be true to their understanding of the case and their responsibilities as jurors, they must risk being seen by others as the holdouts who contribute to a mistrial. In addition, from the perspective of justice writ large, I suggest that the hung jury should also be seen as a hand-brake on the punishment component of the criminal justice system, a component widely documented to be vexed by racial and socioeconomic inequality. When a system is as flawed as the U.S. criminal justice system, an outcome that may at first seem like a mistake of inefficiency (and worthy of explicit remedy such as the Allen charge) might better be thought of as a type of immanent resistance delivered at precisely the moment the state has the greatest leverage over the defendant—the moment of the guilty verdict.

NOTES

1. In contrast to the secrecy surrounding the power of the jury to nullify, the recitation of the Allen charge is meant to give jurors an even more potent sense of their power. When a judge says, "No other twelve people can do a better job than you," jurors realize how critical each of their voices is and the authority of their decision. The fears of anarchy, so present in fears surrounding jury nullification, are not present in concerns regarding the Allen charge or the concerns raised by a hung jury. Nancy Marder, "The Myth of the Nullifying Jury," *Northwestern University Law Review* 877 (1999). Alan W. Scheflin, "Jury Nullification: The Right to Say No," *Southern California Law Review* 168 (1972). Christopher C. Schwan, "Right up to the Line: The Ethics of Advancing Nullification Arguments to the Jury," *Journal of the Legal Profession* 29 (2004–5).

2. *Thaggard v. United States*, 354 F.2d 735 (1965).

3. Mark Lanier and Cloud Miller III, "The Allen Charge: Expedient Justice or Coercion?" *American Journal of Criminal Justice* 25, no. 1 (2000).

4. For the American Bar Association's concerns surrounding the Allen charge, see American Bar Association, "The Allen Charge Dilemma," *American Criminal Law Review* 10 (1972).

5. I also share with Burns the tone of my analysis: it is explicitly interpretive and normative, and not meant as an account of the law as understood by its practitioners or in the case law. Robert Burns, *A Theory of the Trial* (Princeton: Princeton University Press, 1999).

6. Gary J. Jacobsohn, "The Right to Disagree: Judges, Juries, and the Administration of Criminal Justice in Maryland," *Washington University Law Review* 4(1976): 572.

7. I agree with Martha Merrill Umphrey's critique that Burns underestimates the fragility of such an idealized interpretation of the trial. Yet, I still suggest that an appreciation of the legitimacy of the hung jury decision and of the conditions that threaten it highlight the fragility of jury decisions, while preserving a complex understanding of their judging power. Martha Merrill Umphrey, "Fragile Performances: The Dialogics of Judgment in a Theory of the Trial," *Law and Social Inquiry* 28, no. 2 (2003).

8. The impossibility of consensus on a variety of central issues of concern, especially to those of the good life, leads critics like Moon to prefer bracketing them as well as paying attention only to those who are affected by a particular issue. Habermas himself makes the distinction between moral and political questions more defined in his later work. J. Donald Moon, "Practical Discourse and Communicative Ethics," in *Cambridge Companion to Habermas*, ed. Stephen K. White (Cambridge: Cambridge University Press, 2006).

9. Jürgen Habermas, *Moral Consciousness and Communicative Action* (Cambridge: MIT Press, 2001); *Between Facts and Norms: Contributions to a Discourse Theory of Law and Democracy* (Cambridge: MIT Press, 1998).

10. James Bohman, "Critical Theory and Democracy," in *Handbook of Critical Theory*, ed. David M. Rasmussen (Oxford: Blackwell, 1996), 203.

11. Habermas, *Moral Consciousness and Communicative Action*, 66.

12. For a discussion on jurors' ability to understand highly technical subject matter, see Neil Vidmar and Valerie P. Hans, *American Juries: The Verdict* (Amherst, NY: Prometheus Books, 2007), 153.

13. Wellmer has critiqued Habermas for suggesting that the formal requirements of the Ideal Speech Situation are erroneously posited as resulting in truth (and captured by the consensus theory of truth). I am sympathetic to these concerns and they are picked up in a different guise with proponents of a revised majority decision rule for juries, but the concerns do not derail the more important legitimizing function of Habermas's framework. Fundamentally, it is not some abstract truth that is sought through jury deliberation, but an adjudication of the evidence relevant to the charge at hand as the basis for the state's suspension of the rights of the defendant. How a jury of one's peers contingently determines justice in a particular situation is more important than confidence in the consensus theory of truth. Allbrecht Wellmer, "Ethics and Dialogue," in *The Persistence of Modernity: Essays on Aesthetics, Ethics and Postmodernism* (Cambridge: Polity Press, 1991).

14. Compare *Apodaca v. Oregon*, 406 U.S. 404 (1972). *Johnson v. Louisiana* 400 U.S. 356 (1972). Unanimous juries do, however, need at least six jurors. *Ballew v. Georgia*, 435 U.S. 223 (1978).

15. Gary J. Jacobsohn, "The Unanimous Verdict: Politics and the Jury Trial," *Washington University Law Quarterly* 39 (1977). Michael Saks, "The Smaller the Jury, the Greater the Unpredictability," *Judicature* 79 (1996).

16. Peter J. Coughlan, "In Defense of Unanimous Jury Verdicts: Mistrials, Communication, and Strategic Voting," *American Political Science Review* 94, no. 2 (2000).

17. "Juries required to reach unanimity deliberating longer and in more ideal fashion than juries that were not required to reach complete agreement. Specifically, unanimous juries discussed key facts to a greater extent, touched on more case facts than two-thirds quorum juries, corrected mistaken assertions by members more often, elicited the participation of minority-view jurors to a greater extent, and ultimately produced a higher level of member satisfaction." Dennis D. Devine, *Jury Decision-Making: The State of the Science* (New York: NYU Press, 2012), 45.

18. It is reported that 10 percent of trials result in a verdict that is the opposite of a jury's original preferences, and this suggests the substantial influence of the process of

deliberation on assessments jurors had made individually during the trial. For discussion of the implications of a verdict-driven jury style versus an evidence-driven one, see John Gastil et al., *The Jury and Democracy: How Jury Deliberation Promotes Civic Engagement and Political Participation* (New York: Oxford University Press, 2010), 95.

19. I acknowledge that a Habermasian dissent based on (U) would assert that the proposal in question does not advance the interests of all and the interest of the speaker, and this standard is at odds with what juries are asked to do.

20. D. Graham Burnett, *A Trial by Jury* (New York: Alfred A. Knopf, 2001).

21. Chambers suggest that the demand for closure, in the form of a vote, formal decision, and so forth, always dramatically reduces the opportunity for nonstrategic deliberation. She does not see any way to bridge the gap but rather suggests that a balance be struck between deliberation and closure. Simone Chambers, "Discourse and Democratic Practices," in *Cambridge Companion to Habermas*, ed. Stephen K. White (Cambridge: Cambridge University Press, 2006).

22. Iris Marion Young, "Impartiality and the Civic Public: Some Implications of Feminist Critiques of Moral and Political Theory," *Praxis International* 5, no. 4 (1986): 394.

23. William Rehg, "Habermas's Discourse Theory of Law and Democracy: An Overview of the Argument," in *Handbook of Critical Theory*, ed. David M. Rasmussen (Oxford: Blackwell, 1996). Stephen K. White, *Recent Work of Jurgen Habermas: Reason, Justice and Modernity* (Cambridge: Cambridge University Press, 1988). James Bohman, ""System" and "Lifeworld": Habermas and the Problem of Holism," *Philosophy & Social Criticism* 15 (1989).

24. Habermas, *Moral Consciousness and Communicative Action*, 138.

25. The situation of disagreement when there are shared lifeworlds is a liminal case for the interpretation I am suggesting. It may not be a mistake in the sense of failed good-faith deliberation, nor a politically significant impasse (because of lifeworld conflict), but rather a situation where reasonable jurors disagree on how to weight the evidence or to index the different norms.

26. Nicholas Rescher, *Pluralism: Against the Demand for Consensus* (Oxford: Oxford University Press, 1995). Lynn Sanders, "Against Deliberation," *Political Theory* 25, no. 3 (1997). Seyla Benhabib, *Situating the Self* (Cambridge: Polity Press, 1992).

27. Jürgen Habermas, "Civil Disobedience: Litmus Test for the Democratic Constitutional State," *Berkeley Journal of Sociology* 30 (1985).

28. Ibid.

29. Stephen K. White and Evan Robert Farr, "'No-Saying' in Habermas," *Political Theory* 40, no. 1 (2012).

30. Ibid., 51.

31. Lasse Thomassen, "Communicative Reason, Deconstruction and Foundationalism: A Response to White and Farr," *Political Theory* 41, no. 3 (2013).

32. Ibid., 486.

33. In her writing about jury sentencing, Iontcheva sees great value in the Habermasian deliberative model for thinking about the purposes of punishment. While decisions about guilt, she argues, are more technocratic in how they expect jurors to line up evidence with legal calculations about doubt, the purpose of punishment and its manifestation in sentencing requires much more of a juror's individual worldview, or in my application of Habermasian language, the inherited and imbibed perspectives of a particular lifeworld that speak to rehabilitation and retribution. Jenia Iontcheva, "Jury Sentencing as Democratic Practice," *Virginia Law Review* 89, no. 2 (2003).

34. Jeffrey Abramson, *We, the Jury: The Jury System and the Ideal of Democracy* (Cambridge: Harvard University Press, 2000), xi.

35. Judith Butler, "Endangered/Endangering: Schematic Racism and White Paranoia," in *Reading Rodney King/Reading Urban Uprising,* ed. Robert Gooding-Williams (New York: Routledge, 1993).

36. Ibid., 19.

37. Young, "Impartiality and the Civic Public."

38. Burns might be skeptical about the direct relationship I am asserting between lifeworld and juror decisions in the case of a hung jury. His interpretation suggests that there are many other areas of consideration before a juror makes a decision, not to mention the fact that experiencing the trial in all of its complexity challenges the lifeworlds of jurors in a multiplicity of ways. However, Burns highlights that part of a juror's role is to decide between competing norms and ways of judging, and it is plausible to see how jurors might disagree on this because of lifeworld expectations. Burns, *A Theory of the Trial.*

39. Nancy Fraser, "Rethinking the Public Sphere: A Contribution to the Critique of Actually Existing Democracy," in *Habermas and the Public Sphere,* ed. Craig Calhoun (Cambridge: MIT Press, 1992).

40. Vicki L. Smith and Saul M. Kassin, "Effects of the Dynamite Charge on the Deliberations of Deadlocked Mock Juries," *Law and Human Behavior* 17, no. 6 (1993).

41. Martin F. Kaplan and Charles E. Miller, "Group Decision Making and Normative versus Informational Influence: Effects of Type of Issue and Assigned Decision Rule," *Journal of Personality and Social Psychology* 53, no. 2 (1987).

42. Smith and Kassin, "Effects of the Dynamite Charge on the Deliberations of Deadlocked Mock Juries," 642.

6

Law's Mistakes, Legal Pluralism, and the Significance of Systemic Justice

Paul Schiff Berman

It has long been recognized that, for a judge, following the law and doing justice may sometimes be two very different pursuits. Often this dichotomy is invoked in order to criticize law. Law is so concerned with obeying rigid procedural rules or formalistic distinctions, we are told, that there is no room for seeking justice in the individual case.

But is that a weakness of law or a potential strength? After all, the same rules or distinctions that seem unconcerned with doing individual justice may at the same time be serving other, more systemic, justice values. For example, consider the rule of res judicata, which prevents the relitigation of a case that has previously been adjudicated. On the one hand, such a rule means that an unjust verdict (perhaps issued by a biased judge or jury) is allowed to stand. But on the other hand, res judicata serves broader systemic interests in finality and repose, the idea that at a certain point the parties need to move on, regardless of whether or not the outcome was just. Indeed, endless relitigation leads to injustice of a different sort, imposing significant costs on the parties without a real guarantee that subsequent adjudications will actually render greater justice than the first.

It is the same with law's mistakes. At first blush, it might seem anathema to the whole idea of law that we could countenance a wrong-headed or mistaken judgment. But again, even a mistaken judgment must sometimes be allowed to stand, if only because eventually those same interests in finality and repose will mean that systemic justice trumps concerns about accuracy. Likewise appellate review, though it is explicitly focused on correcting errors of law committed during trial court proceedings, often grants a very wide scope for decisions by trial judges deemed to be erroneous. Thus we have doctrines of abuse of discretion, clear error, harmless error, and so on, all of which sometimes allow judgments to stand even when the appellate court judges believe that errors were committed below. These doctrines provide scope for exercise of judgment by a trial judge who is closer to the case than appellate judges reviewing a cold record. And though there is no denying that some or all of these doctrines are controversial (and sometimes misapplied), that does not mean that such doctrines are necessarily unjust solely because they allow scope for mistakes.

Do these various doctrines undermine the idea of law as justice, or do they preserve systemic integrity? Certainly it can be either. For example, when a court interposes a procedural timeliness rule to prevent an appeal proposing new evidence of actual innocence in a capital case, the court may literally be imposing erroneous death by execution upon an innocent person all because of a rule designed to preserve an orderly court docket. But that is perhaps the most extreme case. More often, the claims of justice are more balanced, and it may be that the claims of systemic justice, though perhaps not so obvious or so obviously sympathetic, are sufficient to outweigh the justice claims made in the individual case.

This essay focuses on a different sort of example where claims of individualized versus systemic justice may conflict. These are cases that involve not necessarily an obvious legal or factual mistake, so much as the inevitable pluralism of values that arise when legal systems interact with other systems that may operate based on different laws and principles of justice. Because people and corporate activities cross borders, because actions in one location can have consequences elsewhere, and because assets are often spread throughout the globe, we see many situations in which a tribunal in one legal system is asked to recognize and enforce the judgment of a tribunal in a different legal system. In those cases, there may be a legal decision that is correct in one system, but the question is whether that judgment should be recognized and enforced by a different system that sees the decision as mistaken according to its own laws or norms.

In such judgment recognition scenarios, a judge's sense of individualized and systemic justice can easily conflict. The dictates of individualized justice seem to require a judge to consider how he or she would have decided the case had it been brought in that judge's court as an original matter. Yet, as with res judicata, such an outcome reopens the merits of a case that, by definition, was already adjudicated elsewhere. Moreover, in an interlocking world of multiple legal systems, perhaps a court asked to recognize a foreign judgment should refrain from imposing its opinion on the merits and its own set of legal rules and values on a dispute that may have little connection to its legal system. Thus the idea of a global system that navigates legal pluralism harmoniously may run counter to the impulse to resolve an individual case pursuant to one's own sense of the right outcome. If, as Robert Cover so famously noted, we live in a jurisgenerative world where normative systems are constantly contesting with each other to articulate visions of alternative futures,[1] how do systems manage these plural interactions without simply calling one vision "the law" and the other vision "mistaken"? Recognizing that there can be no rigid lines to be drawn or hard and fast rules available, nevertheless might there be a less jurispathic approach?

For cases brought in the United States, Article IV, section 1 of the U.S. Constitution does seem to provide a hard and fast rule: "Full faith and credit shall be given in each state to the public acts, records, and judicial proceedings of every other state."[2] But even then the question becomes whether the clause means that literally *any* judgment of another state must be enforced, even one that contradicts the laws of the enforcing state? And what about if the prior judgment was actually based on a mistaken reading of the enforcing state's laws?

Let us consider what appears to be an extreme example of the Full Faith and Credit Clause in action. In the 1908 decision *Fauntleroy v. Lum*,[3] the U.S. Supreme Court addressed a case involving two Mississippi residents who had entered into a gambling transaction based on cotton futures. Such a transaction was actually illegal in Mississippi, but because the defendant happened to be in Missouri, the plaintiff sued in Missouri to collect the debt, serving the defendant there. The Missouri court appeared not to have realized that the transaction would have been illegal under Mississippi law and entered judgment for the plaintiff. Accordingly, the question for the Supreme Court was whether the erroneous Missouri judgment was enforceable back in Mississippi, where issuing such a judgment would have been illegal.

By a 5 to 4 vote, the Supreme Court ruled that the Full Faith and Credit Clause required enforcement even in this circumstance. Justice Holmes, writing for the majority, acknowledged that the Missouri judgment might well have been mistaken: "In this case the Missouri court no doubt supposed that the award was binding by the law of Mississippi. If it was mistaken, it made a natural mistake."[4] But he suggested that such "[m]istakes will be rare," and he concluded that the Full Faith and Credit

Clause required enforcement in order to preserve systemic integrity and harmony.[5] According to Holmes, enforcing this erroneous judgment "is not a matter to arouse the susceptibilities of the states, all of which are equally concerned in the question and equally on both sides."[6] Thus, the systemic value to the states of mutual enforcement was enough to override the obvious error in this individual case.

In contrast, the four dissenting justices focused on both the magnitude of the error and the gamesmanship underlying the case. Justice White, writing for the dissent, pointed out that the contract that was the subject of the suit was unenforceable in Mississippi, and the plaintiff was essentially seeking a backdoor way of obtaining a judgment in Mississippi by suing in Missouri, getting a judgment there, and then using Full Faith and Credit to get the Missouri judgment enforced in Mississippi. White argued that this chain of events stretched the idea behind the Full Faith and Credit Clause: "Although not wishing in the slightest degree to weaken the operation of the due faith and credit clause as interpreted and applied from the beginning," he wrote, "it to me seems that this ruling so enlarges that clause as to cause it to obliterate all state lines, since the effect will be to endow each state with authority to overthrow the public policy and criminal statutes of the others, thereby depriving all of their lawful authority."[7] Yet, this argument did not carry the day, and so a Missouri judgment resting on a mistaken understanding of Mississippi law (and one that could not legally have been issued in Mississippi) was nevertheless enforced by Mississippi courts under the Full Faith and Credit Clause.

Note that both the majority and the dissent ultimately framed their arguments in terms of systemic justice. The majority focused on the need for states to reciprocally enforce each other's judgments as a matter of course without reopening or reconsidering those judgments. And the dissent worried that applying Full Faith and Credit in this case would allow litigants to undermine the general criminal and civil statutes of a state by enforcing otherwise unenforceable judgments through the mechanism of Full Faith and Credit. The question for all the justices, in short, was which rule would allow the *system* of justice to function most harmoniously. The individuals involved in the case and the question of justice as between them disappeared from view.

Almost ninety years later, in *Baker v. General Motors,*[8] the Supreme Court again took up the question of how exacting the Full Faith and Credit Clause should be when courts are asked to enforce a prior problematic judgment from another court. *Baker* concerned a stipulated injunction submitted to and signed by a Michigan court in settlement of a lawsuit between General Motors (GM) and Ronald Elwell, a former GM employee.[9] Among other terms, the stipulated injunction purported to prevent Elwell from testifying against GM in subsequent legal proceedings. The question posed before the Supreme Court was whether, in a separate wrongful death suit brought in a Missouri federal court by the Bakers against GM, Elwell could be called as a plaintiff's witness or whether instead the Michigan injunction blocked Elwell from testifying. And while it was clear that the Michigan judgment could not preclude the Bakers, who were not parties to the Michigan proceedings, the difficult question was whether it could bind Elwell, who obviously had been a party in Michigan, and therefore keep him from testifying.[10] The Missouri federal district court judge ruled that allowing such a result would run counter to public policy and therefore invoked a public policy exception to the Full Faith and Credit Clause, whereby rendering courts would be free to ignore prior court judgments anathema to the rendering court's local policies.[11]

Thus the U.S. Supreme Court appeared to be faced with a binary choice. On the one hand, the Court could endorse the Missouri district court's ruling and allow courts to extricate themselves from the Full Faith and Credit Clause simply by deeming a sister jurisdiction's judgment contrary to public policy (and in the process over-ruling *Fauntleroy v. Lum*). On the other, the Court could enforce the Michigan court's order, thereby allowing Michigan's ruling to prevent any other court in the country from hearing Elwell's testimony in cases against GM. The interests in individual versus systemic justice seemed squarely presented as opposing options.

However, Justice Ginsburg, writing for the majority, ultimately rejected both of these options. First, citing *Fauntleroy*,[12] she made it clear that, although choice-of-law doctrines permit courts to use public policy objections in choosing the *law* to apply in a cross-jurisdictional case, the command of the Full Faith and Credit Clause with regard to prior *judgments* is far more "exacting" and permits no such set of broad exceptions: "A final judgment in one State, if rendered by a court with adjudicatory authority over the subject matter and persons governed by the judgment, qualifies for recognition throughout the land."[13] Thus the Missouri court could not simply ignore the Michigan judgment based on assertions of public policy, and the systemic rationale underlying *Fauntleroy v. Lum* was reaffirmed.

At the same time, the Court did not countenance denying the Bakers relevant evidence in their case and ruled that the Michigan court judgment was improper and could not automatically block the adjudication in

Missouri. "Michigan's judgment," Ginsburg wrote, "cannot reach beyond the Elwell-GM controversy to control proceedings against GM brought in other States, by other parties, asserting claims the merits of which Michigan has not considered."[14] The problem with the Michigan order, according to the Court, was that "Michigan lacks authority to control courts elsewhere by precluding them, in actions brought by strangers to the Michigan litigation, from determining for themselves what witnesses are competent to testify and what evidence is relevant and admissible in their search for the truth."[15]

Thus Ginsburg focused on maintaining a system of legal pluralism in which neither court trumped the other fully, and instead both were required to respect each other's authority and judgments. Michigan's judgment could not silence Missouri in matters that Missouri had a right to adjudicate, just as Missouri could not simply ignore a lawful Michigan judgment by interposing local public-policy concerns. A Full Faith and Credit Clause without a public policy exception helps ensure an interlocking system of justice whereby parties cannot evade legal judgments simply by fleeing the jurisdiction. But at the same time, Ginsburg called on courts to be restrained in the kinds of judgments they issue, remaining mindful of the prerogatives of other courts to pursue their own proceedings unfettered by foreign judgments. As a result, the need for both interdependence and independence within a federalist court system can be maintained. Her decision therefore seeks to preserve pluralist, intersystemic interaction. And though she too—like the justices in *Fauntleroy*—focuses on the *systems* of justice, one also senses that the *Baker* Court was uneasy about the injustice that would be done to the Bakers if they were barred from calling Elwell to testify. Accordingly, the decision balances the dictates of systemic and individualized justice, walking a tightrope between the two.

As noted above, in the domestic context the recognition of judgments is constitutionally commanded through the Full Faith and Credit Clause. Moreover, within a single, relatively homogenous country, the idea of one state enforcing another state's judgment does not seem quite so controversial because the legal variations among states are likely to be relatively minor. On the other hand, the Full Faith and Credit Clause derives from the Articles of Confederation,[16] which were drafted when the colonies were less homogenous and more akin to separate nation-states than they are today.

Nevertheless, it is not surprising that judges would be less solicitous when deciding whether to enforce what they consider to be mistaken or inappropriate judgments issued by a tribunal in another *country* rather than another *state*. Yet, while the decision to enforce a foreign judgment (especially a mistaken one or one that derives from a different value system) is surely less automatic, many of the same principles might still be relevant. In particular, the systemic values that underlie the Full Faith and Credit command are still part of the judgment recognition calculus. Judges can see themselves as part of an international network of normative communities and the parties before them as potentially affiliated with multiple such communities. Those various communities might legitimately seek to impose their norms on such affiliated parties.[17]

Thus, when faced with an enforcement decision regarding a foreign judgment, courts need not necessarily assume that their own local public policies trump the dictates of the foreign judgment. Instead, courts can undertake a nuanced inquiry concerning whether the affiliations of the parties render the original judgment legitimate. Although the local policies and sense of justice in the forum country are not irrelevant, those policies can be weighed against the overall interest in creating an interlocking system of international adjudication. Recognizing a judgment becomes an effective hybrid position because it allows communities to maintain different norms while creating a space for cooperation. Indeed, as in the domestic context, deference to other normative communities will have long-term reciprocal benefits and will potentially contribute to a more tolerant, jurisgenerative world order. And, particularly when the parties have no significant affiliation with the forum state, there is little reason for a court to insist on following domestic public policies in the face of such competing systemic values.

This is not to say that foreign judgments should always be enforced. Even if the systemic values of reciprocal enforcement are considered, one would expect that decision makers might nevertheless sometimes interpose local public policies where they would not in the domestic state-to-state setting. But if we acknowledge the importance of the systemic values effectuated by strong judgment recognition, we will necessarily reject the idea that, because a judgment could not have been issued by a decision maker in the first instance, that decision maker is simply *unable* to enforce the judgment. Instead, we will appreciate that enforcing a foreign judgment is fundamentally different from issuing an original judgment. Indeed, judgment recognition implicates an entirely distinct set of concerns about the role of law in a multistate world.

In most areas of law, U.S. courts have generally invoked these systemic values and enforced foreign judgments as a matter of comity.[18] As far back as 1895, in *Hilton v. Guyot,* the U.S. Supreme Court made clear that comity "is the recognition which one nation allows within its territory to the legislative, executive, or judicial acts of another nation, having due regard both to international duty and convenience, and to the rights of its own citizens, or of other persons who are under the protection of its laws."[19] The Second Restatement of Conflict of Laws codified this idea, noting that a "judgment rendered in a foreign nation . . . will, if valid, usually be given the same effect as a sister State judgment."[20] Moreover, validity is based only on whether the court that rendered judgment had proper personal jurisdiction over the parties and utilized procedures that were not inherently unfair.[21]

In addition, while courts enforcing foreign judgments (as opposed to domestic ones) have at times applied a public policy exception to avoid enforcing particularly egregious rulings, the exception has been construed very narrowly.[22] Accordingly, courts refuse to enforce only "where the original claim is repugnant to fundamental notions of what is decent and just in the State where enforcement is sought."[23] Likewise, the UN Convention on the Recognition and Enforcement of Foreign Arbitral Awards and the Uniform Foreign Money-Judgments Recognition Act require that a U.S. court enforce a judgment or arbitral award unless there is fraud or if doing so would be repugnant to the public policy of the enforcing forum.[24] Thus, in most recognition of judgments cases, "[c]ourts consistently have enforced foreign judgments even if they would have refused to entertain suit on the original claim on grounds of public policy."[25]

But what if the foreign judgment seems incurably wrong-headed from the point of view of the rendering court? Or what if it is based on a very different set of fundamental values or policy preferences? In such cases, it may be difficult for judges to resist the urge to block the enforcement of what they view as a mistaken judgment. For example, in stark contrast to the general policy of respecting foreign judgments, U.S. courts have often assumed, at least where U.S. constitutional values seem to be at stake, that enforcing an "unconstitutional" judgment is itself a violation of the U.S. Constitution. As a result, courts have effectively imposed U.S. constitutional norms onto foreign disputes, even in circumstances where the dispute has little connection with the United States.[26]

Consider *Telnikoff v. Matusevitch,*[27] a case decided by the Maryland Court of Appeals. This was a libel action between two British citizens concerning writings that appeared in a British newspaper. After a complicated sequence of proceedings in the United Kingdom, a jury ruled for the plaintiff and ordered damages. However, Matusevitch moved to Maryland and subsequently sought a declaratory order that the British libel judgment could not be enforced in the United States, pursuant to the First Amendment. The Maryland court ultimately ruled that, because British libel law violates the speech-protective First Amendment standards laid out by the U.S. Supreme Court in *New York Times v. Sullivan*[28] and its progeny, the British judgment violated Maryland public policy and could not be enforced.[29]

But is it actually true that the First Amendment is necessarily implicated in an enforcement action? First, it is debatable whether the simple enforcement of a judgment creates the requisite state action to generate constitutional concerns.[30] Second, with regard to interstate harmony, a refusal to enforce the British libel judgment effectively imposes U.S. First Amendment norms on the United Kingdom. Such parochialism in judgment recognition is potentially cause for concern. Third, while it is true that constitutional norms could conceivably create sufficient public policy reasons to refuse to enforce a judgment, the libel dispute in *Telnikoff* does not seem to implicate U.S. public policy because neither party had any particular affiliation with the United States at the time of the events at issue. Thus, even if the British judgment is mistaken from the point of view of U.S. constitutional values, that alone might not be a sufficient reason to deny enforcement.

Indeed, even if U.S. constitutional values or public policy considerations might *sometimes* require a court to refuse to enforce a mistaken judgment, it is not at all clear that the appropriate response is to create a categorical rule preventing enforcement in *all* cases, and one might think there is little reason to refuse to enforce a foreign judgment absent significant ties between the dispute and the United States. Instead, courts might take seriously the systemic values that would be effectuated by enforcing the foreign judgment, weigh the importance of such values against the relative importance of the local public policy or constitutional norm, and then consider the degree to which the parties have affiliated themselves with the forum. Only then can courts take into account the multistate nature of the dispute and the flexible nature of community affiliation in a multivariate world.

The rise of the Internet, of course, makes it far more likely that content posted online by a person in one physical location will violate the law in some other physical location. In such circumstances, there is an inevitable problem of extraterritoriality. Will the person who posts the content be required to conform her activities to the norms of the most restrictive community of readers? Or, alternatively, will the community of readers, which has adopted a norm regarding Internet content, be subjected to the proscribed material regardless of its wishes? The answers to these questions depend both on whether the community of readers asserts the jurisdictional authority to impose its norms on the foreign content provider and whether the home country of the content provider chooses to recognize the norms imposed.

The celebrated case involving Yahoo!'s content in France raised such issues. On May 22, 2000, the Tribunal de Grande Instance de Paris issued a preliminary injunction against Yahoo.com, ordering the site to take all possible measures to dissuade and prevent access in France of Yahoo! auction sites that sell Nazi memorabilia or other items that are sympathetic to Nazism or constitute Holocaust denial.[31] Certainly, selling such merchandise in France would violate French law,[32] and there was little dispute that Yahoo.fr, Yahoo!'s French subsidiary, must comply with requests that access to such sites be blocked. What made this action noteworthy was the fact that the suit was brought not only against Yahoo.fr but also against Yahoo.com, an American corporation, and the fact that the court sought to enjoin access to non-French websites stored on Yahoo!'s non-French servers.

Yahoo! argued in response that the French assertion of jurisdiction was impermissibly extraterritorial in scope because Yahoo!, as a U.S. corporation transmitting material uploaded in the United States, was protected by the First Amendment of the U.S. Constitution. But of course the extraterritoriality charge runs in both directions. If France is *not* able to block the access of French citizens to proscribed material, then the United States will effectively be imposing First Amendment norms on the entire world. And whatever the solution to this problem might be, a territorial analysis will not help because the relevant transaction is both "in" France and not "in" France simultaneously.[33]

Here we have an intractable problem of law's mistakes. The French court issues what in U.S. constitutional terms is surely a mistaken judgment (though the French hate-speech law is entirely defensible in France given French history with anti-Semitism and the Holocaust). And, unlike in *Telnikoff*, where a British party moves to the United States, Yahoo! was and is a U.S. corporation. So, what should happen when Yahoo! files suit in a U.S. federal court in California seeking a declaration that the French judgment is categorically unenforceable in the United States?

Faced with the question of whether or not to enforce the French court's order, the district court started from the assumption that U.S. law (and U.S. constitutional norms) must apply. Thus, the court framed the issue for decision solely in U.S. constitutional terms: "What *is* at issue here is whether it is consistent with the Constitution and laws of the United States for another nation to regulate speech by a United States resident within the United States on the basis that such speech can be accessed by Internet users in that nation."[34]

Conceptualized in this way, the district court had little difficulty determining that enforcement of the French court order would violate the First Amendment, concluding that the French judgment constituted impermissible viewpoint discrimination and that it was impermissibly vague. The court therefore concluded that a U.S. court could not have issued such an order in the first instance without violating constitutional free speech norms.[35] But of course, in a judgments recognition case, that is not the appropriate inquiry. Indeed, as discussed above, in the domestic context the Full Faith and Credit Clause *requires* recognition of judgments that might be illegal in the state where recognition is sought. Thus the real question is whether this is the type of judgment that should be *recognized,* not whether the court could have issued the ruling *as an original matter.*

To its credit, the District Court did include a brief discussion of the judgment recognition issue in a section titled "Comity."[36] And the court acknowledged that "United States courts generally recognize foreign judgments and decrees unless enforcement would be prejudicial or contrary to the country's interests."[37] Yet, after reiterating that the French judgment "clearly would be inconsistent with the First Amendment if mandated by a court in the United States,"[38] the district court judge concluded that, because the foreign order would unconstitutionally chill speech occurring within U.S. borders, "the principles of comity are outweighed by the Court's obligation to enforce the First Amendment."[39] Accordingly, though the Court recognized France's "sovereign right to regulate what speech is permissible in France," it nevertheless decided that "this Court may not enforce a foreign order that violates the protections of the United States Constitution by chilling protected speech that occurs simultaneously within our borders."[40]

Interestingly, to support this conclusion, the district court cited the Maryland *Telnikoff* decision.[41] Yet that case had nothing to do with "chilling protected speech that occurs simultaneously within our borders" because the speech at issue in *Telnikoff* was an article published in a British newspaper. Accordingly, it is unclear whether the *Yahoo!* Court was making a categorical judgment that *no* foreign judgment can be enforced by a U.S. court if that court could not constitutionally have issued the judgment, or rather making a more nuanced argument that *certain* foreign judgments—those that chill U.S. speech—should not be enforced. Obviously, those two formulations are very different ways of analyzing how to deal with foreign "mistaken" judgments.[42]

So, how does a court adopting a more systemic understanding of judgment recognition approach the question of whether to recognize the French judgment? To begin, we must recognize that this is a difficult case. To the extent that local public policies should have any valence in an international judgment recognition decision, here the U.S. public policy is particularly strong. Not only is the First Amendment a constitutional command, but it goes to the heart of American self-identity and arguably helps to define American democracy. Moreover, unlike the *Telnikoff* case discussed previously, Yahoo! is a U.S. corporation based in the United States. Thus, Yahoo!'s entitlement to First Amendment protection is far stronger than was Matusevitch's.

On the other hand, in weighing the relevant systemic values, it becomes clear that this case is not merely a matter of France simply imposing its norms onto an entity with no affiliation in France. Rather, Yahoo! was and is a sophisticated, multinational operator. At the time, Yahoo!'s explicit business plan aimed at reaching web users worldwide, with a strategy focused on attracting and maintaining "as large a global audience as possible,"[43] and a French subsidiary in which it owned a 70 percent ownership stake.[44] Indeed, Yahoo! exerted substantial control over this subsidiary, dictating some of the links and content of the French site and requiring the subsidiary to maintain links to its U.S.-based site. Moreover, Yahoo! routinely profiled French users in order to target them with advertisements written in French. Given these efforts to take advantage of the French market and affiliate itself with France, Yahoo! had less cause for complaining of France's "extraterritorial" judgment.

Thus the *Yahoo!* case falls within two extremes. At one pole is *Telnikoff*, in which the relevant community affiliations of both the parties and the dispute were exclusively British, and therefore enforcing the British libel judgment would be appropriate. At the other pole is a hypothetical case in which a small, local website based in the United States is prosecuted in France solely because of material available on its website. The company's utter lack of community affiliation with France would likely mean that the French judgment should not be enforced in the United States. In that instance, the strong First Amendment values would outweigh the need to enforce the judgment in order to remain a cooperative member of an international community of courts. In *Yahoo!*, there is both significant affiliations with the United States and significant affiliations with France. In the end, under a more nuanced approach, I think that the extent of Yahoo!'s business activities abroad justify the French judgment and should make it enforceable in the United States. But regardless of the final outcome, it is clear that courts should not simply cite the First Amendment and refuse to enforce a "mistaken" foreign judgment without actually considering the systemic values implicated by the enforcement decision.

In short, mistaken judgments are in some ways an inevitable artifact of a world in which multiple legal systems interact. Because procedures, values, histories, biases, and judgments are different from place to place and system to system, the resulting legal pluralism will mean that judgments rendered in one legal system will need to be enforced by other systems that view those judgments as mistaken or wrong-headed. But in an interconnected world, it seems unworkable simply to refuse categorically to enforce *any* foreign judgment that appears mistaken or based on an alternative value system. At the same time, automatically enforcing all judgments can lead to injustice or gamesmanship (as in *Fauntleroy*). Perhaps then the best we can do is to seek nuanced inquiry regarding whether the prior judgment overstepped its bounds (as in *Baker*) or whether the prior judgment unduly impacts actors who have taken no steps to affiliate themselves with the system rendering the initial judgment.

In these inquiries, however, the focus inevitably shifts from the mistake itself to the proper way to preserve a multijurisdictional system of justice. In a fundamental sense, then, mistakes are not unjust; they are an inevitable result of a world of legal pluralism run by fallible human beings. Justice may be found to lie more in the system than in the individual result.

NOTES

1. Robert Cover, "The Folktales of Justice: Tales of Jurisdiction," in *Narrative, Violence, and the Law: The Essays of Robert Cover*, ed. M. Minow, M. Ryan, and A. Sarat (Ann Arbor: University of Michigan Press, 1995), 173–201.
2. U.S. Constitution, Art. IV, sec. 1.

3. 210 U.S. 230 (1908).
4. Ibid. at 238.
5. Ibid. at 237–38.
6. Ibid. at 238.
7. Ibid. at 239 (White, J., dissenting).
8. 522 U.S. 222 (1998).
9. Ibid. at 228–29.
10. See ibid. at 237 n. 11.
11. Ibid. at 230.
12. Ibid. at 233–34.
13. Ibid. at 233.
14. Ibid. at 238.
15. Ibid.
16. The Articles of Confederation contained a provision similar to article IV, section 1: "Full faith and credit shall be given in each of these States to the records, acts, and judicial proceedings of the courts and magistrates of every other State." U.S. Articles of Confederation, Art. IV. For a concise history of full faith and credit, see Robert H. Jackson, "Full Faith and Credit—The Lawyer's Clause of the Constitution," *Columbia Law Journal* 45 (1945): 1.
17. For an extended discussion of judgment recognition in the context of globalization, see Paul Schiff Berman, *Global Legal Pluralism: A Jurisprudence of Law beyond Borders* (Cambridge: Cambridge University Press, 2012): 294–322; Paul Schiff Berman, "Towards a Cosmopolitan Vision of Conflict of Laws: Redefining Governmental Interests in a Global Era," *University of Pennsylvania Law Review* 153 (2005): 1819, 1868–82.
18. See Mark D. Rosen, "Exporting the Constitution," *Emory Law Journal* 53 (2004): 171, 176 (noting that, since the nineteenth century, "the United States has been at the vanguard of enforcing foreign judgments").
19. 159 U.S. 113, 164 (1895).
20. Restatement (Second) of Conflict of Laws §117, cmt. c (1971).
21. Ibid. §92.
22. See Rosen, "Exporting the Constitution," 177–79 (surveying U.S. case law on enforcement of foreign judgments).
23. Restatement (Second) of Conflict of Laws § 117, cmt. c (1971).
24. See, for example, Convention on the Recognition and Enforcement of Foreign Arbitral Awards, June 10, 1958, 330 U.N.T.S. 38 (requiring courts to enforce the judgment or arbitral award unless there is fraud or if doing so would be repugnant to the public policy of the enforcing forum); Unif. Foreign Money-Judgments recognition Act §4, 13 pt. II U.L.A. 58–59 (2002) (discussing situations where foreign judgments need not be recognized).
25. Rosen, "Exporting the Constitution," 178–79.
26. For an insightful critique of this practice, see ibid., 227–32.
27. 702 A.2d 230 (1997).
28. 376 U.S. 254 (1964).
29. *Telnikoff*, 702 A.2d at 249.
30. In *Shelley v. Kraemer*, 334 U.S. 1 (1948), the U.S. Supreme Court ruled that the Equal Protection Clause precluded a court from enforcing a private, racially restrictive covenant. In so doing, the Court determined that, although the covenant itself was entered into by private actors who were not subject to the commands of the Fourteenth Amendment, the action by the courts in enforcing the covenant was sufficient state action to trigger constitutional scrutiny. See ibid. at 14. *Shelley*, therefore, appears to block judicial enforcement of a private agreement (or a foreign order) that would be

unconstitutional. Indeed, courts, in refusing to enforce foreign "unconstitutional" judgments, have explicitly relied on *Shelley*. See, for example, Yahoo!, *Inc. v. La Ligue Contre Le Racisme et L'Antisémitisme*, 169 F. Supp. 2d 1181, 1189 (N.D. CA 2001), *rev'd on other grounds, Yahoo!, Inc. v. La Ligue Contre Le Racisme et L'Antisémitisme*, 433 F.3rd 1199, 1202–3 (9th Cir. 2006). However, since the time *Shelley* was issued, courts and commentators have backed away from the sweeping ramifications of *Shelley*. This is because, under *Shelley*'s reasoning, any private contract that is being enforced by a police officer or court would be transformed into state action. See Laurence H. Tribe, *American Constitutional Law*, 2nd ed. (St. Paul, MN: Foundation Press, 1988), 1697 (arguing that *Shelley*'s approach, "consistently applied, would require individuals to conform their private agreements to constitutional standards whenever, as almost always, the individuals might later seek the security of potential judicial enforcement"). Although generations of legal realists and critical legal studies scholars have articulated similarly sweeping conceptions of state action—see Paul Schiff Berman, "Cyberspace and the State Action Debate: The Cultural Value of Applying Constitutional Norms to 'Private' Regulation," *University of Colorado Law Review* 71 (2000): 1263, 1279–81 (surveying these critiques)—courts have largely resisted *Shelley* and have limited its holding to only the context of racially restrictive covenants. Indeed, even in cases implicating the First Amendment, "with virtually no exceptions, courts have concluded that the judicial enforcement of private agreements inhibiting speech does not trigger constitutional review, despite the fact that identical legislative limitations on speech would have." See Rosen, "Exporting the Constitution," 192–95 (collecting cases). Thus, it is not clear how robust *Shelley* still is and whether it would truly pose a constitutional bar in an action to enforce a foreign judgment. For further discussion of *Shelley* and its implications for judgment recognition, see Rosen, "Exporting the Constitution," 186–209.

31. See *Yahoo!, Inc. v. La Ligue Contre Le Racisme et L'Antisémitisme*, 433 F.3rd 1199, 1202–3 (9th Cir. 2006) (summarizing French court order).

32. See Code pénal [C. pén.] art. R. 645-1 (Fr.) (prohibiting the public display of Nazi memorabilia except for the purposes of an historical film, show, or exhibit).

33. For further discussion of the *Yahoo!* case, and cross-border jurisdictional issues more generally, see Berman, *Global Legal Pluralism;* Paul Schiff Berman, "The Globalization of Jurisdiction," *University of Pennsylvania Law Review* 151 (2002): 311.

34. Yahoo!, *Inc. v. La Ligue Contre Le Racisme et L'Antisémitisme*, 169 F. Supp. 2d 1181, 1186 (N.D. CA 2001), *rev'd on other grounds, Yahoo!, Inc. v. La Ligue Contre Le Racisme et L'Antisémitisme*, 433 F.3rd 1199, 1202–3 (9th Cir. 2006).

35. Ibid. at 1189–90.

36. Ibid. at 1192–93.

37. Ibid. at 1192.

38. Ibid.

39. Ibid. at 1193.

40. Ibid. at 1192.

41. Ibid.

42. The Ninth Circuit ultimately reversed the district court's *Yahoo!* decision, but it did so on jurisdictional grounds, without reaching the judgment recognition issue. See *Yahoo!, Inc. v. La Ligue Contre Le Racisme et L'Antisémitisme*, 379 F.3d 1120, 1121 (2004). The appellate court decision did include some language suggesting skepticism about Yahoo's position. Indeed, the court went so far as to observe that, because Yahoo! "obtains commercial advantage from the fact that users located in France are able to access its website" and because Yahoo! even displays banner advertisements in French to French users, the company is obtaining "benefit from the fact that its content may be viewed around the world" and should therefore not be shielded from the concomitant

costs of such activities. Ibid. at 1126. However, the court refused to reach the issue of recognition, deciding instead that, until the French plaintiffs actually sought enforcement of the order in the United States, they had insufficient contacts with the United States to justify jurisdiction. See ibid. at 1123. Thus, though framed in the language of jurisdiction, the appellate court ruling seems to rest primarily on the idea that Yahoo!'s request for a declaratory judgment was not ripe for review in the absence of any indication that the French plaintiffs were actually seeking to enforce the order. See ibid. ("Jurisdiction may be obtained, and the First Amendment claim heard, once [the French parties] ask a U.S. district court to enforce the French judgment. As of yet, the organizations have declined to do so.")

43. See "Yahoo! Inc. 1999 Annual Report" ("We set out five years ago to build Yahoo! into the only place anyone in the world would have to go to find and get connected to anyone and anything. Our goal was to attract and maintain as large a global audience as possible"). Yahoo! Inc., http://files.shareholder.com/downloads/YHOO/3387322613x0x28475/17CA3BAB-DE4C-4900-B142-2A805253F066/yahoo_99ar.pdf.

44. See "Yahoo! France License Agreement," November 1, 1996. Yahoo!, Inc., www.techagreements.com/agreement-preview.aspx?title=Yahoo!%20-%20Yahoo!%20France%20License%20Agreement&num=4001.

About the Contributors

PAUL SCHIFF BERMAN is Vice Provost for Online Education and Academic Innovation at the George Washington University and Manatt/Ahn Professor of Law.

SONALI CHAKRAVARTI is assistant professor of government at Wesleyan University.

LAWRENCE DOUGLAS is James J. Grosfeld Professor of Law, Jurisprudence, and Social Thought at Amherst College.

JODY LYNEÉ MADEIRA is professor of law at the Maurer School of Law at Indiana University.

STEWART MOTHA is reader in law and director of Postgraduate Research and Intensive LLM Programs at Birkbeck School of Law.

KUNAL M. PARKER is professor of law and Dean's Distinguished Scholar at the University of Miami School of Law.

AUSTIN SARAT is associate dean of the faculty, William Nelson Cromwell Professor of Jurisprudence and Political Science, and professor of Law, Jurisprudence, and Social Thought at Amherst College.

JORDAN M. STEIKER is Judge Robert M. Parker Endowed Chair in Law at the University of Texas.

MARTHA UMPHREY is director of the Center for Humanistic Inquiry and Bertrand H. Snell 1894 Professor in American Government in the Department of Law, Jurisprudence, and Social Thought at Amherst College.

Index